The Making of
the Second Cold War

First published, 1983
© Fred Halliday, 1983
Second impression, 1984

Verso Editions and NLB,
15 Greek Street, London W1

Filmset in Garamond by
Comset Graphic Designs

Printed by
The Thetford Press Ltd.
Thetford, Norfolk

ISBN 0 86091 752 5

Contents

Preface

The purpose of this book is to describe the causes and development of the Second Cold War. It is therefore about the 'making' of this Cold War in both senses of the word—about how it was brought into being, and how it has been sustained. It is an attempt to establish the main parameters of international politics since the late 1960s, and to provide a rival interpretation to that which is conventionally presented, in both east and west.

Part of the impetus to writing this work has come from the peace movement, which has recently pushed the issue of nuclear weapons to the centre of political debate in such a rapid and decisive manner. Many within the peace movement will disagree with what is written here, but I hope that it may nonetheless be received as part of the discussion that animates and guides the campaign against nuclear weapons. By studying how the Cold War has been made, it may be the easier to unmake it. I have also been stimulated by the need to examine the analytic issues underlying this Cold War: the relationship between the arms race and general political events; the influence of domestic changes upon foreign policy; the relative weights of east-west, north-south and west-west conflicts. The situation is so complex and so fluid that any answers must be tentative, but given the importance of the questions involved, that is no reason for not attempting to give any answers at all.

Throughout the writing of this book I have been given sustained and invaluable encouragement by *New Left Review* and the Transnational Institute. The book itself began as an essay that was included in *Exterminism and Cold War*, a volume edited by NLR and published in 1982. Both the original draft of the essay and that of the book drew heavily on the ideas and advice of NLR editorial board members. My first ideas on the whole subject were developed in a series of TNI seminars held in 1979 and 1980, and there is much in this book that could not have been written without the vivid trans-Atlantic stimulation and sustained research assistance provided by TNI.

Amongst the many who helped me, I would first like to thank all those who read the manuscript, in whole or in part, and who have given me comments upon it: Perry Anderson, Anthony Barnett, Neil Belton, Bob Borosage, Mike Davis, Jon Halliday, John Hampson, Saul Landau, and Maxine Molyneux.

Amongst those who gave up their time to discuss the issues raised in this volume, in person or in correspondence, I would especially like to thank: Eqabal Ahmad, Bill Arkin, Cynthia Aronson, Richard Barnet, Elizabeth Becker, Hedley Bull, Noam Chomsky, Alexander Cockburn, Andrew Cockburn, Bruce Cumings, Tamara Deutscher, Carlos Fernandez Espeso, Edmund Fawcett, Andre Gunder Frank, Jeff Frieden, Susan George, John Gittings, Charles Glass, Peter Gowan, Selig Harrison, Phil Hearse, John Helmer, Natalia Jimenez, Mary Kaldor, Michael Klare, David Leech, Larry Lifschultz, Simon Lund, Meg Luxton, Zhores Medvedev, Judith Miller, Dev Murarka, Mathew Nimetz, Jim Paul, Vladimir Posner, Marcus Raskin, Jim Ridgeway, Barry Rubin, John Saul, Stuart Schram, Wally Seccombe, Teodor Shanin, Holly Sklar, Dan Smith, Rick Stanwood, Jonathan Steele, Joe Stork, Marek Thee, Tony Thomas, Peter Thompson, Diana de Vegh, Pedro Vilanova, Paul Walker, Cora Weiss, Philip Windsor, Alan Wolfe, and Claudia Wright. I trust that, as much as they will recognise the contributions which they have made to different sections of this book, they will be assured that they are in no way responsible for the final result.

Fred Halliday   London 2 April 1983

1
Cold Wars,
Old and New

From the middle 1970s the world witnessed the onset of a Second Cold War, a period of east-west hostility and of international focus upon this conflict that was comparable, in its essentials, to the First Cold War of 1946–1953. Whatever accommodations Reagan and Andropov were to seek after this Cold War had been launched, the gravity of this development was plain enough from the very tone in which international relations were being conducted. In contrast to the more co-operative and cautious tone of east-west relations evident during the Detente of the early 1970s, we could now hear Moscow and Washington engage in threat and challenge, self-justification and vilification of the other. In the years from 1979 to 1982 at least, an emphasis upon the search for common ground gave way to one of strength and military preparedness as the bases of international order; an earlier acceptance of the complexity of world affairs, and of the fact that responsibility for problems was distributed between different countries, was replaced by a straightforward indictment of the opposing side.

The crisis attendant upon Cold War II was, however, not just a matter of the tone of east-west relations, but was given special importance because of the role played within it by the nuclear arms race and the dangers which are rightly seen as flowing from this military competition. It is indeed too simple to present the nuclear arms race and east-west conflict as just two parts of the same process, and very few people believe that the present leadership of either east or west would seek suddenly to launch an all-out nuclear attack on the enemy. But the two are so closely interwoven that a worsening in political contacts between east and west is perceived as increasing the danger of war and making it all the more necessary to discover some means of halting and reversing the arms race.

2

Cold Wars involve an erosion of confidence in the mechanisms of peace-making and in the ability of politicians to find solutions to world problems; at the same time, they increase fear of the opponent and the drive towards competition. There is a greater danger of nuclear war developing from local conflict or diplomatic miscalculation. It is here in the reduction of political control as well as in the quantitative and qualitative increase of modern weaponry, that the tensions of Cold War contain the seeds of a possible future nuclear conflict.[1]

Those who seek to comprehend periods of Cold War face, therefore, a double problem. There is first of all the *moral* problem, of reacting to and opposing the forces that bring war nearer and which threaten humanity with nuclear destruction. There is, at the same time, an *intellectual* problem of strengthening moral outrage with an analysis, as accurate and as comprehensive as possible, of what the causes of this international tension are. The latter without the former can become an arid exercise, a probing detached from the hope of human survival that has in recent years come to animate so many people in the cause of peace. The former without the latter can, however, contain dangers of equal force, since a protest without perception of what causes that against which one protests can remain an empty cry; it can be valid in its outrage and concern, but ultimately powerless in its ability either to identify the roots of the problem or to convince sufficient numbers of people of its validity. The urgency of a political response to the arms race is bolstered, not diluted, by such an analytic accompaniment.

The discussion that follows is a product of this dual, moral-intellectual, concern, and is part of a wide-ranging debate that has been in train for a number of years on the nature of the current international crisis. Many writers—journalists and academics, activists and researchers, peace campaigners and politicians—have offered their explanation of Cold War II. This book joins in that discussion in the full knowledge that there are many who have already staked their claim to a solution. Amidst the

---

[1.] 'The risk of a world conflagration arises not so much when a state deliberately provokes a general war—that is hardly ever the case—as when the great powers' willingness to compromise and find peaceful solutions has been eroded by a growing sense of crisis and the sudden emergence of problems to which the traditional solutions provide no answer. This is the situation today. What we are witnessing, as people were witnessing in 1911, is the crumbling of a system, the crisis of a society in the throes of irresistible change.' Geoffrey Barraclough, *From Agadir to Armageddon*, London 1982, p. 168.

many issues which have arisen in this context, three are given particular attention in the ensuing pages. The present chapter seeks to set the terms of discussion, by analysing what a Cold War is, and the similarities and differences between the Second and First Cold Wars. Chapter Two outlines a set of underlying factors, 'constituent elements'. These structure the course of world politics and provide a means of relating the specific issue of the arms race to other political trends in the contemporary world. It is here, in pressing beyond the individual events of world politics, that I discuss the other theories, explicit and implicit, which have been offerred as explanations of Cold War II. The remaining chapters cover the causes and course of the Second Cold War, beginning with the Nixon-Brezhnev initiatives of the late 1960s and ending with Reagan's and Andropov's policies in the early 1980s.

Phases of Postwar History

Cold War II is the most recent of four major phases into which post-1945 history can be divided. In the broadest terms, it can be said that postwar politics have gone through these major phases, which are defined primarily by the character of Soviet-US relations at each stage. They are: Phase I, the First Cold War, 1946-1953; Phase II, the period of Oscillatory Antagonism, 1953-1969; Phase III, Detente, 1969-1979; Phase IV, the Second Cold War, 1979 onwards.

The first phase, that of Cold War I, lasted from 1946 to 1953. Strains between the Allies had been growing during World War II itself—over the Second Front, postwar arrangements for Germany, and plans for eastern Europe. In 1945 there were substantial conflicts on Germany, Poland and Iran and in March 1946 Churchill gave voice to a much wider sentiment in the west when he talked of an 'Iron Curtain', running from the Baltic to the Adriatic. The term 'Cold War', popularised by one of its critics, the columnist Walter Lippmann, came into common use in 1947. In the Truman Doctrine, announced in March of that year, the USA declared its willingness to organise anti-communist forces in Greece and Turkey but this commitment signalled a US support to potential allies anywhere else such aid was needed; the Marshall Plan proclaimed in June 1947 aimed to revive European capitalism under US influence. No substantive progress in east-west negotiation was made from early 1947 onwards, and the London Foreign Ministers Conference of

December 1947 marked the end of meaningful talks between the former allies. Six year of almost complete breakdown of communication between east and west then followed. In Europe, the height of the Cold War was the Berlin blockade which began in June 1948; but it was accompanied by forcible takeovers of power by communist parties in much of eastern Europe, and by the destruction of communist forces in Greece. They had already in 1947 been removed from governments in Italy and France. NATO was established in 1949, the year when the division of Germany into two rival states was confirmed.

By 1949 the focus of international conflict had shifted to the Far East: in October 1949 the Chinese communists came to power in Peking, in June 1950 the North Koreans tried to unify their country by invading the pro-American south, and the Indo-China communist guerrillas, emboldened by the victory of their Chinese allies, intensified a struggle that was to culminate in the defeat of the French expeditionary force at Dien Bien Phu in 1954. Cold War I ended as a result of two developments: one, the death of Stalin in March 1953, and the attendant 'Thaw' in Soviet policies at home and abroad; two, the election of Eisenhower, who promised to end the Korean war. Together these led to the cessation of hostilities in the Far East, with the Korean Armistice of July 1953 and the ceasefire in Indo-China in 1954. If the initiative came from the USSR, it met a favourable response in the west. By 1954 substantive east-west negotiations had begun again, covering Germany, Austria, Korea, and Indo-China. In one case, Austria, a solution was found by declaring the country neutral in return for a complete evacuation of Soviet forces. In two others, Korea and Indo-China, military hostilities ended and partition of disputed countries, Korea and Vietnam, was accepted by both sides, in practice if not in theory. No solution was found in Germany, and some initial Soviet willingness to bargain away the East German state was rebuffed by the west; but the very easing of east-west tension overall did enable a lowering of conflict in this central European theatre as well. No-one thought that east-west hostilities had ended, and the unfinished agenda of Cold War I was later to be reactivated with delayed force—most remarkably in Vietnam. But the easing of confrontation meant that, while east-west contestation continued, Cold War I had come to an end.

The originator of the term Cold War, the fourteenth-century Spanish writer Don Juan Manuel, who was writing of the conflict between Christians and Muslims at that time, remarks that hot and cold wars are distinguished by, among other things, the manner in which they end. 'War that is very strong and very hot ends either with death or peace, whereas cold war neither brings peace nor gives honour to the one who makes it...'[2] Don Juan Manuel's observation applies equally to the Cold War of the nuclear age, for it cannot be said that Cold War I brought either peace or honour to those who waged it. Neither east nor west was able to prevail over the other, and the very partitions that accompanied its end—in Germany, Korea and Vietnam—symbolised the inconclusive character of its termination. Yet if there were no clear winners, both sides can be said to have gained in some measure from it. On the Soviet side, the leadership could see that their alliance system was now established from Berlin to Peking and Hanoi, an extraordinary contrast with the situation prevailing in 1945, let alone with that in existence before World War II. The terrible devastation of the war had given way to an outburst of reconstruction and development in eastern Europe and the USSR as, behind almost sealed frontiers, the 'construction of socialism' went ahead apace. This dynamism was later in the decade to find expression in the expansive visions of Khrushchev and in the scientific achievements of Sputnik and the first manned space flight.

Washington, for its part, had constructed a new alliance system. This was world-wide, in a way that the Soviet one was not, and the dynamism of the US economy, as it emerged unscathed from World War II, enabled US capitalism to exert a hitherto unseen international predominance. The USA oversaw the rearming of Germany, the revival of the economies of western Europe and of Japan, and the projection of a 'Free World' ideology in which it was the military, political and cultural leader. If, therefore, neither the USSR nor the USA won honour or peace from Cold War I in the manner in which they had anticipated, they both gained strategic influence and confidence from this First Cold War of the nuclear age.

[2.] As translated from *Escritores en Prosa Anteriores al Siglo XV*, Biblioteca de Autores Españoles de Rivadeneira, Madrid 1952, p. 362. Don Juan Manuel (1282-1348) was a member of the Castilian royal family who took part in the capture of Algeciras from the Arabs in 1344. The discussion of 'Cold War' comes from his *Libro de los Estados*, a dialogue in which a wise man gives moral advice to a young prince on the conduct of warfare against the Muslim foe.

6

Cold War I gave way to a period of Oscillatory Antagonism, which lasted from 1953 to 1969, and to Detente, which ran from 1969 to 1979. The period of Oscillatory Antagonism was one in which attempts were made to lessen confrontation and reach agreement, and to detach some of the tensions internal to each camp from the east-west confrontation. But each of these attempts failed, because of the impact of other forces and tensions upon the east-west conflict itself[3]. Thus the Geneva conference on Indo-China, the Korean agreement of 1954, and the Geneva Summit of Soviet and western leaders in 1955, the first since Potsdam in 1945, gave way to the twin crises of 1956, the Anglo-French-Israeli invasion of Egypt and the Soviet invasion of Hungary. A second pursuit of negotiation, epitomised in Khrushchev's visit to the USA in 1959, and the 'Camp David Spirit' developed between himself and Eisenhower, was overtaken by the breakup of the Paris Summit in 1960, the Berlin and Laos Crises of 1961, and the Cuba Missile Crisis of 1962. The latter occasioned the gravest threat to world peace since 1945. This period of crisis was quickly followed by a third round of negotiations, which led to the Nuclear Test Ban Treaty of July 1963, to the establishment of a 'Hot Line' between Moscow and Washington, and to a series of Summits lasting up to 1967.

Events to which the great powers felt compelled to respond again halted this process of negotiation. In 1965 US forces went into Vietnam and the Dominican Republic, and in 1967 the Third Arab-Israeli War provoked renewed tensions between the two sides because of their involvement with the conflicting parties. East-west relations were already bad when in 1968 Warsaw Pact forces invaded Czechoslovakia. Only in 1969, with the advent of the Nixon Administration to office in Washington, did Phase III, that of consistent negotiation or Detente, properly begin.

The period of Detente, lasting for a decade until 1979, was one of relatively concerted pursuit on both sides of a negotiated framework on major issues of dispute between them. It was the period of the SALT-I Agreement in 1972, the 35-Nation Helsinki Conference on Europe in 1975, of rising east-west trade and of a belief that Soviet-US rivalry did

---

[3] This period of Oscillatory Antagonism combined elements of Cold War with those of Detente. Thus it was not a period of static confrontation, as in the First and Second Cold Wars, or of sustained negotiation, as during Detente.

not need to be the major axis of world affairs. The Paris Accords of 1973, between the USA and North Vietnam, enabled America to withdraw its forces from Indo-China and so to resolve the most pressing issue on its foreign policy agenda. Overall, the relaxation of tensions between the two camps went together with a loosening of the links between the east-west and other conflicts. There were, certainly, major crises in this period—the 1973 Arab-Israeli war, the Angola crisis of 1975—but these did not prejudice negotiation in the manner characteristic of Phase II. It was only the accumulation of tensions later in the decade which finally ended Detente and ushered in the Second Cold War.

Defining a Cold War

At this point, it can be asked what exactly a 'Cold War' is in the sense in which this term is used to describe the 1946-1953 period and that which began in 1979.[4] The term 'Cold' is used in a double, contradictory, sense: (a) to mean that relations between east and west are cold, frozen, paralysed, frosted and so forth, i.e. are not warm; and (b) to mean that although relations are bad and warlike, they are to some extent restrained and have not reached the point of 'hot' war. This double significance is clear from what the two contraries are. In the first sense, the opposite of Cold War is Thaw. In the second it is all out or Hot War, pure and simple. Although formally, it is the second sense which is predominant, i.e. a state of bad relations short of hot war, Cold War has historically been evoked more in the first sense, to denote a coldness bordering on war and to mark a deterioration from periods of greater warmth, such as the Alliance of the early 1940s and the Detente of the early 1970s. Hence Cold Wars are periods when war is regarded as being more, not less, likely than in the preceding period. Whilst nuclear weapons may stay the hands of politicians and generals and prevent a hot war, they invest the period of confrontation with greater dangers. Thus they make the period of Cold War all the riskier and more menacing. And this proximity to war is the more evident because Cold Wars between the major powers are often accompanied by bloody hot wars between their respective allies in the third world.

---

4. The *Oxford English Dictionary* defines cold war as 'a state of hostility consisting in threats, obstruction, propaganda, etc. without physical violence'.

Six characteristics above all marked the First Cold War and provide the historical elements of what constitute modern Cold Wars.

1. The feature most evident to the inhabitants of both blocs was that there was a military buildup with special emphasis upon nuclear weapons, the purpose of such buildups being to prevent advances by the other side along certain publicly identified fronts—in the earlier case Europe. During Cold War I the USA deployed nuclear weapons in Europe, and the Russians for the first time acquired them.

2. The First Cold War was accompanied by a particularly intense propaganda campaign between the two camps, in which each side sought maximally to denigrate the other. The west sought to berate the USSR for its 'totalitarian' qualities, and to establish a homology between the natures of Soviet society and Nazi Germany on the grounds that both were repressive and warlike. The Russians sustained their critique of the exploitation inherent in capitalism and accompanied this by stressing the warmongering character of imperialism, both vis-à-vis the USSR itself and in the colonial world, where a considerable number of conflicts were raging. This ideological conflict often rested upon a suppression of accurate or balanced information about the opposite camp.

3. There were no successful negotiations between the USA and USSR on issues of mutual concern, whether bilateral, in Europe or in the rest of the world. Polemics and mutual denunciation replaced compromise and negotiated agreement. The inability to find common ground on major issues was marked by tense confrontation along an 'Iron Curtain' in Europe and by armed conflict in the Far East.

4. The conflict between capitalism and communism found expression in third world revolutionary situations, in which the west sought to reverse and contain local movements that were presented as instruments of Soviet policy. This took place in Korea and Vietnam, Malaya and the Philippines.

5. There was a tightening of controls within the capitalist and communist camps, a construction of military blocs, a repression of those suspected of sympathies for the other side (persecution of Titoists in eastern Europe, McCarthyism in the USA).

6. While conflict, even confrontation, between east and west has con-

tinued throughout the postwar period, as have conflicts within the two blocs and between metropolitan and third world countries, in the periods of Cold War greater emphasis was placed upon mobilising for the east-west confrontation than at other times. This does not just mean that the stress was upon such confrontation rather than upon negotiation: it meant above all that all other conflicts were viewed in the context of this overriding one and were subordinated to it. The stress was upon the dominance, and if possible exclusivity, of the east-west confrontation.

This analysis of Cold War I rests upon a certain restriction of the term that is not always accepted. Historians do tend to treat the First Cold War as a self-evident period ending at some point in the 1950s, but the term Cold War is now often used to denote the very process of east-west conflict itself, or the situation of arms buildup without outright wars.[5] In these latter usages, the term is co-extensive with the whole postwar period, the phases of which are all regarded as part of the Cold War. However, although the east-west conflict and the nuclear arms race are indeed co-extensive with the period since 1945, they are also distinct from each other and both can be distinguished from the Cold War in its original, historically specific sense. This refers to a particular period of globalised conflict, namely one in which the emphasis is upon military and strategic confrontation and in which negotiation is minimal or non-existent.

The conflict between east and west, i.e. communism and capitalism, has been a feature of world politics since 1917 and has been globalised, i.e. geographically and politically dominant, since 1945; but it has also known periods of greater or lesser intensity. It is this fluctuation that explains the phases of postwar history and which suggests a use of the term 'Cold War' to denote a *particular* phase of globalised social conflict, one intermediate between the two extremes of allout or 'hot' war, and of maximised accommodation. Those, on either left or right, who assert that there has been Cold War continuously since 1945 or even 1917 are right in arguing that international social conflict has been continuous;

[5.] As in, for example, E.P. Thompson's writings in *Exterminism and Cold War* and *Beyond the Cold War* and André Fontaine, *History of the Cold War*, New York 1969. I am not arguing that the equation of the term cold war with the east-west conflict cannot be justified, only that, if it is used in this extended sense, then some other means of identifying the periods of greater tension has to be devised.

but they tend to understate the degree of *fluctuation* involved in this process. Hence they undervalue the specific nature of the more intense conflicts experienced in the late 1940s and early 1980s. In this restricted sense, Cold War is not an inevitable concomitant of globalised social conflict, whilst the latter conflict is an inevitable consequence of the existence of two rival social systems.

Characteristics of Detente

Defined in this manner, it becomes easier to identify the peculiarities of those periods that have come between the two Cold Wars, that of Oscillatory Antagonism and that of Detente. If the latter marks the clearest contrast, the former is an ambiguous period containing elements and phases of Detente followed by reversion to the characteristics of the Cold War. The six features of Detente contrast with those already seen as characterising Cold War.

Detente was marked by a retreat from the allout arms race, by a rhetoric of peace and a pursuit of agreed levels of armament. While Detente was not accompanied, on either side, by substantial disarmament, i.e. by a net reduction of weapons levels, some limitation of the arms race, i.e. arms control, was a prominent aim and achievement in the Detente period. During Detente, there was greater tolerance of the other social order, more interest in and more accurate information about its character. Indeed, there was sometimes a tendency for analysts on one or other side to minimise the failings of the other side even when these were well known in both camps, and to downplay the degree of conflict between the two systems. Detente involved agreements on arms, on third world conflicts, on Europe. There were summits, long-running conferences and visits of heads of state, all in contrast to the paralysis of the Cold War.

Detente was marked by the desire of the west to extricate itself from third world confrontations and by so doing to draw the line in the face of the revolutionary forces it had been combatting. It was preceded by some loosening of political controls in the eastern bloc—by the Thaw internally in 1954-5 in Russia—and it led to looser emigration controls in the 1970s. At the same time it reflected a lessening of anti-communist sentiment in the capitalist countries, and the growth of social movements contesting various dimensions of established order. Detente was marked by the attempt to separate or disentangle the different international tensions which are in periods of Cold War bound together by the conflict of east and west. All the world's problems were not seen as part of a single overriding antagonism, as they tend to be during Cold Wars.

Cold War II

Cold War II developed, like its predecessor Cold War I, from the breakdown of relations between the major capitalist states and the USSR that were to some degree more co-operative. On the basis of its first four years, 1979–1982, it can be seen how it partook, with some significant variations, of the characteristics that marked off Cold War I as a distinct period of postwar history.

The most obvious index of Cold War is a greater sense of the danger of war. Cold War II involved an increased emphasis by both sides upon the likelihood of war and on the need for military preparations against possible attacks from the enemy. The rise of the peace movement certainly served to draw greater attention to this issue, and it, for the first time, achieved a significant audience inside the USA. But the development of resistance to nuclear weapons policies in the west from 1979 onwards was not only a response to the sustained accumulation of weapons over the past two decades. It was also a reaction to the specific increases in military expenditure and changes in weapons deployment associated with the late 1970s, i.e. to a military buildup that got under way at the start of Cold War II.

Western governments had, since 1978, been calling for a new military capacity, stressing the need to expand military expenditure and highlighting the legitimacy of the use of force in international relations. Carter pledged himself in 1978 to a 3 per cent real increase in US military spending; the Republican Party Manifesto of 1980 committed itself to restoring US military superiority. Speaking to cadets at the US military academy of West Point in 1981, on the dangers of the 'Treaty Trap', Reagan promised to expand America's military strength: 'No nation that placed its faith in parchment or paper while at the same time it gave up its protective hardware ever lasted long enough to write many pages in history,' he said. Reagan's first Secretary of State, Alexander Haig, stated on many occasions during the first months after coming into office that the Administration's priority was, in his phrase, 'the restoration of

US economic and military strength'. He told one audience that some things were more valuable than peace. This emphasis upon the need for a new military capacity vis-à-vis the USSR went together with greater belligerency in third world policies—with increased preparations for intervention there, with warnings about a renewed US willingness to intervene in key states (e.g. Saudi Arabia) and with threats of force against such targets as Libya, Cuba and Nicaragua.[6] The increased level of US military readiness, imitated to a greater or lesser degree by its European allies, was the most evident practical symbol of the changes in the west attendant upon the Second Cold War.

There was not a commensurate hardening of policy on the Soviet side. Indeed western politicians justified their shift as a response to a continuous Soviet buildup over the 1970s. But force came to play a more prominent part in Soviet foreign policy, most notably in the Soviet intervention in Afghanistan of December 1979, the first time Soviet troops were used in combat outside the Soviet sphere of influence since 1945. The Soviet Union attained a level of military preparedness never seen before and had introduced new missiles into the European theatre, the SS-20s. In response to the declarations of the Reagan Administration Soviet leaders increasingly stressed that they were prepared to match western military innovations and, if necessary, to fight to defend their interests when attacked. Whilst not overtly bellicist in tone, as US statements often were, Soviet foreign policy statements certainly became distinctly more martial with the onset of the Second Cold War.[7] Soviet

---

6. An excellent account of new US conceptions of international relations which stress the use of force is given by Diana Johnstone in 'Une Nouvelle Stratégie Imperiale', *Le Monde Diplomatique*, December 1980. Johnstone stresses the importance of the thought of George Liska, long a conservative critic of detente. In his *Quest for Equilibrium* published in 1977 Liska calls for 'a not inherently illiberal, but confidently conserving, corrective' to recent US policies. This would involve selective uses of force in the third world. Despite the complexity of the sentence, the thought is clear: 'An occasional employment of force and demonstration of resolve in the peripheries will help more than can any feasible central-systemic military buildup, compensating for systemic inaction, to reduce to a practically irrelevant minimum the likelihood of major conflict with the Soviet Union' (p. 216). The evolution of US thinking on the use of force in the third world is documented in Michael Klare, *Beyond the 'Vietnam Syndrome'*, Institute for Policy Studies, Washington DC 1981.

7. In a book published in early 1982, *Always Ready to Defend the Fatherland*, Soviet chief of staff Nikolai Ogarkov stressed the need for the whole nation to mobilise its resources in readiness for war. This was more necessary than ever before, he wrote,

officials also, on occasion, adopted a hectoring and minatory tone in addressing public opinion in countries that were seen as particularly facilitating the US buildup—Japan and West Germany.

Cold War II was also accompanied by new waves of that ideological contestation so characteristic of the earlier period. In the west, this involved emphasis upon such questions as the weakness of the Soviet economy, the plight of dissidents, the rate of Soviet arms expenditure and production, and the global implications of Soviet foreign policy. These are all serious issues meriting discussion; but the manner in which they were conventionally discussed was of a highly speculative and polemical kind, one that often bore little relationship to the truth or to historical proportion. With the advent of the Reagan Administration the USSR was repeatedly accused of backing 'international terrorism', and even of attempting to assassinate the Pope. Reagan's remark that the Russians 'are prepared to lie, cheat and steal' to further their goal epitomised this mood.[8] Very few commentators associated with the Reagan Administration appeared to know much about Soviet society, or to seek to understand the motivations of Russia's leaders or population.[9] What is striking is that many of the problems identified in this propaganda had, if anything, been alleviated in the 1970s. They could not justify the *intensified*

---

because of the need for quick mobilisation and transition to a war-footing in the event of war *(International Herald Tribune*, 12 March 1982). Leonid Brezhnev's last speech before his death in November 1982 was a call to the Soviet armed forces to increase their vigilance.

[8.] *The Economist*, 3 May 1981. Many of the attempts to prove Soviet involvement with 'terrorism', as in El Salvador, were unsubstantiated; others involved the use of the term 'terrorism' to designate nationalist movements aided by the USSR, such as the PLO or SWAPO, which had on occasion used terror against civilians, but which had legitimate national aims.

[9.] Thus the former US Ambassador to Moscow George Kennan speaking in the language of establishment admonition: 'This endless series of distortions and oversimplifications; this systematic dehumanization of the leadership of another great country; this routine exaggeration of Moscow's military capabilities and of the supposed iniquity of Soviet intentions; this monotonous misrepresentation of the nature and the attitudes of another great people—and a long-suffering people at that, sorely tried by the vicissitudes of this past century. . . these, believe me, are not the marks of the maturity and discrimination one expects from the diplomacy of a great power; they are the marks of an intellectual primitivism and naivete unpardonable in a great government' *New York Review of Books* 21 January 1982.

vilification to which the USSR was subjected in the climate of the Second Cold War.[10]

The Soviet side did, for different reasons, show less of a change in tone. One factor was that in the Detente period, Soviet writers were less accommodating to the capitalist viewpoint than many western writers were to the USSR, and the switch back to a more polemical tone involved less drastic changes. Another factor is that greater control of the press means that if Soviet writers reveal less of the truth about their opponents, they also retail less untruth and abuse. But the US Administration did not continue to enjoy the favour shown to it in the period of Nixon and Ford, and the USA was now held responsible for a wide range of militaristic initiatives towards the USSR. Whereas US foreign policy was treated more indulgently in the past, it was now charged with counter-revolutionary activities in Afghanistan, Cambodia, Central America and Poland in a replay of the polemics characteristic of the earlier Cold War.

Cold War II was accompanied by a dramatic cooling in bilateral relations between east and west, and in particular in negotiations between the USSR and the USA. There was certainly a contrast with the First Cold War, when no talks at all took place and discussions on arms control were completely blocked. In 1982, three years into the Second Cold War, east-west talks were taking place in Geneva, on intermediate-range

---

[10.] One indication of this mood is the Cold War novel, that sets out to depict the USSR in unremittingly hostile terms and to stress the east-west conflict. Two prime functions of Cold War novels, supportive as they are of a body of non-fiction work, are to discredit critics of western foreign policy as agents of the KGB, and to make the prospect of nuclear war less frightening. A suitably degenerate instance of the first was *The Spike*, by Robert Moss and Arnaud de Borchgrave (London 1980), a spy story in which opponents of the Vietnam war and of US militarism are pictured as Soviet collaborators. The prime example of the second is *The Third World War* (London 1978) by General Sir John Hackett, a former commander of the British Army of the Rhine. Hackett alleges that his is but an attempt to tell a moral story, a cautionary tale for the nuclear age, but his novel is a flamboyant encomium to the possibilities of a limited and, for the west, victorious nuclear exchange. Hackett's theses are essentially three: (1) that the USSR poses as great a threat to the west as did Nazi Germany; (2) that the ability of the west to wage this war rests upon a strengthening of political will and traditional social values as well as upon military preparedness; (3) that nuclear war is winnable—the book ends with the incineration of Minsk and Birmingham after a limited nuclear exchange that provokes the revolt of Poland and the non-Russian areas of the USSR. The decision to use fiction for ideological ends may in some measure reflect conservative exasperation with what were seen as the ravages, in the 1960s and early 1970s, of pacifist literature. Thus Norman Podhoretz complains, in his *The Present Danger*, New York 1980, pp. 62-3, of the 'Vietnamisation', i.e. discrediting, of World War II by two popular novels of the 1960s, Joseph Heller's *Catch-22* and Kurt Vonnegut's *Slaughterhouse Five*.

nuclear weapons and on strategic arms reductions, in Madrid, at the
Conference on Security and Co-operation in Europe, a sequel to the
Helsinki Agreement of 1975, and in Vienna, on Mutual and Balanced
Forced Reductions in Europe. The 'Hot Line' remained in place and data
on space exploration were being exchanged. But on the western side the
political intent of such talks seemed to be as much to reduce criticism
and force concessions on the USSR as it was to seek compromise; and,
whatever the outcome of these talks, the fact remained that there was
from the mid-1970s onwards, i.e. before the onset of Cold War II proper,
a standstill in east-west negotiation. SALT-II did not follow on from SALT-I
signed back in 1972. The CSCE and MBFR discussions appeared to be going
nowhere and were used primarily as occasions to pillory the other side.
In strategic matters a similar lack of agreement was evident—on such
issues as the Arab-Israeli question, security in the Persian Gulf, the
Horn of Africa, Afghanistan and the Indian Ocean. Economic ties between east and west were maintained and there was not a complete shut-
ting off of the financial and commercial bonds built up in the 1970s; but
as far as the USA was concerned, trade itself became an area of conflict. A
series of boycotts and cancellations of agreements in the period from
1979 onwards served to subordinate economic links to the dictates of
Cold War.

Overall, the flow of meetings and talks during Cold War II served to
mask the similarity with Cold War I whereas the underlying reality of
bilateral impasse served to confirm it. Cold War I involved a standoff in
Europe, with the exception of Greece, but major conflicts in the Far East.
Cold War II has not led to any direct conflict in Europe either, but during
the 1970s there were massive social upheavals in all three continents of
the third world and these helped both to cause and to sustain Cold War
II. As will be discussed later in Chapter Four, one of the main reasons for
Cold War II was the wave of third world revolutions which from 1974
onwards engulfed the South, from Saigon to Managua, and thereby provoked deep anxiety in the advanced capitalist states. The response of the
USA and its allies was to blame these developments on the USSR, and to in-
stigate counter-attacks in Central America, Western Sahara, the Persian
Gulf, Afghanistan and Cambodia.[11] None of these third world crises

---

[11.] Thus Ronald Reagan: 'Let's not delude ourselves. The Soviet Union underlies all the
unrest that is going on. If they weren't engaged in this game of dominoes, there wouldn't
be any hot spots in the world', as quoted in *New York* magazine, 9 March 1981.

equalled the high point of Cold War I—the Chinese Revolution of 1949—in scale, but once again the massive but paralysed tensions of Europe, the 'Central Front' of NATO designation, were displaced onto third world theatres where no such paralysis was to be found.

The USA and the USSR sought to accompany the heightened level of confrontation with each other by greater controls on dissent within their own ranks, both within their own societies and within their own alliance systems. Within western society the previous two decades witnessed a substantial erosion of traditional ideological and social systems of domination—along lines of class, race, sex and age. The Second Cold War was linked to a wide-ranging conservative rollback in most spheres of social policy, both in the USA and Europe. In economic matters this took the form of monetarist macroeconomic policies and the devastations of supply-siders. In social policy, this rollback involved the reversal through fund-cutting and legislation of the gains made by trades union organisations and by movements of women, gays and blacks during the 1970s. A combination of direct confrontation and unemployment was also used to undermine trades unions.[12] The reassertion of internal unity and hegemony was, however, but a concomitant of the re-establishment of a new international unity, with in this case the reassertion by Washington of US hegemony as forcefully as circumstances allowed. This reinforcement of the US position was most evident in military matters—pressure on allies for expenditure increases, stationing of Cruise and Pershing-II missiles in Europe, demands for support for US initiatives in the third world. But it was also extended to encompass inter-capitalist economic policy, aid and trade policies towards the third world, and negotiating postures towards the USSR.[13] In both internal and inter-

---

[12.] Hackett, pp. 45-8, looks forward to a conservative shift in British public life—away from trade union power and the welfare state, towards law and order, discipline and increased military expenditure, i.e. the Thatcherite programme implemented a year after the first edition of his book came out. The ideological instruments of rollback were in place long before Cold War II began. In the USA this involved not only the reassertion of 'traditional' values but the trumpeting of much neo-conservative thought, particularly on economic individualism. Typical of the latter is the best-selling *Wealth and Poverty* by George Gilder, New York 1981, which begins: 'The most important event in the recent history of ideas is the demise of the socialist dream.' Gilder writes: 'The only dependable route from poverty is always work, family and faith.' See also below Chapter Five.

[13.] For an illustrative discussion of these issues, see *Western Security: What has changed? What should be done?* by Karl Kaiser, Winston Lord, Thierry de Montbrial, David Watt, Royal Institute of International Affairs, London 1981. Whilst stressing the need for

national issues, the postulation of an external threat was combined with alarm about the erosion of pre-existing values to foster mobilisation for a new Cold War.

In the USSR the party leadership had, from the early 1960s onwards, brought about a steady reduction in arbitrary and terroristic acts by the state security forces. Only in one area, the use of psychiatric clinics to intern political dissenters, was there a subsequent net deterioration. But the Kremlin accompanied this with an erratic policy towards those outspokenly critical of the system. This suppression of the overtly critical began in the early 1970s and by the late 1970s the dissident movement had to a large extent been driven underground; a few publicised trials had been used both to intimidate critics within the USSR and to demonstrate to their western supporters that the Soviet system was not going to tolerate their interference. The onset of Cold War II nevertheless led to an increase in hostility to internal opposition as contacts between east and west lessened. Jewish emigration was cut by 95 per cent between 1980 and 1982; direct telephone links to western Europe were severed in the latter year, and the mailing of books abroad was impeded. This went together with an attempt to stimulate greater patriotic sentiment in the USSR and with an emphasis on the need to educate the young in the necessities of military discipline. A small independent peace group set up in June 1982 was harassed. In the broader context of eastern Europe, special attention was given by the CPSU leaders to Poland, where opposition was greatest, and in December 1981 martial law was declared there by the Polish army in order to contain and reverse the movement that had grown up around Solidarity. Polemics against 'pluralism', even under socialism, became common. While there was no return in Moscow during Cold War II to the levels of control associated with the Stalin period, involving show trials and political executions, repression of dissent in both the USSR and eastern Europe was notably greater than during earlier periods of tolerance.

Cold War II involved a concerted and sustained attempt by the USA to subordinate the various dimensions of its foreign policy, and that of its allies, to confrontation with the USSR. The image of a 'Soviet Threat' was used not merely to elicit increased vigilance against the Soviet Union,

---

greater understanding on both sides of the Atlantic, this diagnosis, reproducing the conventional wisdom of foreign policy establishments, advocates in practice a strengthening of unity beneath the American banner.

but also to create a strategic framework within which other issues should be seen and given their due proportion and to mobilise the European allies and Japan for economic pressure on the USSR. The emphasis was on facing up to the USSR, rather than on seeking compromise, and on giving priority to this, rather than on the relative distinctness of the different issues dividing the states of the world.

It is relevant to recall how different this was from the dominant tone of western political discourse in the earlier part of the 1970s. Then the Soviet Union was not seen as the *radix malorum,* the root of all international evil, that it was later to become. A revival of the Cold War was no more foreseen than the resurgence of politicised religion, a world-wide recession, or the combative regionalism of western Europe. Speaking in 1974, Secretary of State Kissinger was able to say: 'the biggest problem American foreign policy confronts right now is not how to regulate competition with its enemies . . . but how to bring our friends to a realisation there are greater common interests than simple self-assertiveness.'[14] In a major foreign policy speech at Notre Dame University in 1977 President Carter called on America to 'get away from the unhealthy obsession' with the USSR that had marked previous Administrations. For a while Carter espoused the viewpoint associated with the Trilateral Commission which placed priority on the need to restructure relations between capitalist states rather than on the bipolar US-Soviet conflict.

This disaggregation of the problems of foreign policy was accompanied by a belief that the USA and the USSR could find common ground on the major issues of the day. Thus Kissinger sought to involve the Soviet Union in agreements that would encourage it to reduce its arms production and restrain itself in the third world. Typical of this period was the view of the noted foreign affairs specialist Alistair Buchan, writing in 1973: 'The Soviet Union and the United States will develop a series of specific understandings to keep their strategic relationship stable and to attempt to restrain conflict in areas where they cannot escape commitment, notably Europe and the Middle East.'[15] Similarly, the Washington

---

[14.] As quoted in Mary Kaldor, *The Disintegrating West*, London 1978, p. 25.

[15.] Alistair Buchan, *Change Without War*, London 1974, p. 99. A comparable shift was noticeable in academic theorising on international relations, with the move away from the 'realist' school dominant until the 1960s, which emphasised great power relations, towards 'pluralist' and 'globalist' theories which stressed international interdependence and the possibility of non-military solutions.

correspondent of the *Sunday Times*, Henry Brandon wrote of the USA and USSR as 'confined by a mutual vulnerability of which they have become well aware' and which would ensure that the 1970s would see a lessening of international tensions.[16] This expectation was widely held at the time. Hence, if Detente involved the twin beliefs of a multipolar world and the possibility of compromise with the USSR on the basis of shared interest, in Cold Wars I and II western leaders have laid stress upon the bipolar and antagonistic character of world politics and on the need to marshal all the forces at the west's disposal for a confrontation with the opposite camp.

The First and Second Cold Wars: A Comparison

Despite these similarities, there are arguments which deny that the post-1979 period can legitimately be termed a Cold War. One reason offered for rejecting the comparison is that if the First Cold War had a strong ideological motivation, this cannot be claimed of the Second Cold War, when both camps have been acting much more according to the logic of major powers. The historian Arno Mayer has written: 'The opposing ideological projects that once fired the Soviet-American competition in international politics are exhausted or bankrupt. In that sense, the cold war is over. Now the USSR and the United States are locked into a conventional struggle for power centered in the Third World.'[17] A second argument points to the durability of the agreements negotiated between both sides: SALT-I and even SALT-II were respected, the European talks continued, the Hot Line remained in existence; trade continued to flow; in contrast to the total suspicion and lack of communication of the late 1940s, a system of assumptions about crisis management and arms negotiations had been permanently established. A further reason for questioning the comparison concerns internal repression: if Cold War is accompanied by the control of internal dissent, then however much such control was increased on both sides in the period after 1979, this increase was not at all comparable to that which accompanied Cold War I. There were no executions of people accused of being Titoists in the east, no Red Scare or comparable witch-hunts against the left in the west.

---

16. Henry Brandon, *The Retreat of American Power*, London 1973, p. 345.
17. Arno Mayer, 'The Cold War Is Over', *Democracy* , vol.2, no 1, January 1982, p. 32.

These three counter-arguments can, however, be seen as identifying certain differences between Cold War I and Cold War II, rather than as reasons for rejecting the comparison altogether, for, despite the differences between the two, the deterioration in east-west relations along the dimensions identified remained substantial. There certainly was a variation in the ideological appearance of this Second Cold War, even though the actual ending of political conflict between the two camps was not as great as Arno Mayer implies. This ideological originality is reflected in the political alignments that were created: if the First Cold War was clearly anti-communist, this Second Cold War was more specifically directed against the USSR. On the international level, the world's largest post-revolutionary state, China, aligned itself for the first part of Cold War II with the forces opposed to the USSR. Within the advanced capitalist states, there was less anti-communist hysteria from governments and parties of the right than in the earlier Cold War: on the other hand, much of the left adopted positions that are themselves as opposed to the USSR as those of the right. An eloquent index of this changed political configuration was the kind of support being given by metropolitan forces to third world guerrillas: much of the European and American left supported the Afghan mojahidin, ferociously conservative tribal rebels hostile to socialism, democracy, women's emancipation and liberalism of any kind, while the CIA, under the guise of refugee aid, was stimulating the resistance of the murderous Khmer Rouge, the CIA's former foe, from neighbouring Thailand.

The persistence of negotiations and of a shared framework for crisis management certainly marks Cold War II off from its predecessor, but this may reflect less the degree of confrontation than the shift in the international balance of forces that produced this change. The Second Cold War differed from the First precisely in the new correlation of strategic forces it represented. In Cold War I the USA had overwhelming military superiority over the USSR, and comparable economic superiority over its capitalist allies. The USSR was too weak to negotiate; the USA too strong to need to. Whilst it has not wholly lost superiority in either field, these margins of US dominance were radically reduced in the intervening period. This certainly accounts in part for the vigour with which Washington prosecuted the Second Cold War; but it also explains the greater restraint it was obliged to show, and in particular the willingness to engage in negotiations on arms control demonstrated by both the USSR and the USA. It remained to be seen how far discussions on European and strategic nuclear forces would produce results; but the very fact that both sides consented to such talks and affected at least in public to prosecute them seriously was in marked contrast to the seven years of the First Cold War (1946–1953) when no substantive east-west negotiations at all took place. This difference reflects the greater strength of the Soviet Union, which was now willing to talk, and the reduced confidence of the USA, which now had to talk, as well as the pressure upon the latter by its NATO allies. It does not invalidate the fact that a Second Cold War began in the late 1970s.

The argument that the post-1979 period is not a Cold War because the level of internal repression has been much lower again underlines a difference, rather than establishes the invalidity of comparison. For although accompanied by less intense suppression of opponents in east and west, Cold War II certainly involved a widespread ideological counter-offensive against dissenting forces on both sides. This led, in the west, to a reassertion of what are said to be traditional 'Judaeo-Christian' values, and a fostering of that suspicion of criticism which is so important in intimidating and disconcerting opponents at home.

In enumerating the differences between Cold Wars I and II, there is, however, a much more important distinction which serves not to annul the similarity but to highlight the force of Cold War II: this is the changed role played within it of both the third world and Europe. The First Cold War was concentrated initially on Europe—on the German question and on conflicts over Poland, Greece, and the communist parties of western Europe. It was later extended by the crises of the Far East—the Chinese, Korean and Vietnamese revolutions, and the guerrilla movements in the Philippines and Malaya. Yet even with the prominence of the Far East, Europe remained a theatre of dispute.

The onset of the Second Cold War owed little to conflict in Europe. The Berlin issue was dormant while Cold War I began in Europe and then shifted to the Far East. The events that precipitated Cold War II lay in the third world, in, for example, the Arc of Crisis, the region running from Afghanistan, through Iran and the Arab world, to the Horn of Africa. Yet Europe re-entered the Cold War in another manner. In western Europe the imposition of new strategic policies by NATO generated opposition that turned these countries into a political battleground of immense significance. This coincided with the emergence of mass opposition to communist party rule in Poland. Albeit in a quite different way, Europe therefore remained a theatre of the Cold War, not because military conflict between east and west was an imminent possibility, but because of the increasing rejection of strategic hegemonies by political movements in both camps—by the peace movement in the west, and by the opposition movement in Poland in the east.

So far, the discussion has focussed on three reasons why it might be thought that Cold War II was less intense than Cold War I, and may not merit application of the term 'Cold War'. These reasons for denying the analogy were the decreased ideological motivation of the two sides, the durability of agreements between them, and the lower level of repression in both camps. But there are other differences between the two Cold Wars which suggest that, if anything, Cold War II was more serious than Cold War I. The first such difference is that Cold War II coincided with a general economic recession in the capitalist world, as well as with a slowing down of growth rates in much of the Soviet bloc as well. It is not necessary to posit any one-to-one connection between these two processes, Cold War and recession, to realise that in a situation of economic difficulty, which threatens the authority of governments and disrupts the lives of many millions of people, the danger of war increases. Weak government, domestic pressure, and a diffuse loss of confidence can all combine to render leaderships less cautious than would be the case in times of prosperity. If this is true for the developed countries, it is even more so for the third world, where mass hunger and the violence of the recession have important disruptive political effects. Political leaders can see war as a distraction from domestic issues; religious and national hatreds increase; the temptations of destroying an enemy and seizing the opponent's economic resources become greater. Cold War I had no such additional destabilising component.

In the most important of all perspectives, that of the risks involved, the two Cold Wars are also incomparable because Cold War II was far graver: a full exchange of destructive potential between the USA and the USSR during Cold War I would have caused enormous damage to both Russia and the rest of Europe. But both the USSR and USA could have survived as functioning societies and economies. The rest of the world would have suffered by the extension of the combat through conventional war and from nuclear fallout, but would probably have avoided nuclear bombardment. A full exchange of weaponry in Cold War II could destroy humanity as we know it: there are enough nuclear weapons now accumulated to destroy life on the planet twenty times over. The military threat contained within the Second Cold War therefore makes it a far more ominous confrontation than was Cold War I.

Whatever their implications, these distinctive features of the Second Cold War should not, occlude those respects in which it bore similarity to its predecessor, or mask the fact that identifiable historical forces were at the origin of both Cold Wars. Both periods of heightened east-west tension were produced not by impersonal and immanent forces, nor by the mere facts of military accumulation, but by the evolution of that globalised social conflict accentuated by the other constituent elements of world politics. Cold War II reflected the desire of both blocs to retain what they had acquired in the earlier periods of reduced antagonism, together with their determination to deploy the fear of the other as a composite ideological device for guaranteeing unity at home. Above all, it reflected the continued force of long-range goals that were irreconcilable with each other and which determined the strategic plans of both camps. Soviet actions in the 1970s reflected priorities and plans established in the previous decade, particularly in the early 1960s, as well as the outlook of a generation of leaders whose formative period was the 1930s and 1940s. On the US side, just as the First Cold War was a reflection of wartime planning by committees within the Roosevelt Administration, so the promotion of the Second Cold War has been shaped by discussions and decisions among strategic planners and foreign policy advisers that have been under way in Washington and New York since the early 1970s or before. The Second Cold War was neither an accident, nor the product of some neat conspiracy: it reflected conscious, long-term decisions taken by people in power with limited control over world events. Theirs was a response to a changing world situation which provided new challenges to their system of domination and new opportunities for prosecuting the globalised conflict with the opposing bloc. The aim of the chapters which follow is to identify the factors underlying and aggravating this conflict and, more precisely, those changes in the world situation and the threats and opportunities involved which served to occasion the emergence of the Second Cold War at the end of the 1970s.

2.
Constituent Elements
of World Politics

It might, at first sight, appear fruitless to search for underlying factors which shape the course of international relations: a system involving over one hundred and sixty states, many non-governmental forces, and several levels of interaction, allows of no simple explanation. But if it is intellectually implausible to reduce world politics to being the expression of some single cause, a Hegelian essence or a *primum mobile*, it may be less outrageous to suggest that there are certain theoretical approaches which can, without undue simplification, provide coherent explanations of recent world history by highlighting deep trends within it. Rather than proferring one single cause of the current Cold War, analysis of such theories suggests that it can be explained by reference to a set of constituent elements which, in their interaction, profoundly shape world affairs.

Theories of Cold War

It is remarkable how many of those who practise or comment upon international politics do, in fact, make assumptions about what its constituent elements are. These assumptions may be presented explicitly, and justified by reference to recent events, history or what is said to be common sense. They may be implicit, but known to both exponent and audience. At the risk of some condensation of the argument, it is possible to identify at least eight major schools of thought, each of which purports to offer an explanation of contemporary world politics and hence of why Cold War II began.

1. *Soviet threat theorists* place the blame for the current world crisis on the policies of the USSR. It is, they argue, Soviet expansionism and ag-

gressiveness which underlie the major problems of the contemporary world, and which have ruined Detente. Whether such a Soviet orientation is due to the workings of Marxist-Leninist theory or to more embedded features of Russian society that predate 1917 is of secondary importance: the fact of Soviet actions being primarily responsible for the crisis of world politics is said to be evident whichever explanation is accepted.

2. *US Imperialism theorists* produce what is, in some respects, a mirror image of the Soviet threat account. Again, responsibility is ascribed to the actions of one major state, and the actions of the other innocent one are not seen as having contributed to the deadlock. US imperialism theorists locate the aggressiveness and belligerence of the west in the workings of a social system, capitalism, which they argue requires confrontation and military production for its survival.[1]

3. The *super-power theorists* place the blame on the two major powers together, arguing that the USA and the USSR have conjointly subordinated the world to their common interests and to their remaining differences.[2] Popularised by China in the 1960s, the 'superpower' theory identifies

---

[1.] Throughout this essay the terms 'capitalism' and 'communism' will be used to denote the social systems prevailing in, respectively, the USA and USSR and in their corresponding alliance systems. The use of the term 'communism' is not intended to suggest that the Soviet Union has attained what Marx or Lenin have described as the communist organisation of society. It is rather used as a means of designating a form of society that is not capitalist because of collective ownership, which has, whatever its precise character, a different form of organisation from that prevailing in western Europe and the USA and where communism is a proclaimed goal.

[2.] The term 'superpower' was orginally used in the 1940s, and has since become common in both political and analytic discussion. It is not, however, used in this essay. It is true to say that the USSR and USA are 'super' in the sense that they possess the means of 'super'-destruction. They are also the two most influential states in the world. But the term 'superpower' in many of its usages has other, somewhat misleading, connotations. First, it exaggerates the extent to which either state is able to influence other states, i.e. exert power in a multi-state world. The term encourages the belief that world events are the result of the actions of one or other protagonist, usually the one to which the speaker is opposed. Secondly, the term implies that the two major states have a common interest as against all the other states of the world, a view that obscures the alliance systems and social systems clustered around each. Thirdly, it implies an equivalence in the main dimensions of political and economic power: politically, as argued here, the two operate, at home and abroad, according to different logics; economically they are not comparable.

the two major powers as, in Peking's phrase 'colluding and contending' to dominate the world. This explanation has won particular support amongst those who see themselves as building a third alternative in world politics, be they European conservatives, anti-Soviet Marxists, or third world nationalists. It has the attraction of avoiding identification with one or other of the major blocs and of suggesting that, were the world to be rid of these two disputant and dominant states, then other problems and tensions could the more easily be resolved.

4. *Arms race theorists* single out the stockpiling of weapons, and particularly of nuclear weapons, as the central factor in recent world politics. The danger of potential destruction of much of the social, economic and cultural fabric of the world by nuclear weapons, and the apparent lack of control over the arms race, are seen as of such overriding importance that they are invested with the power of explaining the course of world events. The stopping and reversing of this arms race is therefore seen as the key to reducing international tensions. Such theories tend to a considerable extent to equate the political and social impact of this arms race in east and west.[3] They abstract the problem of arms from other, it is argued, secondary and distinguishing, features of these societies, be they political intentions or social interests.

5. *North-south theorists* present the dynamic of world politics as lying primarily in the conflict between rich and poor nations, between imperial and colonial, dominant and dominated states.[4] The great importance

---

[3.] A cogent statement of the arms race theory is given by E.P. Thompson in *Exterminism and Cold War*, NLB 1982. A popular variant of the arms race theory is what might be termed its psychologistic variant, according to which the rush towards mass destruction reflects some underlying but universal human urge towards collective annihilation (e.g. Nicholas Humphrey, 'Four Minutes to Midnight', *The Listener*, 29 October 1981). Attractive as this psychological approach may be, it serves a limited analytic function: its vaults over all the historical, political, social and economic factors that influence state policy.

[4.] The importance of the third world in the 1960s and 1970s was reflected in theories of international relations giving primacy to issues of domination and development. The latter, often borrowing more or less explicitly from Marxist theories of imperialism, tended to run the risk of ignoring the issues of relations between industrialised states in the search for an alternative perspective on international affairs.

which this issue has attained since 1945 and the continuing immisera-
tion and subordination of hundreds of millions in the third world are factors that, it is argued, override morally and strategically the east-west and
other conflicts and provide the motor for these. The production of
weapons and the disputes of richer states are, in the first instance, seen as
motivated by the intention of consolidating their influence over weaker
and poorer countries. In a north-south perspective it is the difficulty of
maintaining this control over third world peoples and a competitive advantage over rival dominating states that underlies the deterioration of
international politics in the late 1970s.

6. The *west-west theorists* argue that world politics is determined by the
conflict between richer capitalist states, just as it was in the period before
1914.[5] For them, the conflict with the USSR is but a pretext used by the
USA for waging conflict with its major capitalist rivals—the EEC and Japan.
It is the sharpened rivalry between these OECD countries which has produced the Second Cold War.[6] Military buildups are a means of reimposing US control over its competitors; the Soviet Threat is the only ideological tool available for reuniting the major capitalist states; the turmoil
in the third world is fuelled and aggravated by these intercapitalist
rivalries.

[5.] The application of the term 'west' to the major capitalist states is vitiated by the fact
that one of the most dynamic examples thereof, namely Japan, is further 'east' than any
communist country. For reasons of convenience, the term will nonetheless be used here
to denote the advanced capitalist states. 'East-west' conflicts have also been of considerable significance in the postwar epoch, most notably that between the USSR and
China. The term 'New Cold War' was even used in the 1960s to refer to the Sino-Soviet
dispute. However, although important, east-east conflicts have not been such as to present themselves as candidates for explaining world politics as a whole. The place which
the Sino-Soviet and Sino-Vietnamese disputes in the evolution of the Second Cold War is
discussed below, in chapter eight.

[6.] In the words of André Gunder Frank: 'The Soviet Threat is an instrument to blackmail
western Europe into accepting US economic conditions and to prevent Europe from
liberating itself economically from the USA's (Transnational Institute Seminar, Amsterdam, 26 November 1982). Noam Chomsky has stressed in his writings that Europe and
Japan, not the USSR, are 'the real rivals' of the USA, (Chomsky, Jonathan Steele, John Gittings, *Superpowers in Collision*, London 1982, p. 20). Mary Kaldor has written of the
conflict between the west and the Soviet Union as a 'ritual', designed to mask tensions
between western states (*The Disintegrating West*, London 1978, p. 10). Dan Smith and
Ron Smith see the new Cold War as a means by which the USA can re-establish hegemony
over its allies and 'offset' inter-capitalist rivalries ('The New Cold War', *Capital and
Class*, no. 12, Winter 1980/81.)

7. The *intra-state theorists* locate the primary causes in the inner workings of the major world powers. Thus international relations are seen as fundamentally the expression of domestic factors. Changes in foreign policy are related to shifts in internal power structures, new economic weaknesses or strengths, and changes in the social composition of the country concerned. The politicians in charge of foreign policy may pretend to their respective constituencies that they are responding to the actions of forces and states outside their own countries; but they are above all using these international events to resolve internal tensions and to gain ground over domestic competitors.[7]

8. *Class conflict theorists* see international politics as determined by the ebb and flow of social revolution, and of the conflict between capitalism and communism, on a world scale. In such a perspective, it is the simultaneous unity and variety of the world as transformed by capitalism which accounts for the turmoils of the postwar epoch. This conflict may at times be expressed primarily in rivalry between the major states of each bloc. But this is not necessarily so. At other times class conflict is reflected in the spread of revolutionary activity in the third world, at others still, at least potentially, in the level of class conflict within the major capitalist states.[8]

All of these eight theories claim to provide some plausible explanation of world events. They all identify factors which must be taken into account in explaining the onset of the Second Cold War. Yet each also raises certain difficulties. The *Soviet Threat* and US *Imperialism* theories can only be sustained by denying an active role, any responsibility, to the other, exempted, state and by suppressing discussion of the rivalry between the two. Both powers helped to bring on the Second Cold War, as

---

[7.] This view is cogently advanced in Alan Wolfe, *The Rise and Fall of the 'Soviet Threat'*, Washington 1979.

[8.] For example, see Mike Davis, 'Nuclear Imperialism and Extended Deterrence', in *Exterminism and Cold War*, p. 44. 'It is necessary, in my opinion, to reinstate the revolutionary Marxist conception of the modern epoch as an age of violent, protracted transition from capitalism to socialism. From this perspective the Cold War between the USSR and the United States is ultimately the lightning-rod conductor of all the historic tensions between opposing international class forces, but the bipolar confrontation is not itself the dominant level of world politics. The dominant level is the process of *permanent revolution* arising out of uneven and combined development of global capitalism.'

they did the First, albeit in different ways. The *super-power* approach overstates the degree to which the USA and USSR actually share common interests and exaggerates their ability to influence the course of world events: the USA and USSR 'contend' far more than they 'collude', and there are many factors in world affairs which are beyond the control of Moscow and Washington. This is indeed why the two major powers have been persistently unable to reach a negotiated settlement of their main differences. The *arms race* clearly constitutes a major factor in world politics, but it is itself fuelled by other tensions and purposes which must themselves be addressed: rather than being irrational or beyond human control, the arms race reflects conscious aims pursued by political actors, and it is these that have to be identified. Important as the *north-south* issue has become it cannot on its own explain the course of world politics, since so much of the power—industrial, political, military—which influences the conflicts of the south and those tensions between north and south is located outside the third world. The north-south conflict has not been waged in isolation from the east-west and west-west conflicts, but it has rather articulated with them and has been greatly accentuated, and rendered more lethal, precisely by this articulation.

The misleading attraction of the *west-west* theory is that it dispenses with the need to account for Soviet behaviour at all: yet in so doing it implies that the USSR, and the third world revolutionary movements associated with it, play no active instigatory role in the course of world politics. Not only does this go against the rather substantial evidence of a deep concern in western states about the policies and actions of the USSR, but it also downplays the importance of recent Soviet involvement in third world revolutionary advance. The *intra-state* theory has similar intellectual seductions in that it avoids the problem of analysing east-west conflict itself; but it reproduces the limitation of the *west-west* approach. World events do impinge on individual states—however strong the latter are—through military and economic challenges, through political threats, through ideological influence. Whilst the internal plays a more significant part than foreign policy experts usually admit, the course of international relations cannot be reduced to the domestic alone. The *class conflict* theory has the special merit of seeking to relate state and class politics within one approach. But it can suffer from two limitations.

First, it downplays the importance of the conflict between rival *states*; in particular it underestimates the manner in which the US-Soviet conflict takes effect in other countries. Secondly, in its unrevised reassertion of a classic Marxist perspective on international affairs, it runs the risk of neglecting the degree to which the introduction of nuclear weapons has altered the nature of world politics in the postwar epoch.[9]

East-west Rivalry and the Arms Race

There is no need to deny the importance of any of these theories and the elements to which they draw attention. It is, rather, possible to explore more carefully how such elements interrelate and how, in any particular period, one or other of the main factors in world politics comes to play a leading role. It is in this connection that an attempt will be made here to suggest what the constituent elements of recent world politics have been, so that the course of events leading up to the Second Cold War and the articulation of these different constituents can become somewhat more intelligible. It is these elements which, in their individual evolution and their mutual interaction, have generated the crisis and the changes of direction that have marked the postwar epoch, and it is they which can explain the causes and course of Cold War II.

The starting-point for such an investigation is 1945, the end of the Second World War, for it was then that the international political system as we know it today was born. Since that time two elements have above all else dominated international relations, to such an extent that they have often been elided with each other. These are the conflict between two rival social systems, capitalist and communist, what Isaac Deutscher termed 'the Great Contest' and the nuclear arms race. The one has come to form the structure within which international relations are

---

9. Thus Ernest Mandel in 'Peaceful Coexistence and World Revolution' (in *Revolution and Class Struggle*, Robin Blackburn ed., London 1978) argues that the major capitalist countries are made more belligerent by *defeats* of revolutions, not by their *victories*. Mandel underestimates the degree to which the development of nuclear weapons has invested the international situation with much greater risks and difficulties than was previously the case, and he plays down the extent to which the USA and its allies do respond to successful revolutions by increased militarism.

worked through, the other has introduced an element of potential annihilation that has transformed not only the nature of any future war but also the risks and methods of diplomacy in time of peace. The theory being suggested here is, put simply, an extension of the class conflict theory to encompass both of the single-state theories—the Soviet Threat and US Imperialism variants—and the arms race itself.

Both the Great Contest and the arms race have to be accorded their due importance. To focus only on the conflict of east and west, of Soviet Union and United States, is to diminish the attention which must be paid to these new weapons of mass destruction and to the deep changes in the nature of international relations and political conflict which they have introduced. Yet to see this span of history in terms of the arms race alone is to obscure the very real political and social issues around which international affairs have revolved and which have themselves to a great extent determined the course of that arms race. Tempting as any single-factor analysis may be, it is not one or other of these constituent elements but rather their unpredictable and unprecedented combination which has made the postwar period so unique, and so perilous.

Although these two major constituent elements are all too familiar in the 1980s, it has to be remembered just how novel they are. The competition of the two social systems differs from previous great power rivalries in three respects. First, it is a rivalry that is *globalised*, i.e. it involves the whole world in its political and military dynamics. Whilst unable to control or programme much of world events, the major powers nonetheless tend to impose their own competitive logic upon them. Secondly, the rivalry rests upon a *bipolar* conflict between the USA and the USSR, the two states which emerged as dominant forces in their respective domains at the end of World War II. In the nineteenth century Britain was supreme in its international influence. In the period between the First and Second World Wars a variety of states competed for dominion. The bipolar conflict dates from the period since 1945 and from the emergence of these two and only two great powers of the nuclear age. They are endowed with economic, geographic and political weight at a time when the possession of large nuclear arsenals has given each of them additional superiority over other states within their own camp. Thirdly, this conflict is *systemic*. It is not just one between rival states, a realisation of the prediction made by de Tocqueville in the 1830s that

Russia and America would one day be rivals for world domination. It is a conflict in which aspects of this great power rivalry are grafted onto a rivalry between two social systems that remain, with all necessary qualification, in continuing conflict. However much the leading states do act or appear to act simply like great powers in the traditional mould, there is something more at stake in their competition. There are underlying reasons, inherent in their respective social orders, which dictate that they cannot permanently resolve their disagreements.

The globalised and bipolar nature of the conflict is perhaps evident enough; but there are many who doubt the inter-systemic element, whether out of a belief in the underlying similarity or convergence of capitalist and communist states, or because of scepticism about the rival ideological claims of the two states involved. The right has less difficulty in recognising this reality than the left. With all due caution about believing the claims each camp makes about itself, it is worthwhile summarising the reasons why such a conflict does still have this systemic character. The eminently justified rejection of the way in which the 'Soviet Threat' is presented in much western analysis should not lead to the mistake of denying that an east-west conflict exists.

The fundamental nature of the conflict between the two social systems can be seen in three aspects of their interrelationship. First, these societies are organised on the basis of contrasting social principles: private ownership of the means of production in one, collective or state ownership in the other. This antagonism is, however, rooted not just in the contrast of social organisation but ultimately in the different social interests which they represent. For the capitalist world has, since 1917, faced an opponent where capitalist rule has been overthrown and replaced by a society of a fundamentally different kind. The original hope of those who made the Russian revolution, that a society in which workers' democracy could be established, was belied; instead a system based on the dictatorship of the party leadership, and of a social group tied to it by bonds of power and privilege, emerged. But for all the betrayal of the intentions of those who made the Bolshevik revolution, a contrasted social system, representing different social interests and classes, was produced and it is this difference which above all else underlies the Great Contest as it continues to this day.

This difference is reflected in a second distinction, that both systems stake an ideological claim to be world systems, ideal societies which others should aspire to follow. However hypocritical such proclamations may at times be, and however much each side seeks to find accommodation with the other, there are conflicting appeals embodied in both systems which direct state policy and state responses to events elsewhere. Thirdly, the search for even limited bilateral accommodation between the USSR and the USA cannot proceed smoothly because of the outbreak of the conflicts in other countries which draw the two major powers into antagonistic involvements. Systemic conflicts override attempts at state-to-state accommodation. For the very social interests embodied in the leading capitalist and communist states are present, in a fluid and conflicting manner, in third countries; the result is that the clash of the two blocs is constantly reanimated and sustained by developments in these other states that may be supporters or allies of one or other bloc. While state advantage and competitive opportunity play a part in this, the pull towards involvement in other societies and conflicts has its roots in the systemic imperatives of both camps. It is in these three dimensions that the inter-systemic conflict of capitalism and communism resides; and it is above all this inter-systemic nature of the conflict which marks the era of postwar international politics off from that of inter-state competition in the pre-1945 period.

The novelty in the nature of the conflict also applies to the arms race: competition in weaponry was characteristic of the world before the First and Second World Wars, with much of the suspicion, secrecy, and manoeuvring visible today. Yet because of their destructive power and the inability of states to defend themselves against the missiles of an enemy, nuclear weapons have involved an arms race of a very different character. It is more dangerous and more complex than that associated with heavy cruisers, tanks, or bombers earlier in the century. The development of nuclear weapons in the course of World War II has therefore yielded an element of world politics as fundamental and as new as the inter-systemic rivalry which emerged simultaneously from the defeat of the Axis states.

Yet despite their novelty, neither of these elements sprang *ex nihilo* on the day when the war with the Axis powers ended. The conflict between capitalism and communism began with the Russian Revolution of 1917. Russia was invaded by the armies of fourteen capitalist countries in the period 1918-1922 in an attempt to crush the first post-capitalist state, and containment of Bolshevism was a priority of American as it was of British, German and French policy in the interwar period.[10] The USA did not recognise the USSR until 1933. But in the 1920s and 1930s the main axis of international politics remained that of conflict between the major capitalist states—Japan, Germany and Italy on the one side, Britain, France, America on the other—and it was armed clashes between these capitalist states that precipitated World War II.

With the German attack on the USSR in June 1941 the war in Europe acquired a predominantly capitalist-communist form: it was the Red Army which contributed most to the defeat of Nazi Germany. In Asia, the Soviet Union fought Japan from 1937 to 1939, and the war in China, where Japan had half of her combat forces, was to a considerable extent a capitalist-communist one. But the main axis of conflict was an inter-capitalist one, between Japan and the USA. The Second World War was therefore both a conflict between capitalist states and one between capitalism and communism.[11] What the War marked was the period of transition between a world dominated by inter-capitalist conflict to one dominated by the conflict of competing social systems. This latter has thereby come to characterise international relations in the subsequent period: the international division between two vast geographic, demographic and economic entities, Russia and the USA, has been located within the context of a conflict between two systems, each of which seeks to produce a world in its own image.

[10.] André Fontaine, *History of the Cold War*, Vol. 1.; and William Appleman Williams, 'American Intervention in Russia: 1917-20', in D. Horowitz ed., *Containment and Revolution*, London 1967.

[11.] Anthony Barnett has written: 'In the Pacific the conflict was primarily an inter-imperialist and only secondarily a Capitalist/Communist confrontation. In the European "theatre" on the other hand, the conflict was primarily between Capitalism and Communism, and the inter-imperialist aspect was only secondary' (Note to the author, January 1982). Ernest Mandel (*Revolutionary Marxism Today*, London 1979, p. 164) sees the Second World War as combining five wars in one: 'an inter-imperialist war between plunderers...; a just war of self-defence by the Soviet bureaucratized workers' state against imperialist aggression by Nazi Germany and its allies; a just war of self-defence by semi-colonial China against Japanese imperialism; just wars of national liberation by oppressed colonial peoples against their imperial overlords, whether Japanese, English, or French; and finally, a just war of resistance by the masses of workers and the oppressed in the occupied countries of Europe against...the Nazis'.

Nuclear weapons are, equally, something that predates 1945. They were first developed during World War II in the inter-capitalist domain by German experts on one side, and British and American scientists on the other. These weapons were then used on two occasions in the closing stages of the war by one capitalist state, America, upon another, Japan. Given their discovery, development and use in such an inter-capitalist context, it can be assumed that if conflict between the major countries had continued to dominate world politics then there could have been a nuclear arms race between the major capitalist powers. However, the changed context of international politics, the emergence of the conflict between capitalism and communism into a dominant position, placed the nuclear arms race in a wholly different context, giving it new causes and new implications for military policy, as a means of influencing social change as well as regulating relations between states.

Nuclear weapons have become not just the means for defending the interests of one capitalist state against another, but an instrument for influencing the international social and political conflict between capitalism and communism.[12] The ebb and flow of revolution and counter-revolution, of class conflict and social upheaval, has now been overshadowed and shaped by the far greater risks for both sides which the availability of nuclear weapons has introduced. At times the restraints imposed by nuclear weapons have opened up political spaces for local political forces that might not otherwise have been there, by holding back the major powers of east and west. But the process of social and political change within and between states has been invested with an immanent lethality that has on occasion dictated caution, retreat and fear on both sides. Neither bloc has been willing to risk its own future and that of civilisation as a whole for some tactical advantage. The nuclear threat did not therefore freeze conflict between the systems, but it has constricted its field of operation.

[12.] Mike Davis (*Exterminism and Cold War*, p. 53) has described the strategic arms race as 'a complex, regulative instance of the global class struggle', and has listed several dimensions in which an edge in nuclear weaponry can be used, in his terms, to *regularise* conflicts in the third world. For further discussion of this point, see below Chapter Three.

The course of international relations has not, however, been determined merely by these two constitutive factors, globalised social conflict and the nuclear arms race. As noted, although the two factors have accentuated each other, the dangers involved in nuclear weaponry have also imposed restraints. There has been no war between the USA and the Soviet Union, and the US-Chinese conflict of the early 1950s was confined to the Korean Peninsula. Nor has any major capitalist ally of the USA's been in direct conflict with either the USSR or China. The interlocked dynamic of globalised social conflict and nuclear arms race has, instead, found expression through other dimensions of international conflict, each of which has been moulded and impelled by the way in which the dual dynamic has acted upon it.[13]

An Unequal Contest

The political and economic conflict between east and west points to a fundamental aspect of the Great Contest which is too often ignored in discussions of the conflict on either side, and which constitutes the first of the contributory factors. This is that, for all the appearance of competition between equals, the Contest has been a profoundly unequal one. This remains true of the contemporary situation. The USSR and the USA have enormous destructive potential in their nuclear arsenals, but even here in the military sphere as will be shown in Chapter Three, the USA is considerably stronger than the USSR. In economics, the USSR is far weaker than the USA—its overall GNP is 40%-50% of that of the USA, its GNP per capita is equivalent to that of Ireland, Spain or Greece, and the combined GNP of the Warsaw Treaty states as a whole is at most one third

---

[13.] 'The Cold War has *at least* four structural components, which any adequate account must synthesize: a struggle between capitalist and socialist economic systems, a contest between imperialist and indigenous national systems, a conflict between parliamentary and authoritarian political systems and a confrontation between technologically equivalent and reciprocally suicidal military systems. International class stuggle, defence of democracy, revolt against colonialism, arms race: each slogan indicates one "moment" in the Cold War, and denies the other. The reality is their infinite imbrication and interpenetration', Perry Anderson, 'The Left in the Fifties', *New Left Review* 29, January-February 1965, p. 12. The argument developed here draws upon Anderson's schema, with the addition of a fifth structural component, and the different usage of the term Cold War.

that of the major capitalist states in the OECD. But the contrast is even greater in historical terms. The USSR and its allies have done well to make the advances they have in the military and economic spheres, but in these, as in the political and cultural, they have not been able to overcome the enormous disadvantages with which they began. The differences in historical starting point explain much of the disadvantage which the east still has in the Great Contest. Russia in 1917 was a largely impoverished country, the mass of its population illiterate. Even if other problems—the intervention of 1918-22, the Stalinist dictatorship, the ravages of the Second World War—had not inhibited its later development, it is extremely unlikely that it could have caught up with western Europe or the USA economically in the intervening period. Eastern Europe was, similarly, much poorer than its western counterpart at the end of World War II and the war itself had taken a much greater toll on the eastern fronts. The cultural and political endowments of the blocs were if anything, even more unevenly distributed, since of all the Warsaw Treaty countries only East Germany and Czechoslovakia had any significant experience of democracy prior to World War II. Such historical factors should not be used simply to exonerate the communist party leaderships who have subsequently ruled these countries; but the historical legacies which the post-capitalist states inherited cannot be ignored in an assessment of what these societies have, and have not, achieved in the competition with the west since World War II.

The appearance of equality is, therefore, misleading. It is one which the west sustains in order to draw comparisons that are, overall, favourable to it. The east is trapped into making the same claim, in order to advance its legitimacy as a viable alternative system. The result has been that the record of the east, apparently unfavourable in the economic and political spheres, has provided the advanced capitalist countries with the idiom, vocabulary and justification for the conflict between the social systems. The internal political workings of the communist world determine the form in which the east-west conflict has been presented in the west, namely as a contest between 'totalitarianism' and freedom, between dictatorial communism and a democratic capitalism. This political contrast has been compounded by the economic successes of capitalism in the advanced market countries, and through the manner in which the availability of consumer goods has far outstripped that in the communist states. These political and economic advantages have, in their combination, provided the west with its ideological justification for the conflict with the USSR. The USA has claimed that it is fighting for the 'Free World': the case for capitalism has been that through the unfettering of the individual spirit, both greater political and greater material benefits for all can be attained.

This is a claim which is hollow and pernicious as far as many third world components of the capitalist bloc are concerned: there dictatorship and poverty reign supreme. But when the comparison is between those living in the advanced capitalist and advanced communist states then it acquires greater force. Here, indeed, the importance of 1945 as the founding moment becomes especially relevant, for in the transition from World War II to Cold War I the capitalist states were able to transfer the ideological terms of the former conflict into the disputes of the latter: the image of a 'totalitarian' state, repressive at home and aggressive abroad, was taken from its most recent target, Nazi Germany, and transferred, with considerable ideological success, to the USSR, at the same time as memories of the Stalinist terror in the 1930s were revived after the interlude of wartime collaboration. This apparently clear contrast in the records of capitalism and communism results from the fact that the communist states have so far failed to realise either the political or the economic potential yielded by their transcendence of capitalism. Far from going beyond capitalist political freedom, something for which socialism has the capacity, they have established systems that in most visible dimensions still fail to match their competitors. They have removed many forms of economic, social, racial and sexual oppression characteristic of capitalist societies, but in the realm of political democracy—of voting, publishing, organising, criticising established authorites—these countries have, as yet, failed to produce liberties that compare with those achieved under capitalism. In the language of western political theory, the communist states offer 'substantive' freedoms—to work, housing etc.—but not 'procedural' ones—to vote, criticise and so on. On the economic front, the record of the communist countries has been a rather good one, and certainly far better than most western argument would suggest.[14] But there has still been a great gap between the potential of planned economic growth and the results, and there has been

---

[14.] See pp. 138 ff.

a special gap in the realm of those consumer goods which are the most tangible and universally valued index of individual, family and class enrichment.

TABLE ONE
GNP PER CAPITA 1979

Capitalist States	*US$*
West Germany	11,730
USA	10,630
France	9,950
Japan	8,810
UK	6,320
Italy	5,250
Post-Capitalist States	
East Germany	6,430
Czechoslovakia	5,290
USSR	4,110
Hungary	3,850
Poland	3,830
Bulgaria	3,690

Source: World Bank, *World Development Report 1981*, p. 135.

Conflict in the Third World

If the contest of east and west favours the west in these domains, the balance of advantage is reversed when the emphasis of the debate is moved from the questions of freedom and prosperity to that of peace. This reflects a profound countervailing reality about the postwar world, one that comprises another of these contributory factors in world politics and which provides a great advantage for the communist world. For it has been the west which has played the larger role since 1945 in threatening peace in the world, both, as will be discussed in Chapter Three, by pushing the arms race further and further along its path, and by waging and encouraging a series of bloody wars in the third world against dominated peoples seeking to gain emancipation from metropolitan control. This contrast is evident even in the very language and culture with which war is treated in east and west: the impact of World War II was to make Soviet society deeply patriotic in sentiment, but hostile to anything that smacks of light-minded belligerency and warmongering. The much milder burden born by the western powers in the defeat of fascism, and the complete exemption from war on its own territory by the USA, have enabled their leaders and populations to contemplate war, and to talk about it, with much more insouciance and irresponsibility.

The link between western responsibility for the arms race and actual war is to be found especially in the third world where, since 1945, the advanced capitalist countries have engaged in wars of suppression and conquest on an almost continuous scale, of which the sanguinary combats in Central America during the early 1980s are but the most recent example. Beyond direct intervention, the advanced capitalist countries have also been encouraging local allies to launch wars that stand to benefit the west if these local states prevail. There has been no allout war between the USA and USSR, but through the wars of the third world the east-west conflict has found vivid expression and new arenas of confrontation.

The very category of the 'third world' reflects a certain dubious distinction. For it implies a greater difference between these poorer states of the world and the major components of the eastern and western blocs, and, by the same token, implies a greater unity between the 'third world' countries than in fact exists. One thing these states do share is a certain poverty, although even here there is much to link an Argentina, a Kuwait or a Singapore more to the richer capitalist countries than to Haiti, Upper Volta or Afghanistan. Beyond their poverty, however, the states of the 'third' world belong, by virtue of the social systems prevailing in them, to either the 'first', capitalist, or 'second', post-capitalist worlds, and political movements of the south are similarly ones that seek to establish societies that would themselves follow one or other model. For this reason, the internal diversity of 'third world' states, there is no common character to the movements and states that emerge there and hence to the kind of challenges they pose to the advanced capitalist countries: the conflicts of the USA and Britain with Vietnam or Cuba differ profoundly from those with Saudi Arabia or Argentina. The former seek to challenge the capitalist system as such, the other to negotiate a new position within it. Yet precisely because of the systemic linkage of both the capitalist and post-capitalist components of the third world to the first and second worlds, the rise of new forces and states since 1945 has directly affected relations between the major powers of east and west.

In their own bilateral negotiations, the Soviet Union and the USA have, in different ways, sought to minimise the impact of third world upheavals upon their own relations while taking advantage of each other's difficulties. But the American and more general western attempt to subdue the south and to secure Soviet acceptance of this has failed time and again on the rocks of third world revolution and nationalism themselves. These have defied the terror of metropolitan armies and the diplomatic injunctions of Soviet caution. Thus Stalin's obstinate compromise in Europe after 1945 was dramatically upstaged by the independent initiatives of the Chinese and Korean communists in the Far East. Later Khrushchev's search for agreement with America was stopped by US retaliation against the Cuban revolution of 1959, by Chinese stubbornness over 'peaceful coexistence' and by the renewed determination of the Vietnamese communists to unite their country. Brezhnev's pursuit of Detente in the early 1970s was undermined by the revolutions that swept the third world from 1974 onwards.

Yet while both the Soviet Union and the USA have been affected by the insurgencies of the third world, the two have reacted asymmetrically, since the USSR has to a certain extent made itself the ally of third world emancipation and has provided support—military, economic, diplomatic—for those resisting control by the major western states. In certain countries, the leadership of the nationalist movements has itself been assumed by communist parties or other forces sympathetic on ideological grounds to the USSR. There are many cases where the USSR has not provided significant aid, or indeed any; but, on balance, the USSR has acted and has been perceived as acting in support of third world movements, however reluctant and partial that support has been. This Soviet role has served to link the struggles between metropolitan and dominated third world countries to that between social systems and has, in so doing, provided a political advantage to the USSR, comparable to that provided to the capitalist world in the realm of political and economic achievement. The reason for the USSR's involvement in the struggles of the third world are often said to be great power interest and tactical advantage alone. Such factors and calculations must play a role; yet, on closer examination, these cease to be sufficient explanation. It is certainly true that some of the states aided by the USSR—Egypt and India, for example—have remained part of the capitalist bloc, and that here state interest seems to be primary in Soviet motivation. But other examples of economic and military support, from China in the 1950s to Afghanistan, Cuba, Vietnam and Nicaragua in the 1980s, represent the drive to consolidate these as extensions of the post-capitalist world.

The major capitalist states are also in conflict with each other and have, to some extent, given expression to these conflicts by rivalry with each other in the third world. There has since 1945 been competition between different western European states, the USA and Japan for influence in the Middle East. But this inter-capitalist conflict has had clear limits and is quite distinct from that between the USA and the USSR. No capitalist rival of the USA's has offered to guarantee the security of Cuba against US attack, has armed Vietnam to fight the American intervention forces, or has airlifted weapons to Angola and Ethiopia. There is, in other words, a more fundamental dimension to this Soviet involvement in the third world, one that goes beyond mere inter-state rivalry. It is here that the systemic character of the Great Contest arises again: the Soviet Union is committed by its own ideology and the social interests it represents to competing with the USA in the third world and to supporting those states that have themselves sought to break from the capitalist world order.

Divisions within Blocs

The third, final, contributory factor is one which many writers have seen as the core of contemporary international conflict, namely the desire of the leading powers, the USA and the USSR, to maintain control within their own camps. Its appeal lies behind the 'west-west' and 'intra-state' theories already mentioned. In this perspective, the conflict between camps is a convenient issue around which the maintenance of internal order can be justified. It is a diversion, a ritual, an excuse, which masks the primacy of conflicts within the societies and between the states of both camps. The easiest way to discredit opponents is to accuse them of being agents of the enemy camp. In the early 1980s this was the fate of Solidarity in Poland and the guerrillas of El Salvador, the one accused of working for the CIA, the other of being tools of Soviet expansionism. The easiest way for a stronger state to impose policy on a weaker ally is to remind the latter of the dangers from which the stronger is protecting it. The easiest way to mobilise domestic support for a course of action is to justify it as a response to the threat from outside. As Edward Thompson has argued, such ideological 'bonding' serves important functions in both east and west.[15]

This 'internal' analysis is an approach especially attractive to those who are in opposition within either camp. Those in capitalist societies who seek to focus criticism upon the actions of their own governments can do so the more easily if they ignore the conflict with the communist world, and put all the blame for the world's problems upon their own politicians. Yet this can only be done by suppressing the degree to which the USSR is itself an actor in world politics, with aims and policies at variance with those of the west. No account of the Second Cold War, any more than that of the First, can portray one of the two major constituents as simply a passive element. Those in communist countries, struggling for democratic freedoms, finds it convenient to blame all on their ruling parties and Politburos. Yet, in so doing, they ignore some elementary but significant facts: that the USA has sought since 1945 to maintain military superiority over the USSR and its allies, that the west has used a wide variety of economic pressures to harass the communist states, and that the metropolitan capitalist states have waged a series of barbaric wars in the third world under the justification of fighting communism. On both sides such dissident analysts, in the attempt to criticise their own governments try to portray the official enemy as either politically innocent or analytically irrelevant. It is for this reason that both the opposition in the Soviet bloc and the peace movement in the west have tended to understate the degree of inter-systemic conflict *and* to downgrade the role of third world revolt in international tensions.

There is much to recommend this 'internal' perspective, but its insights can be preserved only so long as it does not exclude the other constituent elements. The intra-bloc conflicts between major capitalist or communist powers, between the USA on one side and the EEC and Japan on the other, have figured prominently in recent years, as has for a longer period the dispute between the USSR and China. Threats to metropolitan control posed by third world resistance of various kinds have often been met by casting all of these as the product of a Soviet grand design. Just as the First Cold War was accompanied by the mobilisation of anti-communist sentiment in a Red Scare, so the Second Cold War has

---

15. E.P. Thompson, *Beyond The Cold War*, London 1982, pp. 18ff.

involved a concerted rollback of social and political changes in the advanced capitalist countries and renewed emphasis upon the need to control the third world. Domestic interests and tension and conflicts between states within one system do play a major role in influencing international relations. They are linked to the conflict between systems both by the rhetoric of those who seek to discredit their opponents by making such links, and by the search of dissenting forces for support from outside their own system.

Yet despite the ferocity of these intra-bloc conflicts, and their contribution to international relations, they cannot on their own account for the course which the latter take. Beyond the disputes of the Russian and American governments with their respective allies and populations, there lies the Great Contest, the ongoing dispute between the two systems itself, to which the maintenance of order within each camp is linked. The inter-systemic conflict is not fought out as its main protagonists claim, and there is much that is ritualistic, diversionary and misleading in it. But this is a long way from saying that the conflict between capitalism and communism is a mirage: it remains the focal point of world politics, the globalised conflict around which other constitutive elements, for all their independence and unpredictability, must develop. If these constituent elements provide the framework within which international politics work themselves out, they do not, on their own, provide explanation of the specific events of any one period. And to explain the onset of the Second Cold War, it is necessary to look in more detail at those developments which combined to alter the east-west climate from one of Detente to one of Cold War. It is this closer examination which the following chapters attempt, concentrating on five major causes of the Second Cold War, from the arms race through to the conflicts between the major capitalist states.

The central role of the Great Contest needs, however, to be underlined once again, because it is easy to lose sight of it in the rush of individual incidents and because there are many who, as indicated earlier in this chapter, deny its importance. For opponents of the arms race, it seems to be a complicating factor, one that can make the abolition of nuclear weapons appear more difficult, and introduce divisive issues into the campaign against them. For the left, critical of the revolutionary pretensions of the USSR and the 'Soviet Threat' rhetoric of the right, it is equally unwelcome. Yet it is also important to stress the unequal character of this Contest, and the continuing superiority, in resources and initiative, of the USA and its allies. It is they who bear the primary responsibility for launching the Second Cold War because of what was seen in Washington and its allied capitals as an erosion of the superiority, military and political, which the west had previously had. The responsibility for Cold War II is shared between east and west, as was that for Cold War I; but it is the west which, precisely because it has the upper hand, took the intiative in introducing a new level of competition which it believes will restore the primacy in world politics which recent developments have taken from it. It is this theme, of the shared but unequal responsibility of east and west for the Second Cold War, which the subsequent chapters discuss.

3.
The Decline
of US Military Superiority

An emphasis upon the need for military preparedness and increased military expenditure is, as discussed in Chapter One, one of the hallmarks of Cold War. And Cold War II has been preceded and accompanied by calls for stronger military forces in both east and west. So important is this feature of Cold War II that in the eyes of many it is the very essence of the Cold War. Yet it has already been suggested that this equation is, in its various forms, a simplification. The Cold War has other features—political, economic, ideological—which are distinct from the arms race, however they are related to it. Moreover, the arms race has been proceeding apace for many years, through the periods of Oscillatory Antagonism and Detente. It may have to some degree been controlled by bilateral agreements between the USA and the USSR, but the level of destructive power available to both sides was rising throughout the 1960s and 1970s, i.e. between the two Cold Wars.

The world did not wake up in the late 1970s to find itself faced with the possibility of nuclear annihilation: that prospect has long faced humanity. What has changed with Cold War II is more the political response to the threat of destruction, and the prominence which the issue of the nuclear arms race has in times of Cold War for both its instigators and its opponents. If one reason for this increased awareness and concern is the drive for even greater quantities of arms and technical refinements in their use, other reasons must lie outside the arms race as such, in those political trends that increase the fear of great power confrontation and a resulting nuclear war. To locate the place of the arms race in Cold War II is above all to find what the link is between the production and stockpiling of arms on the one hand and the broader political context of world politics on the other. It is to see how the arms race intersects with the Great Contest, and with the subordinate conflicts that divide each bloc. Although weapons on their own cannot have direct political effects, especially when like nuclear weapons they are not used, the process of the arms race obviously does have a political logic which analysis may unravel.

Functions of Superiority

The argument developed in the following pages suggests ways in which the arms race and the political dimension do interrelate. If Cold War II has been accompanied by intensified arms production, two reasons above all suggest themselves for this turn of events. First of all, the nuclear balance is perceived as in itself part of the Great Contest, as a means of influencing the rivalry of the USA and the USSR even when the nuclear weapons making up this balance are not used. What has happened over the past two decades is that a pre-existing US superiority has been eroded by the Russians, and the USA is now trying to win a greater degree of advantage back again. The argument about the meaninglessness of superiority is usually confined to cases where war has already been assumed to have broken out: here many people point out that since both sides can destroy each other many times over superiority makes no sense. But what this ignores is the ways in which, short of war, competition and superiority in nuclear weapons have a political appeal. One can say that of all the causes of Cold War II none is more important than this determination in the USA to reach for a new margin over the USSR and to foster a climate in which such a policy appears legitimate and even defensive. The appeal of nuclear superiority rests on much hypothesis and speculation—what some critics have called 'nuclear theology'—yet the force of this appeal is not diminished by lack of definition. Indeed, as an emotional and symbolic attraction, the idea of superiority can be said to benefit from such vagueness.

The appeal can be seen to work in at least four general domains:[1]

[1.] I am particularly grateful to Mike Davis for his unravelling of the logic of nuclear superiority in 'Nuclear Imperialism and Extended Deterrence', *Exterminism and Cold War*, pp. 54-6. In a famous statement in 1977 Henry Kissinger asked: 'What in the name of God is strategic superiority? What is the significance of it, politically, militarily, operationally at these levels of numbers? What do you do with it?' However, he did not mean that strategic superiority had lost all significance; as he went on to explain, strategic superiority had served the USA well for many years after 1945 (*Years of Upheaval*, p. 1176).

1. *Ideology*: The debate on nuclear weapons has an appearance of scientific precision: the assumption is that the rhetoric and charges of public debate are founded on and derive from a set of precise and calmly established theoretical assumptions about what would happen in war. In reality, the reverse is the case. Nuclear weapons policies are in the first instance determined by a set of vague but deeply felt ideological assumptions about the nature of power in the modern world. The theories adduced to legitimate and guide the use of nuclear arms are produced in a subordinate manner. Ever since World War II, when America assumed a leadership position in the capitalist world, nuclear weapons have been seen as the symbol and effective guarantee of that role, as the bastions of US security in the conflict with the USSR[2]. Paranoia is common in US politics, and the experience of the sudden Japanese attack in 1941, combined with the very speed and suddenness of nuclear weapons, have reinforced a fake sense of strategic vulnerability. US security rested throughout the 1950s and 1960s upon a real superiority, and there exists a strong sentiment in the USA in favour of restoring that in the 1980s as far as is possible.

US government officials deny that they are pursuing military superiority. Instead the talk is of 'modernisation', as if weapons grow old independently of human judgement, of 'restoring the balance' when the word 'balance' refers to a previous *imbalance* in the USA's favour, to 'negotiating from strength', and to achieving 'sufficiency', for what it is not specified. But in political rhetoric this superiority claim comes to the fore. Nixon came to office in 1969 calling for the restoration of US superiority—what he called 'sufficiency'. Reagan's election platform of 1980 was clearer: 'We will build toward a sustained defence expenditure sufficient to close the gap with the Soviets, and ultimately reach the position of military superiority that the American people demand.'[3] The leading organiser of the New Right Political Action Committees in the 1980 elections, Richard Viguerie, has stated that the primary goal of the

---

[2.] Frank Schurman argues that national security based on nuclear weapons was developed in the postwar era as an ideology of Presidential power. While nuclear weapons cannot be justified rationally, this is not the central consideration: what predominates is a public feeling in the USA justifying nuclear weapons because they provide a sense of security (*The Logic of World Power*, New York 1974, Chapter One).

[3.] As quoted in *Aviation Week and Space Technology*, 25 August 1980, p. 9.

conservative forces in US politics is to 'regain strategic military superiority without delay'.[4] Such public concerns find their reflection in the
literature on nuclear weapons, where strength in warheads and missiles
is seen as conveying a government's determination to friend and foe
alike, i.e. as being of both symbolic and substantive importance in the
projection of power. In both the 1980 US elections and in the Congressional discussions following Reagan's accession to office on larger
military appropriations, this political importance of superiority, as the
ideological core of US global power, was repeatedly emphasised.[5]

2. *Bargaining Power*: The possession of a margin of superiority is seen
by US policy planners as increasing US leverage in the event of crisis situations, especially in the third world. Threats of nuclear attack can be made
either against local, non-nuclear, third world countries, or against the
power seen as encouraging the third world challenge, namely the USSR.[6]
The core of Kissinger's concern about the revolution produced by the

---

[4.] Richard Viguerie, *The New Right-We're Ready to Lead*, Falls Church, Virginia, 1981,
Chapter Ten.
[5.] Thus an unnamed senior official of the US Defense Department stated in August 1981
that the aim of the US expansion of its strategic nuclear deterrent forces was 'to enable the
United States to regain nuclear superiority over the Soviet Union within this decade' (*International Herald Tribune*, 8-9 August 1981). In March 1981 Secretary of Defense
Weinberger stated: 'We must have naval superiority. Control of the seas is as essential to
our security as control of their land border is to the Soviet Union' (*Time*, 16 March
1981). A singularly clear opinion on the use of nuclear weapons at a time when the US
had a complete monopoly is found in the memoirs of Harry Truman who in June 1946
came up with the following solution to the problems he was facing: 'Adjourn Congress
and run the country. Get plenty of atomic bombs on hand—drop one on Stalin, put the
United Nations to work and eventually set up a free world' (*International Herald
Tribune*, 6 April 1982).
[6.] Thus Reagan's Assistant Secretary of Defense for International Security Policy,
Richard Perle: 'I'm always worried less about what would happen in an actual nuclear exchange than the effect that the nuclear balance has on our willingness to take risks in local
situations. It is not that I am worried about the Soviets attacking the United States with
nuclear weapons confident they they will win that nuclear war. It is that I worry about an
American President feeling he cannot afford to take action in a crisis because Soviet
nuclear forces are such that, if escalation took place, they are better poised than we are to
move up the escalation ladder' (quoted in Robert Scheer, *With Enough Shovels*, p. 13).
This theory has been categorised as a form of 'strategic mercantilism' by one historian of
the arms race, Michael Mandelbaum. He talks of the psychological protection which
superiority in nuclear weapons can give in crisis situations:...short of 'victory' in a
nuclear exchange, asymmetries in the nuclear arsenals the United States and the Soviet
Union deploy can lead to significant political consequences even when both sides possess
the capacity for the assured destruction of the other' (*The Nuclear Revolution*, Cambridge 1981, p. 124). For further discussion of the political and psychological dimension

Soviet attainment of strategic parity was that this had enabled the USSR to play an active role in the third world which US nuclear superiority had previously prevented. It is known that on nineteen occasions since World War II the USA has deployed nuclear weapons in situations of international tension. In four of these an actual threat was made: the paradigmatic instance was the crisis of October 1962 when, in a humiliating defeat, the USA forced the USSR to withdraw its missiles from Cuba.[7]

Table Two

Incidents in Which US Strategic Nuclear Forces Were Involved

Incident	Date
U.S. aircraft shot down by Yugoslavia	November 1946
Inauguration of president in Uruguay	February 1947
Security of Berlin	January 1948
Security of Berlin	April 1948
Security of Berlin	June 1948
Korean War: Security of Europe	July 1950
Security of Japan/South Korea	August 1953
Guatemala accepts Soviet bloc support	May 1954
China-Taiwan conflict: Tachen Islands	August 1954
Suez crisis	October 1956
Political crisis in Lebanon	July 1958
Political crisis in Jordan	July 1958
China-Taiwan conflict: Quemoy and Matsu	July 1958
Security of Berlin	May 1959
Security of Berlin	June 1961
Soviet emplacement of missiles in Cuba	October 1962
Withdrawal of U.S. missiles from Turkey	April 1963
Pueblo seized by North Korea	January 1968
Arab-Israeli War	October 1973

Source: B. Blechman and S. Kaplan, *Force without War*, Washington 1978, p. 48

---

of nuclear superiority see Lawrence Freedman, *The Evolution of Nuclear Strategy*, London 1981, pp. 363-9.

[7.] For analysis of the nineteen instances see B. Blechman and S. Kaplan, *Force Without War*, pp. 47-49. They divide these cases into different groups: four cases when 'an overt and explicit threat was directed at the USSR through global actions of US strategic forces' (Suez 1956, Lebanon 1958, Cuba 1962, Arab-Israeli war 1973). In three of these the US move was intended to deter the USSR *from doing* something, i.e. from intervening

Given the setbacks which the USA faced in the third world in the 1970s, US planners see the restoration of relative superiority as an essential part of the drive to reimpose control on the south, and even the introduction of new TNFs, Cruise and Pershing, into Europe stations them nearer the Middle Eastern battlefields which could develop in the 1980s. So much of the military programmes of the Reagan Administration is, in fact, concerned with developing new capacities for conventional intervention in the third world; but the buildup of a nuclear superiority enhances this drive to check the tide of revolution there.

3. *Burdening the Enemy*: The drive for superiority and the increases in US defence expenditure make another contribution to the conflict with the USSR, namely the cost which they impose on the Soviet Union itself. Even if not used, weapons cost money, and the expenditure burden which the USSR, carries, with a GNP less than half that of the USA , has enormous debilitating consequences for the rest of the economy. The USA has been ahead in almost all areas of military technology since World War II, and, given the Soviet desire to match US capabilities, US advances have imposed new expenditures on the USSR. The development of the MX missile and of Cruise and Pershing in the 1980s will force further expenditure on the USSR and will thereby create new problems for the Soviet economy. Some US officials, such as Secretary of Defense Caspar Weinberger, have been particularly clear about the impact of US military development upon the USSR: without any of the weapons being used, they nonetheless serve to weaken the enemy camp. The nuclear arms race

---

directly in the Middle East; only in one case, that of Cuba, was it designed to force the Russians *to do* something. In ten cases, US strategic bombers were moved nearer the USSR or China, placed on alert or had their withdrawal postponed in a situation of US-Soviet or US-Chinese tension. No less than six of these cases occured in Europe; the other four involved deployment of aircraft to the Western Pacific. In two incidents (Jordan 1958 and Berlin 1958-59) Sixth Fleet aircraft carriers were deployed. In two cases US bombers were sent to Latin American countries to reassure allies-the second case involving the despatch of bombers to Nicaragua to bolster the Somozas during the crisis over Guatemala in 1954. In one case a US nuclear submarine was sent to Turkey, in 1963, to reassure the government there when US missiles were being withdrawn. Former Chairman of the US Joint Chiefs of Staff, General Maxwell Taylor, has doubted whether US nuclear superiority played a role in the 1962 Cuba crisis: in his view the stakes were too small, and US conventional superiority was overwhelming, *International Herald Tribune*, 13 October 1982. This is not what later US strategists have believed, and may not be what the Russians believed either—as their response to the Cuba humiliation was to show.

therefore plays an important part in the globalised conflict between the systems, even while conditions of peace prevails.

4. *War-Winning theories*: Horrendous as it may appear, there is a quite widespread belief in US military circles that nuclear war is winnable. The speculation on a possible US surrender after a Soviet first strike is in part a projection of what US expectations are, namely that a nuclear exchange with the USSR would be won, and that accurate targeting could break the political will of decision-makers. Here the import of the current 'counterforce' doctrine becomes evident: this argues that selective strikes against key Soviet decision-making centres and strategic weapon systems would force a Soviet surrender.[8] Behind this lies the prospect of an absolute victory through a successful first strike made possible by the increased missile accuracy and submarine detection capacities of the late 1970s and early 1980s. For the advocates of this policy, Mutually Assured Destruction is an outdated concept, no longer valid because of the new technologies. Nuclear wars can, it is said, be won. Absolute superiority is therefore attainable, as it was until the Soviet advances of the mid-1960s. The Reagan Administration officials who deny that tend to give the USA the capacity to win, not deter, a nuclear exchange.[9]

However, nuclear weapons make up only a small part of the total military expenditure of the major powers—around 10% in the case of the USA. The rest goes on spending for conventional weapons, much of

---

8. 'The United States should plan to defeat the Soviet Union and to do so at a cost that would not prohibit US recovery. Washington should identify war aims that in the last resort would contemplate the destruction of Soviet political authority and the emergence of a postwar world order compatible with western values. The most frightening threat to the Soviet Union would be the destruction or serious impairment of its political system. Thus, the United States should be able to destroy key leadership cadres, their means of communication and some of the instruments of domestic control. The USSR, with its gross overcentralization of authority, epitomized by its vast bureaucracy in Moscow, should be highly vulnerable to such an attack...Judicious US targeting and weapon procurement policies might be able to deny the USSR the assurance of political survival' (Colin Gray and Keith Payne, 'Victory is Possible', *Foreign Policy*, No. 39, Summer 1980). While the authors of this article were not, at time of writing, government employees they later became so and their 'war-winning' ideas reflected an increasingly influential view within the US defence establishment.

9. In a characteristic statement to a BBC interview in September 1981 Weinberger said that the concept of superiority 'has no validity and is not related to what we are talking about'. But he went on to say: 'We are talking about achieving the renewal of *the degree*

which can be used in local wars short of an allout nuclear one. The high levels of US defence expenditure in the 1960s and early 1970s were due to the demands of the Vietnam war. The political logic of this expenditure needs much less explanation: the arms produced can be used, and are designed to maintain influence in countries where allied governments face rebellion or revolution. In a climate where the nuclear threat of the Soviet Union is given special prominence, it is easier to secure public support in the west for this kind of conventional expenditure, the purpose of which is, so it is argued, to contain Soviet influence wherever it may arise in the third world.

The US drive for a new superiority is a response to changes in the balances, nuclear and conventional, over the last two decades. For many years after World War II, the USA maintained visible military superiority over the USSR in most spheres. In strategic nuclear forces, the USA enjoyed overwhelming superiority over the USSR. It was only in 1957 that the USSR acquired the capacity to hit US territory at all and only in the late 1960s that the Russians began to draw closer to American levels in delivery systems, numbers of warheads and megatonnage. In tactical nuclear weapons, there appeared for much of the 1960s to be rough parity in the European sphere, but America had advantages in accuracy and mobility. In the third world, the Soviet Union had until the mid-1960s a minimal conventional presence and projection capability, and it had no base system at all to match the world-wide US base network. The one exceptance to this imbalance was in Europe, where the USSR has always had a conventional military superiority, in numbers of men under arms and in tanks. What has happened from the mid-1960s onwards is that the USSR began to reduce the gap in the different spheres of military com-

---

of strength that we used to have that could and will maintain the peace by deterring any Soviet attack' (Department of Defense, *Current News*, 16 October 1981, my italics). Many of the statements by Weinberger and his military advisers stressed the need for the USA to have a 'war-winning' capacity, i.e. more than just a deterrent force. Thus Weinberger to the Senate, 3 November 1981: 'We set out to...achieve improved capabilities to enhance deterrence and US capabilities to prevail should deterrence fail.' And Deputy Defense Secretary Frank Carlucci on 13 January 1981: 'I think we need to have a counterforce capability. Over and above that, I think we need to have a warfighting capability.' And Navy Secretary John Lehman to the Senate, 5 February 1981: 'You have to have a war-winning capability if you are to succeed' (*Centre for Defence Information News Release*, 21 January 1982).

petition where it was inferior, to lessen, and in a few cases overtake, the preexisting US superiority. In overall nuclear and conventional terms the USSR remains inferior to the USA; but the very fact of Soviet approximation has detonated the alarmist response in the USA that is so central to the dynamic of the Second Cold War.

The most important component of this military balance is the strategic nuclear one, the changing character and political implications of which have been summarised by Henry Kissinger, himself an unctious exponent of Cold War politics, as follows: 'Until the early Fifties we had an atomic monopoly enabling us to substitute strategic power for conventional inferiority without fear of retaliation. Until the Sixties we were in a position of such superiority that in a first strike we could probably have destroyed the Soviet retaliatory force, and the Soviets had no comparable capability. In any event the Soviets, calculating the worst-case scenario, would not risk it. Until the early Seventies, in fact, the worst-case scenario analysis of the Soviets was bound to be a significant restraint on adventurism. Therefore, our loss of strategic superiority was a strategic revolution even if the Soviets did not achieve a superiority of their own. For that, to some extent, freed the Soviet capacity for regional intervention.'[10] 'It was not necessary to postulate a Soviet advantage in strategic weapons to be concerned about the altered military balance. Even US-Soviet equality in strategic weapons implied a revolutionary change in the assumptions on which the West's security had been based in the entire postwar period.'[11]

It is, first of all, this shift in the military balance that underlies the current US drive for increased military expenditure and Washington's Second Cold War emphasis upon the need for confrontation with the USSR. Much of the US response has indeed consisted of the charge that the USSR has attained superiority and that it is incumbent upon the west to counter this. Stated in these terms, the US position is, however, quite unfounded. The claim made by Nixon that the USA could become a 'helpless, pitiful giant' is but one, grotesque, instance of the strategic self-pity that American leaders expressed as the 1970s wore on. It is in a similar vein to the accusation frequently made in the 1980 election that Carter

---

[10] Henry Kissinger, *Year of Upheaval*, London 1982, p. 1176.
[11] Ibid., p. 258.

had 'dismantled' US military power. The call, enunciated by Reagan, for America to 'rearm' is a similarly misleading one, since it rests upon the pretence that the USA has in some measure *dis*armed. The same can be said for the torrent of analysis of American weakness, inferiority and vulnerability which came out in the late 1970s, playing upon the figures of the military balance to induce a sense of inferiority and legitimate a new burst of arms expenditure. Yet for all the factual distortion involved, this ideology of US weakness was not only widely believed, but reflected certain real changes in the international situation to which the call for new military expenditure was a reaction. In other words, however ideological the public debate in the west on Soviet-US military comparisons, there lay behind it substantive and identifiable political and military concerns which found expression in this myth of American 'disarmament'. The following analysis attempts, first to establish the real nature of the US-Soviet military balance in the early part of Cold War II, and then to suggest what the reasons for the alarmist US response may have been.

The charge of Soviet superiority covers a number of fields, the four major ones being expenditure, conventional forces, intermediate nuclear weapons and strategic nuclear weapons.

Expenditures: the Myth of a Soviet Lead

One of the central accusations of western leaders is that the USSR outspends the west on military matters, and that it is therefore incumbent on NATO , and the USA in particular, to 'catch up' on this Soviet lead. This is not, however, a valid claim. Estimates of military expenditure by both major powers vary enormously according to the methods used. The Soviet figure for 1980 military expenditure is 17 billion rubles, or around $26 billion; the US government figure for Soviet spending in the same year is $185 billion. The Soviet figure is obviously far too low: by its very definition, it omits wages, housing costs and Research and Development. There are however reasons for doubting the US figure, since the method of accounting, known as the 'CIA Dollar', is one that leads to a lot of exaggeration. In essence, it calculates Soviet costs by stating what it would cost to produce the same equipment or muster the same forces in the USA. But since Soviet costs may be lower, and since its conscript army is paid at only 20 per cent the rates of the US volunteer force, such calculations are highly inflationary.[12]

It is not just US estimates of Soviet costs however, that are, debatable: the accounting methods used by US government sources to estimate their own costs are also questionable. According to one analysis US military expenditures are up to 200 per cent higher than the figure given in official statistics.[13] The official 1980 figure of $127 billions represented 5.2 per cent of GNP. But this omitted several categories of military expenditure that should have been included: obligations incurred in previous fiscal years and actually disbursed in 1980; production of nuclear warheads by the Department of Energy; NASA, i.e. space, expenditures;[14] 'International Affairs', i.e. military aid to third world allies; and payments related to previous wars. If these categories are included then the US total rises to $223 billion, or 9.5 per cent of GNP. To this must be added the impact of military expenditures through the employment of over five million people in military-related activities.

The most judicious independent source of information on military expenditure is the Stockholm International Peace Research Institute, SIPRI.[15] Its figures confirm neither of the two main charges levelled against the Soviet Union in this domain: that Soviet expenditure has overtaken US expenditure, and that there was in the mid-1970s a sudden increase in the rate of Soviet military expenditure growth. SIPRI figures for the 1970–1980 period, calculated in constant 1978 prices, show that at

---

[12.] On the manipulation of Soviet military expenditure figures see Arthur Macy Cox, 'The CIA's Tragic Error', *New York Review of Books*, 6 November 1980. As Cox points out, the CIA's increased estimation of Soviet expenditure reflected a judgement that Soviet production was less efficient.

[13.] James Cypher, 'Rearming America', *Monthly Review*, November 1981.

[14.] For example, despite priority given in publicity to civilian tasks much of the work assigned to the US Space Shuttle is for military missions. It costs $18 million to position a spy satellite by shuttle, as opposed to $100 millions by a Titan rocket.

[15.] *World Armaments and Disarmament*, SIPRI Yearbook 1981, p. 156. Even if one takes the figures of the International Institute for Strategic Studies in London, which reflect a consensual western view, the overall balance of expenditure is in the west's favour. Thus in 1980 the USSR spent $185 b. (the CIA figure in current prices) compared to a US figure of $142 b; but the rest of the WTO spent only $16.7 b. compared to an 'other NATO' figure of $98 b. Once the Chinese ($56 b.) and Japanese ($8.9 b.) figures are added in, the overall balance becomes $201.7 b. for the USSR and its allies, as compared to $305 b. for the USA and its associates.

no point did the USSR outspend the USA, and that the rate of Soviet expenditure increase rarely rose above 2 per cent in any one year, i.e. it grew less than Soviet GNP over the same period. In 1980 the USA still outspent the USSR, by $111 billion to $107 billion.

Table Three

Soviet and US Military Expenditures 1970-1980

Figures are in US $mn, at 1978 constant prices and 1978 exchange-rates

	1971	1972	1973	1974	1975	1976	1977	1978	1979	1980
USA	120 655	121 105	114 976	113 666	110 229	104 261	108 537	109 247	109 861	111 236
USSR	93 900	95 400	96 900	98 300	99 800	101 300	102 700	104 200	105 700	107 300

Source: *SIPRI Yearbook 1981*, p. 156.

This comparison of expenditure on a bilateral basis is, nonetheless, the one most favourable to the USA's case. If it is not just the two major powers, but also their respective allies which are taken into account, then the expenditure balance is even more against the USSR. The USSR's Warsaw Pact allies are in overall economic and population terms far weaker than in the USA's NATO allies, and this disparity is reflected in the much greater contribution which the NATO states makes: total alliance expenditure figures for 1980 show NATO (including France) spending $194 billions to the WTO's $120 billions. If the strategic dimension is widened, then the Soviet disadvantage becomes still greater. For outside of the WTO the USSR had no military allies capable of making a significant military expenditure contribution: Vietnam and Cuba both rely on Soviet economic and military aid. The USA, on the other hand, had major economically independent allies who must be included in any balance-sheet of the forces favourable to it: Japan and South Africa, to name but two military effective powers. Added to these are Israel and the Arab states tied to US strategic concerns. The USSR must also face the possibility of war with China. Even if the Middle Eastern states are excluded in transpires that the 1980 military expenditures of the USSR and its allies were at most half those of the USA its associates and China.

Table Four

1980 Military Expenditures: the Strategic Balance

Figures in US $mn. at current 1978 prices.

USA	111 236
Other NATO	82 674
Japan	9 200
China	40 000
TOTAL	243 110
USSR	107 300
Other WTO	12 250
TOTAL	119 550

Source: *SIPRI Yearbook 1981*, pp. 156-7.

The western charge that Soviet military expenditure is an index of its belligerency must therefore involve other elements, and this turns out to be the case: a combination of semantic slippage and accounting devices serve to produce the impression of Soviet superiority. One common charge is that the Soviet levels of expenditure are 'unprecedented'. This is a true enough charge if it is taken, literally, as meaning that these levels are unprecedented for the USSR; but it is a misleading statement when, as is normal, this is said to be an unprecedented level *for any state*, i.e. to mean that Soviet spending is greater than American. Similarly it is often claimed that Soviet military expenditure represents a much higher percentage of GNP than US military expenditure. This is certainly true, since Soviet GNP is less than half US GNP: to achieve a similar amount of military expenditure the USSR would have to spend over twice the US GNP percentage. If, of course, the relevant criterion were taken to be military expenditure per head of population then quite different results would be achieved; since the USSR had in 1980 a population of 265 millions compared to a US population of 225 millions, the relevant figures, for military expenditure on a per capita basis, would be $404 (USSR) to $494 (USA), a US excess of around 25 per cent.

The issue of Soviet military expenditure is therefore one in which selected figures have been used to convey a picture that is substantially at variance with the facts. The allegation of Soviet outlays being at higher levels than the USA is, however, a convenient one in debates within the

USA on the need to raise arms spending there. The actual figure of military expenditure in any one fiscal year has been invested with immense importance in public debate within the USA, and there is no more appropriate means of advocating an increase than to brandish some version of what Soviet spending has been.

Far from confirming the argument of a sudden shift in Soviet policy in the mid-1970s, of a Soviet outspending of the USA, the figures show a lower rate, but one that has over the years brought Soviet expenditure to near American levels. The real leaps in Soviet expenditure came not in the 1970s, but in the 1960s, at a time when the Soviet leadership appears to have decided to attempt to achieve parity with the USA[16]: the outlays attained by the late 1970s reflect these longer-run Soviet decisions and tendencies, which were evident even before Detente, not some sudden change of policy in the mid-1970s which might legitimate a similar increase on the US side.

Conventional Forces: European and Third World Balances

A comparable, if more differentiated, picture emerges in the analysis of conventional forces. Here again the USSR is alleged to have recently acquired superiority over the USA and it is this conventional buildup, in Europe and in the third world, which is said to justify recent US force increases in both spheres. The reality is that the USSR has always had a certain conventional superiority in Europe, an advantage which geography alone would convey. In the third world, on the other hand, the USA continues to enjoy overwhelming superiority: what changed in the 1970s is that for the first time the USSR acquired a certain conventional capacity where previously it had had virtually none.

The argument over Soviet conventional superiority and in particular over its lead in the European theatre covers three areas—armies, air and sea power. While the USSR has always had a larger number of men under arms than the USA, this has been partly a reflection of the greater Soviet proportional contribution to the WTO, partly a compensation for US advantages in other fields, and partly a reflection of the USSR's greater population and the continuance of conscription. 1981 figures give Soviet armed

---

[16.] In constant 1960 prices, Soviet military expenditure rose from $22 b. in 1960 to $33 b. in 1963 and $40 b. in 1968 (SIPRI Yearbook 1968/9, pp. 200-1).

forces of 3.7 millions, as against US forces of 2.0 millions. But overall numbers of NATO military forces are still larger than those for the WTO: in 1981, 4,934,000 as compared to 4,778,000. Secondly, there is the fact that the USSR must face a foe on its eastern front, namely China: of a total of 171 Soviet divisions there are 44 facing China, as compared to only 31 facing NATO. These troops stationed in the east could obviously be moved; but the eastern front means that, short of massive redeployment, NATO does not face the full might of the Soviet forces. If the Chinese and Japanese totals are added, then the WTO faces a combined opposition of nearly 10 million compared to its total of under 5 million.[17]

These numerical calculations of troop strength omit any consideration of qualitative factors. Although hard to measure, these are of great importance in military calculations. The USA has experienced many problems in troop morale and combat readiness in recent years, but so too has the USSR. According to US intelligence in 1980 97 out of 150 Soviet divisions are at less than 50 per cent of their authorised strength and 134 are, on US criteria, not combat ready. If the US forces are affected by drug problems, the Soviet forces are negatively affected by high rates of alcohol consumption. Skill weaknesses are also widespread: if the US forces complain about the quality of their officer corps in an all-volunteer army, Soviet commanders have major problems with a conscript intake. Many Asian soldiers do not have an adequate understanding of Russian, and a significant difference in skills is the fact that most Soviet conscripts have to be taught to drive, and to read maps.[18]

One of the major arguments used by NATO commanders for expanding their European capabilities, both nuclear and conventional, is the Soviet advantage in tanks on the Central Front, in Europe, and there is no doubt that in numerical terms the USSR has a considerable lead in the European theatre: NATO has 17,000 main battle tanks in Europe, as opposed to 26,300 WTO tanks in eastern Europe and another 19,200 in the

---

[17.] *The Military Balance, 1981-2*, International Institute for Strategic Studies, London, pp. 112-13.
[18.] National Public Television, USA channel 12 'The Red Army', 6 May 1981. According to one military consultant, James Dunnigan, the USA is 'miles ahead' of the USSR in all major respects. 'Our forces are better trained and better equipped... American tanks, planes and ships are more sophisticated and more reliable' (*International Herald Tribune*, 21 November 1982).

western parts of the USSR. This gives the WTO a superiority of almost 3:1 in tank numbers. This Soviet lead in tanks is one of the factors most invoked in justifying the development of the neutron bomb and in legitimising the drive for theatre superiority in Europe itself. Yet even before the decision to deploy the neutron bomb as a battlefield anti-tank weapon, NATO commanders were confident that they had superiority over the WTO in this field.

The west has an enormous arsenal of sophisticated anti-tank guided missiles, an estimated 240,000 in all by October 1980.[19] These are a much cheaper way of countering any possible Soviet tank offensive than the deployment of a comparable number of tanks. Moreover the Soviet tanks and tank crews are noticeably inferior to those of NATO; while the Russians have begun to introduce a new battle tank, the T-72, Soviet tanks deployed in Europe are still in their majority T-62s, equipped with external fuel tanks which are highly vulnerable, and capable of firing only 6 rounds per minute compared to the NATO M-60 tanks' 30 per minute. The Soviet crews operate in much more cramped conditions, and receive only one tenth the annual firing practice of NATO crews, a conservation measure of great importance for reducing later battlefield accuracy and speed.[20] The apparent quantitative superiority of WTO over NATO forces in this much publicised field is therefore offset by a qualitative superiority on the west's side that predates the current measures designed to enhance NATO's European battlefield capability. While only a full battlefield confrontation could settle the matter, it appears from the importance of sophisticated electronic guidance mechanisms in the Lebanon and Falkland wars of 1982 that this dimension, in which the west leads, will be of even greater importance in the future.

The expansion of the Soviet airforce in recent years has provoked claims of superiority; here the main items listed have been the Backfire bomber and the WTO's fighter interceptor force. The Backfire, known to the WTO as the Tupolev 22M, is a supersonic plane that carries five

---

[19.] Dan Smith, 'The European Nuclear Theatre', in *Protest and Survive*, London 1980, p. 121; Andy Mack 'The Soviet Threat: Reality or Myth?', *Politics and Power* no. 4, 1981.
[20.] NATO General Ferdinand von Singer as quoted on BBC Radio 4, 'World This Weekend', 20 June 1981.

nuclear bombs and is capable of avoiding most forms of radar detection by flying at low altitudes. It is not, however, capable of hitting targets in the USA: it has a range of 2,500 miles. It is therefore in no way a compensation for the overall strategic possessed by the USA as a result of its Poseidon submarine fleet and its strategic force which can hit targets in the USSR. Indeed as part of the SALT-II agreements the Russians committed themselves to maintaining the current range of the Backfire and not extending it to give it a western hemisphere capability.

The Soviet superiority in interceptors is real enough, a ratio of 2.6:1; but interceptors are essentially defensive planes and it is NATO which has superiority in fighter ground attack aircraft, the most vital in modern offensives. Again, qualitative factors are of equal importance and here the NATO forces are in a far more favourable situation. The top Soviet fighter, the Mig-25, is made of steel, as compared to the F-14s and F-16s of the US airforce which are made of the much lighter titanium. The Mig-25 has bad visibility, a maximum speed of 2.8 Mach, and an effective range of only 200 miles. The F-16 is a proven all-weather fighter, and has an effective range of 500 miles. The top US fighter, the F-15 Eagle, has a range of over 1,500 miles. US advances in microelectronics, computers and precision-guided munitions all give the NATO air forces a sustained qualitative superiority over the WTO.

The Soviet development of improved combat capacity has been accompanied by the establishment of new long-range transport forces. In 1972 Soviet planes were able to move 25,000 soldiers from one end of eastern Europe to another in 40 days: by 1976 they moved 100,000 in less than 10 days. In 1967 and 1973, and again in 1977, they organised major airlifts of supplies to embattled allies—in the first two cases to Egypt and then to Ethiopia. In the second and third cases they used around 225 transport planes, or about 15 per cent of all available military cargo planes. The Soviet Union has certainly improved its air transport position, now possessing a limited capacity it did not have in the early 1960s; but this remains notably inferior to that of the USA. The Soviet long range air transport fleet has no in-flight refuelling capacity, and has therefore a far shorter range than that of the USA. The USSR has also restricted the growth of this air fleet: the largest plane, the Antonov-22, the only Soviet carrier capable of transporting tanks and heavy artillery, went out of production in 1974, when 50 had been constructed. The

Soviet forces do include substantial numbers of airborne troops, roughly equal in number to those available to the USA. But these can operate only where there already exists a ground support system, i.e. in eastern Europe, not in the third world.[21]

A more visible increase in the Soviet Union's relative strength has been in the naval field. This is one particularly relevant to Russia's third world projection. The Cuba missile crisis of 1962, in which the USA successfully blockaded the Caribbean island, illustrated Russia's lack of a global naval capacity. The next year, however, Soviet warships began deep-water deployments. The Soviet Union has had a permanent squadron in the eastern Mediterranean since 1964. In 1967 Soviet ships anchored in Egyptian ports helped deter Israeli attacks. In 1968 the first Soviet warships paid visits to Indian Ocean ports. In 1975 they provided an off-shore backup to the Cuban expeditionary forces in Angola, and in 1977 they performed a similar function during the Cuban intervention in support of Ethiopia. Whereas until the 1960s the Soviet fleet was confined to waters near friendly territory, and played an insignificant role compared to the army and airforce, it has since become an instrument of Soviet projection further from home, a change associated with the energetic naval commander, Admiral Gorshkov.

As a result of a major shipbuilding programme organised by Gorshkov in the 1960s, the USSR had by the end of the 1970s 900 warships to NATO's 700, and about 360 submarines to NATO's 260. The Soviet naval expansion has therefore given the WTO numerical superiority over the west and the USSR's strategic projection beyond its own coastal waters has greatly increased over the past two decades. But the appearance of superiority is deceptive, since NATO has a clear qualitative lead. In larger ships, frigates and above, NATO outnumbers the WTO by 460 to 195 ships: the majority of the WTO vessels are smaller and more obsolescent.[22]

Much mileage is made out of the claim that the US navy's complement has declined by about half in the period since 1965, but this calculation

---

[21.] Michael Klare, 'The Power Projection Gap: A Comparison of US and Soviet Long-range Intervention Capabilities', in *Beyond the 'Vietnam Syndrome'; US Intervention in the 1980s*, Washington 1981, pp. 110-33.

[22.] 'NATO and Warsaw Pact', *The Economist*, 8 August 1980.

omits the more important facts of qualitative expansion, achieved by
building larger and more sophisticated ships: since 1960 the USA has outbuilt the USSR in warship tonnage by three to one and NATO has outbuilt
the WTO by nine to two.[23] The WTO superiority in submarines is again offset by quality: whereas the Russians have, under SALT-I, 50 per cent
more missile–carrying submarines than the USA, they are only capable of
keeping about half of the US number at sea at any one time. In other key
areas there is still no contest. The first Soviet aircraft carrier, the *Kiev*
launched in 1975, can be used only by helicopters and the three other
carriers are used only by submarine detection helicopters: the USA has
fourteen aircraft carriers capable of launching fighter planes with a deep
penetration capability, three of them nuclear-powered, and the European
members of NATO have six more. Since navies are particularly relevant in
projecting power in third world situations, much US alarm has centred on
the Soviet naval expansion but NATO outnumbers the WTO three to one,
in troop-landing craft, and in deployable naval troops the US advantage is
overwhelming: its Marine Corps has 188,000 men, compared to the
USSR's 12,000-strong naval infantry.[24] Despite all the expressions of
western alarm at the increased level of Soviet deployment in waters far
from home, the numbers of Soviet ships in the Indian Ocean, Caribbean,
Mediterranean and Pacific remain below those of the west.[25]

These advantages in equipment are compounded by three additional
factors which militate against the USSR's gaining even remote equality in
the naval field. The first is geography. The USSR has only six major naval
bases, all of them in the Soviet Union itself and liable to closure in the
event of war by western blockades. The only Soviet base with
unhindered acccess to the open seas is that of Petropavlovsk on the Kam-
chatka Peninsula in the Far East, and it itself has to be supplied by sea
from the port of Vladivostok. The USA has dozens of naval bases, many

[23.] Barry Posen and Stephen Van Evera, 'Overarming and Underwhelming', *Foreign Policy*, No. 40, Fall 1980, p. 115.
[24.] *The Military Balance*, 1981-2, pp. 8, 13.
[25.] For example, figures for April 1981 give the USA 17 combat ships patrolling the Indian Ocean as against 5 Soviet combat ships. These figures omit British and French ships also in the area (*International Herald Tribune*, 21 April 1981).

of them outside the USA and it has unhindered access to the oceans.[26] It is a reflection of the different deployment of their two navies that whereas almost half of all US ground combat units are overseas, 80% of Soviet divisions are inside the USSR. A second US advantage in naval competition comes from history: the Soviet navy has very little combat experience since it played only a tiny role in World War II and has only expanded within the space of the last generation. Thirdly, working conditions in the Soviet navy appear to be very unsatisfactory. Soviet crews may receive as little as ten days' leave in three years; the mutiny in the Baltic in 1976 when fifty-four crew members reportedly tried to hijack a cruiser to Sweden was probably an indication of how far tensions within the Soviet fleet can develop. Whether these problems are greater than those faced by western navies is debatable: what cannot be disputed is that the rapid numerical expansion of Soviet naval forces since the early 1960s has met with substantial manning problems that qualify the apparent statistical increase in maritime capacity.

The conventional military balance is normally treated as of less dramatic significance than the nuclear one, despite the fact that it is non-nuclear forces which absorb the greater part of military budgets and it is these forces which will be the first to be used, whether in conflicts in Europe or in third world crisis situations. Yet, if the stress upon nuclear weapons often has a primarily ideological and symbolic function, since they would only be used in the last instance, that on conventional forces can have a much more immediate political import where the states involved are confronted with threats within their own spheres of influence. The NATO alarm about Soviet conventional force developments in the 1970s is therefore two-edged: it is partly a response to changes in Soviet capabilities, but it is also a reaction to political problems in the third

---

26. One of the consistent aims of US policy has been to prevent the USSR from acquiring permanent naval facilities abroad at all. A Soviet attempt to base submarines in Cuba in 1969 was blocked by US pressure. Soviet success in securing bases in Egypt and Somalia in the late 1960s was soon reversed by the offer of substantial economic aid by Saudi Arabia to both sides. The USSR lost its submarine base at Vlöre in Albania when the split between the two erupted in 1961. Much of the debate skates over what is involved in a 'base', a term which can cover anything from the occasional use of facilities to the stationing of personnel and equipment in a sovereign area; but even on the loosest 'facility' definition, the USSR's bases network in the third world is far smaller than that of the USA. While the USA has dozens of overseas naval bases and facilities, the USSR has no full bases and a handful of facilities.

world for which the west now feels it is less prepared than it previously was. The irony is that in the European theatre, the balance has, if anything, shifted in NATO's favour during the 1970s, with the deployment of anti-tank weapons, while the USSR has for the first time established a limited third world capability. Yet it is in the European theatre as much as anywhere that Cold War alarm has been generated, partly by continued emphasis on Soviet tank superiority, and partly by linking this to the issue of the theatre balance which has provided the third of the major themes upon which the argument on the military balance is conducted.

Theatre Nuclear Forces in Europe: Pretexts for 1979

The focus of debate on the east-west military balance during the latter part of the 1970s was on nuclear weapons, both strategic, i.e. for use in a direct US-Soviet exchange, and theatre, i.e. for use in Europe, whether in intermediate-range exchanges, from one country to another, or in shorter-range battlefield conditions. It has, in particular, been the NATO contention of an underlying inferiority in TNFs—Theatre Nuclear Forces—which has been used to legitimate the 1979 decision to install Cruise and Pershing II missiles in Europe by 1983. Two main arguments are used: first, that the Soviet Union has a superiority or even monopoly in delivery systems; secondly, that the USSR has superiority in the number of warheads targeted for use in Europe. In fact, the USSR long had a marked inferiority in TNF delivery systems and only began, in 1977, to overcome this by installing the SS-20s. The USSR has always had a great overall inferiority in TNF warheads, but it has had superiority in certain categories of these. What NATO is trying to achieve is a new comprehensive superiority in both delivery systems and warheads. To clarify this, a bit of history may be of some relevance.

Although it sprang into public view in 1979, the issue of TNFs in Europe is not a new one.[27] NATO decided in 1954 to install them as a way of compensating for its overall weakness in conventional forces on the Central Front. From that time onwards, when the first bombs were on

---

[27.] Chris Paine, 'Pershing II: the Army's strategic weapon', *The Bulletin of the Atomic Scientists*, October 1980; Myra Struck, 'Theater Nuclear Weapons and Europe', *SAIS Review*, No. 2, Summer 1981; William Arkin, 'Nuclear Weapons in Europe', in Mary Kaldor and Dan Smith eds, *Disarming Europe*, London 1982.

planes stationed on aircraft carriers in the Mediterranean, the use of nuclear weapons in theatre operations, i.e.short of an allout war, has been part of NATO fighting doctrine. It has always been assumed that NATO forces would move rapidly to the use of such weapons in the event of conflict with the Soviet Union.

The current pattern of TNF deployment in Europe came into being in the late 1950s when the first missiles were installed. The USA stationed Thor and Jupiter TNFs in Europe and Turkey, as well as 7,000 short-range nuclear weapons for use in battlefield or 'theatre' situations. For their part, the Russians deployed the SS-4 and SS-5 missiles, the equivalent of the Thors and Jupiters, as well as thousands of battlefield weapons, mounted like the American units on tanks, artillery units and rockets. There has, therefore, been European theatre nuclear deployment of missiles for two decades. As in the strategic nuclear domain, the major changes were made by the Americans: from 1962 onwards they began to pull out their land-based missiles and replace them by submarine-launched Polaris weapons. From 1970 onwards the US Polaris submarines were replaced by the Poseidons, each with 16 missiles carrying ten or more MIRVed warheads.

This qualitative improvement in the US position in Europe was matched by an even greater US advantage, the deployment from 1967 onwards of ICBMs based in the USA which could also hit the USSR, the Minutemen. This opened up the possibility of the USA being able to fight a nuclear war in Europe while keeping its ICBM force intact. Despite the availability of Minutemen, the USA did not decrease its TNF commitment to NATO, and this US component was supplemented by smaller British and French nuclear missile contingents. The latter was, despite Gaullist reservations about NATO from 1966 onwards, an effective part of the western military alliance. The USA, Britain and France all retained a bomber-carried nuclear capacity, and the French maintained their own land-based missile system.

Not content with the advantages it already had in the quality of its TNFs, however, NATO had from the early 1970s begun considering other improvements, and in particular the deployment once again of improved land-based missiles. These would be of a less vulnerable character, because mobile, and with much higher accuracy, thus permitting of attacks against selected military targets in the east rather than against the cities targeted in more indiscriminate periods. It was in this context, in the early 1970s, that the first plans for the deployment of Cruise and Pershing II were made. The reasons for such a programme were essentially two: first, the desire to implement a new strategic doctrine, the 'counterforce' policy, now made possible by developments in microelectronics which rendered these missiles more accurate; and secondly, to offset the advantages of the WTO in conventional and geographic terms by an added nuclear capability. The US army also wanted its own missiles and so pushed ahead with research on the Pershing II from 1969 onwards. These plans long predated the deployment of SS-20s. The imbalance in land-based missiles was not a major factor: the US had itself voluntarily created this by withdrawing its Thor and Jupiter rockets in the 1960s, and the process of MIRVing produced a balance overwhelmingly in the west's favour since this had been introduced by the Poseidon in 1970. NATO always held the initiative and it was only in 1977, after waiting for the west to accept negotiation on European missiles, that the USSR began to respond by introducing the SS-20 as a replacement for the 700 or so SS-4s and SS-5s.[28]

The SS-20's advantages over earlier Soviet rockets have often been mis-stated. Its range of 2,500 miles is only slightly greater; its accuracy is no greater than that of the Pershing–I deployed in the early 1960s; and although it is mobile, this is not an absolute mobility, since, as US Department of Defense officials have made clear, the sites for SS-20s have to be surveyed and prepared in advance. By 1982 US reconnaissance satellites had been able to identify the thirty-nine bases and surrounding sites in the USSR where the SS-20s were located. The real advantages of the SS-20 over its predecessors lie elsewhere: first, instead of the single one-megaton warhead of the earlier missiles, it has three warheads, of 150 kilotons each; secondly, each SS-20 launcher is equipped with one refire missile which can be used in a matter of hours after the first missile has been launched. The SS-20 therefore increases Soviet firepower in the European theatre considerably: although it has decreased the number of

---

[28.] The Soviet installation of SS-20s came only *after* the west had *for several years* refused to include the TNFs in the SALT talks. NATO first detected SS-20 deployment in western Russia in October 1977.

missiles, it has increased the number of warheads, and as of July 1981 175 SS-20s had been deployed against NATO.[29]

The SS-20's basic function is to serve as a retaliatory weapon—it is not accurate enough to serve counterforce functions. It has increased Soviet capacities to some extent, but it has not reversed the balance in Europe: it is being used as a pretext to justify a US advance that was mooted long before the Russians deployed this new missile. The Russians, by introducing MIRVed and less vulnerable SS-20 missiles in 1977, have begun to catch up on US advantages gained in the 1960s and early 1970s: hence the US-proposed 'zero option', of removing Soviet SS-20s in return for a cancellation of the Cruise and Pershing II missiles is designed to return to a pre-existing US advantage and to confirm NATO superiority. The alleged Soviet superiority in land-based missiles is an irrelevancy, given NATO's other forces, and is a fact with which NATO has been happy to live for over a decade.

A greater degree of proportion can be introduced by bringing in other NATO delivery systems which can also send nuclear warheads to the USSR. First there are the submarine-based missiles of the USA, Britain and France: the USA has put 400 warheads on Poseidon submarines at the disposal of NATO; there are four British Polaris submarines, with a total of 64 A-3 missiles, each with three warheads; and France has five nuclear submarines, with a total of 80 missiles. In addition, NATO possesses a substantial nuclear bomber capacity, capable of hitting targets in the USSR: 156 US F-111s, stationed in Britain, and around 500 Phantoms, A-6s and A-7s based on aircraft carriers off the European coast, and in the Mediterranean. To these can be added 55 FB-111A bombers, based in the USA but assigned for European deployment, and 55 British Vulcans and 46 French Mirages. The WTO has a much larger number of planes capable of delivering nuclear warheads—around 3,600 of these—but it has only around 550 medium-range bombers of the Badger, Blinder and Backfire variety, the equivalents of the US, British and French nuclear bombers, which total around 1,000 planes.[30]

[9.] On the SS-20 see Andrew Cockburn in *The Nation*, 28 November 1981, and William Arkin in ibid., 24 October 1981. The figure of thirty-nine SS-20 bases is given in *Le Monde*, 7-8 March 1982.

The arsenals of the two sides comprise large numbers of theatre warheads, but in overall terms the advantage is with the west. The USA has 7,000 warheads stationed in Europe and another 10,000 which it could easily bring to Europe. The number of Soviet warheads is disputed, estimates ranging from 3,500 to 6,000: even this higher figure does not give the USSR superiority.[31] The Soviet Union does have one real advantage in the European theatre, but it is the one that it has always possessed, namely that of geography. This is, however, only an advantage in attack, enabling the WTO to deploy all its forces against NATO's western European positions. It is this which gives the USSR a lead in delivery aircraft. But this same immutable factor is also a major disadvantage in defence: it leaves Soviet territory open to attack by NATO's TNFs as much as by the ICBMs stationed in the USA . For the Russians NATO's TNFs are no different from ICBMS since both can hit the territory of the USSR. It is for this reason that improvements in NATO's TNF capacity affect not only the European theatre balance, but the whole strategic balance between the USSR and the USA. The Soviet Union has in recent years sought to improve its European position by introducing changes which NATO had introduced years before; the USA, already intent upon introducing its own qualitative improvements, has taken the Soviet lessening of the gap as a pretext for a new drive towards superiority.

Strategic Nuclear Weapons: Quest for a New Advantage

Strategic nuclear weapons are both the foundation of the two major powers' military capabilities, and the issue around which enormous emotion and concern is generated in military debates. Just as a supposed

---

30. Dan Smith, William Arkin as above.
31. Arkin, op. cit., p. 43. The picture changes, however, when different categories of TN are considered. Between one third and half of NATO's 7,000 TNF warheads are for battle field or short-range use, up to 100 miles. The Russians have deployed the smalles numbers of warheads in this battlefield range, and in one category, that of atomic demoli tion munitions, they have produced nothing to match NATO's capacity. In the range c 1,000 miles and over NATO also has an advantage in warheads of, in 1980, 1,420 as op posed to the WTO's 1,040. Where the USSR has a striking advantage is in the range be tween these two, i.e. in the 100 to 1,000 mile range, and here it has 1,030 to NATO' 390. Similarly, if all warheads other than battlefield ones are totalled up, i.e. the tw

'Missile Gap' in favour of the USSR accompanied the burst of US military expenditure in the early 1960s, at a time when the USA enjoyed in reality overwhelming superiority,[32] so in the late 1970s, when the US advantage had been reduced but not terminated, a similar strategic alarmism was to be found in western discussions of Soviet nuclear strength, this time in the shape of the equally mythical 'Window of Vulnerability'.

As with the expenditure question, much of the argument rests upon a combination of linguistic slippage and debatable systems of measurement. The simplest index is that of strategic warheads, and here a gradual Soviet closing of the gap is evident. In 1960 the USA had a twelve-one lead over the USSR in deliverable strategic warheads. In 1970 the USA had somewhat more than a two-to-one lead (4,000 warheads to 1,800). By 1980 the US lead had fallen to 3:2 (9,200 to 6,000); but it still had an enormous advantage. In the other most important index of comparison, delivery systems, the Soviet Union enjoyed by 1980 a certain advantage, with more ICBM launchers, and more SLBM launching tubes, but fewer strategic bombers. All in all, the USSR had 2,501 delivery systems to the USA's 2,124. But the discrepancy of Soviet superiority in delivery systems with American superiority in warheads points to an underlying US advantage, namely the far higher number of US missiles which have multiple warheads i.e. are MIRVed, a refinement introduced by the USA on its missiles in 1970 and not replicated by the Russians until at least 1974. Both in warheads and in this most important of technical innovations the USSR has continued to develop its capability, but has remained somewhat behind the USA.

---

larger categories are combined, then the WTO has an advantage. It is this lead in long and medium range TNF warheads which NATO officials are particularly prone to stress. When this selection is combined with the omission of the Poseidon submarines, 400 of whose warheads are committed to NATO, then the picture of an overwhelming Soviet superiority in TNF acquires a semblance of plausibility.

32. Daniel Ellsberg, 'Call to Mutiny', in the American edition of *Protest and Survive*, New York 1981.

72

Table Five

us and Soviet Nuclear Arsenals, 1970 and 1980

	1970	1980
ICBMS		
USA	1 054	1 052
USSR	1 487	1 398
SLBMs		
USA	656	576
USSR	248	950
Long-range bombers		
USA	512	348
USSR	156	156
Total warheads		
USA	4 000	9 200
USSR	1 800	6 000

Sources: SIPRI Yearbooks 1979, p. 422, and 1981, p. 273.

There are other measurements of strategic nuclear capability: in some of these the Soviet Union would appear to have gained an advantage over the USA in the 1970s. One of these is throw-weight, the weight of the top stage of the missile, including the warheads, guidance systems and missile casings. By 1977 the Russians had acquired a three-to-one lead in throw-weight. Another index is megatonnage, i.e. the explosive yield of a bomb measured in millions of tons of TNT. In 1977 the Russians enjoyed a three-to-two lead in megatonnage. But on their own these indices, although suitable for frightening an enemy, are not a sufficient guide to military capability, since what is above all necessary for explosive impact is accuracy. Soviet missiles remain heavier, because the technology involved is less advanced than that in us missiles. They have a larger explosive yield, because there are fewer of them. But they are, in general, less accurate:[33] us lethality was nearly three times greater than Soviet in 1980.

---

[33] On comparative Soviet and American ICBM accuracy see Robert Aldrige, *The Counterforce Syndrome*, Washington 1978, p. 60; SIPRI 1981, p. 22. Technical discus-

Beyond these static comparisons of Soviet and US capabilities, much discussion in the USA has focussed on the 'Window of Vulnerability' as a reason for introducing a new generation of US strategic missiles.[34] This is the claim that Soviet missile accuracy has so improved that by the mid-1980s the Soviet Union could launch a successful first strike against the land-based US ICBMs, the most vulnerable but also the most accurate part of the US strategic nuclear triad. Whilst the US forces would be able to retaliate against Soviet cities, they would not do so for fear of inviting a similar response from the USSR and they would not be accurate enough to reply in kind by hitting Soviet military targets. It is this 'Window of Vulnerability' which the development of a new US ICBM capability is allegedly designed to close.

The USSR could, in theory, launch a sudden first strike against the US land-based strategic missiles in the northern plains, and the undoubted improvements in Soviet missile accuracy in recent years would increase the destruction such an attack would bring about. Given the speed with which an attack of this kind could be launched, and given the deep-seated US concern about such an assault, the prospect of Soviet missiles coming through the 'Window' is one that has a certain effect in the USA. But apart from the mere abstract possibility of such a strike, something that has always existed, the 'Window' thesis is quite bogus.

First of all, the opening of the 'Window' in the early 1980s does not signify a Russian strategic *advantage* vis-à-vis the USA: what US commentators completely ignore is that this 'Window', the possibility of a first strike by one power against the other, has been open in the opposite direction for many years. The USA has been able, in theory, to launch such a surprise first strike on Soviet ICBMs since the 1950s. Secondly, the 'Window' thesis rests upon quite unrealistic assumptions of what a Soviet first strike could achieve. Even if 90 per cent of the Soviet missiles did hit their targets, this would leave 10 percent of the US ICBM force, i.e.

---

sions of missile effectivity tend to use the concept of counter-military potential or 'lethality', an index combining both explosive power and expected accuracy. The fact that in 1980 the total lethality of the US strategic forces was nearly three times that of the USSR is given in *Strategic Survey 1980-1981*, p. 14. The US argument rested on the assumption that during the first half of the 1980s Soviet lethality would overtake that of the USA, an unlikely presupposition given the much less sophisticated Soviet delivery systems.

[34.] On the 'Window' argument see Fred Kaplan, *Dubious Specter*: A Skeptical Look at the Soviet Nuclear Threat, Washington 1980, pp. 40-52; Lawrence Freedman, *The Evolution of Nuclear Strategy*, London 1981, pp. 387-92; Kissinger, op. cit., p. 1003.

one hundred MIRVed missiles, intact: more than enough to wipe out all major Soviet cities. Given the possibilities of technical failure and misdirection en route, plus the dangers of 'fratricide', i.e. one missile explosion knocking out another incoming missile, even such a 90 per cent success rate against US ICBMs would be extremely doubtful.

However, the US ability to respond does not rest upon its ICBM force alone, since the two other branches of the strategic triad, bombers and SLBMs, would remain intact. The USA keeps a third of its strategic bomber force on alert at any one time, and could use this to reply to a Soviet first strike. Even more importantly, a Soviet first strike would not hit the USA's submarine-based missile force, and this mobile component of the strategic deterrent forms a much more important part of the US force than it does of the Soviet: fully 54 per cent of the US strategic warheads are submarine-based, compared to only 21 per cent of the Soviet. By contrast the USA has only 25 per cent of its strategic warheads in ICBM sites compared to 79 per cent for the Russians. This simple difference, a further reflection of the greater technical sophistication of US weaponry, makes the Soviet Union still far more liable to a 'Window of Vulnerability' style first strike. It also means that the USA would retain more than enough capacity to destroy major Soviet sites, civil and military, in the event of a retaliation after an initial Soviet strike. The missiles on only two Poseidon submarines could hit over 200 targets in the USSR. The only objectives which the SLBMs are believed to be not capable of destroying, i.e. where the land-based ICBMs are superior, are hardened missile sites.[35] But the SLBMs could hit other military sites in addition to Soviet cities and they thus constitute a more than sufficient deterrent to keep the so-called Window firmly closed.

Much of the supposed appeal of the 'Window' thesis comes from a confusion in the term 'first strike'.[36] Literally, this just means the first use of strategic nuclear weapons in a full-scale attack on the enemy, something either side is capable of doing. But this term also suggests a *successful*, pre-emptive or disarming, first strike, i.e. a sudden attack which prevents the other side from replying. This would be either because all the attacked country's strategic missiles have been destroyed,

[35.] Kaplan, op. cit., p. 45.
[36.] My thanks are due to Bill Arkin for his advice on this point.

or because even if it has some left, it is at such a disadvantage that its political leadership will decide to surrender rather than to pursue the conflict. The combination of inaccuracy and diversification of missile delivery systems, on land and sea, means that this equation of first strike with disarming first strike cannot hold. The Soviet Union, and even more so the USA, is capable of replying to any first strike from its opponent with a devastating response. It is here that the absolute falsity of the 'Window' thesis lies.

US discussion of a supposed strategic inferiority to the USSR also understates the advantages which the USA has in two other significant respects: readiness, and detection. In both submarine and strategic bomber readiness the USA has a distinct lead over the USSR. The USSR has only ten of its missile–carrying submarines at sea at any one time, and the remaining fifty are in harbour positions where they can easily be hit by US missiles. The USA has fewer submarines, but, out of its total of forty-four, twenty of these, i.e. twice as many as the Soviet figure, are at sea at any one time. The Russians keep none of their strategic bombers on runway alert; as noted, the Americans keep a third of their much larger strategic bomber fleet in such a state at any one time, and each plane carries four nuclear bombs.

In the field of detection the United States was able to gain a major lead in the latter part of the 1970s: conventional satellite reconnaissance can identify the location of Soviet ICBMs and strategic bombers, but the problem of identifying the location of missile-carrying submarines was believed to be insoluble. It was these submarines which rendered the strategic deterrent force of both sides most invulnerable to a first strike. However, by the end of the decade the USA had developed the technology for detecting Soviet submarines, using a combination of aerial detection systems and fixed sonar arrays on the ocean beds.[37] Since Soviet SLBMs have a maximum range of 4,500 nautical miles and since there were nor-

---

[37.] On the US led in Anti-Submarine Warfare see SIPRI Yearbook 1981, pp. 23-5, IISS *Strategic Survey* 1980-1981, pp. 31-6; Aldridge, op. cit., pp. 34-43. According to the SIPRI Yearbook 1979, p. 427, 'these combined developments may soon make it possible to detect, locate and destroy all adversary missile submarines within a time period so short as to effectively eliminate the adversary's sea-based retaliatory capability'. Two other components of the counterforce capability are long-range communications and anti-satellite warfare, in both of which the USA also has a marked advantage.

mally four Soviet nuclear submarines within range of the US mainland, the task of keeping track of Soviet missile-carrying submarines was well within US capacities. The Soviet ships were the more liable to detection since they had to reach the open seas from Soviet ports through relatively narrow channels where they could initially be located. How far the USA had yet ringed the oceans of the world with this anti-submarine detection system is not known, but there could be no doubting the US superiority in this dimension: 'Though the Soviets have more submarines, the US can easily detect where they are—whereas the Soviets, so far as is known, have never tracked even one of the 2,000 voyages that US missile-firing submarines have made, some of them very close to the USSR's shores.'[38] The easiest part of the US move against such submarines would be the actual destruction of the submarines, for, once detected, they are relatively slow moving targets that US air- and sea-borne systems could soon eliminate. The temptations of a pre-emptive US first strike have therefore grown through this, more menacing, marine Window of Vulnerability.

The 1970s began with what appeared to be an acceptance by both sides of strategic equivalence: the SALT-I agreement ratified in 1972. This limited the totals of delivery systems—of ICBMs and SLBMs. Both totals were in the USSR's favour, but this Soviet lead in the means of delivery concealed a great US lead in other fields: the USA had at that time twice the number of warheads, and greater missile accuracy. It had introduced multiple warheads on its missiles and taken submarine launching of missiles much further. SALT-I was therefore, as is explained in Chapter Eight, an attempt by the USA to freeze an existing superiority. The decade since SALT-I has seen both sides continue to respect the delivery system totals specified in that treaty; they have sought to develop their forces and gain advantages over the other in those other areas not specified in SALT.

The roots of the instability in strategic weaponry of the early 1980s result from this continued development of strategic nuclear forces on both sides, and the political consequences attendant upon it. Three major trends have contributed to this situation:

1. *Soviet Quantitative Advance:* The USSR has gone some way to reducing the gap in numbers of strategic warheads. Were present trends to

---

38. *Time*, 27 July 1981.

continue, the Soviet Union may at some point in the 1980s draw level with the USA. At the same time, Soviet missile accuracy has increased: the major ICBM, the SS-18, is believed to have an accuracy of 1,500 feet which gives it a 60 per cent chance of knocking out a hardened ICBM silo. Another major strategic development in the Soviet arsenal has been the great increase in the number of submarine-launched missiles, the total of which has risen by almost four times since 1970. These three developments have not, as already noted, given the USSR an overall strategic advantage over the USA. The new Soviet missile, the SS-18, is no more accurate than the upgraded Minuteman already possessed by the USA. The American forces have more warheads; overall US missile accuracy is greater; and the US submarine force is both proportionately larger and more invulnerable than the Soviet one. But the perceived margin of superiority which US strategic forces had enjoyed in the 1950s and 1960s has been substantially reduced. This alone constitutes a major incentive for the US forces to introduce a new round of 'modernisation' that will in some measure restore that earlier margin. Were the MX to be installed, it would have an accuracy twice that of the SS-18.

2. US *Qualitative Advance*: Far more important than these quantitative changes during the 1970s has been the qualitative shift, the improvement of accuracy and detection which, together, encourage the 'counter force doctrine' and theories of war-winning.[39] Although present in US strategic thinking from the 1950s, and enunciated by then Secretary of Defense MacNamara in 1962, this 'counterforce' theory has become more of a practical possibility in the 1970s as a result of technological developments. Counterforce weapons are aimed not at cities but at the military targets of the enemy; they are usually discussed in the context of fighting a limited nuclear war, consisting of controlled exchanges against the military targets of the enemy. Even such an approach, which purports to reduce the dangers of a nuclear exchange, has its inconsistencies: it assumes that the other side will accept the limited nature of the exchange, and that in the heat of battle controls will apply. But the real problem with the counterforce doctrine is that it suggests another possibili-

---

[39.] Allan Krass and Dan Smith, 'Nuclear Strategy and Technology', in Smith and Kaldor, *Disarming Europe*, pp. 3-34; Robert Aldridge, *The Counterforce Syndrome*; Freedman, op. cit., *passim; Strategic Survey 1981*, pp. 12-17.

ty, namely that of a successful pre-emptive first strike. For if accuracy, detection and surprise are sufficient then it may be possible to hit all of the enemy's strategic delivery systems in one go, or at least to disable so many of them that it decides to surrender.

Whereas strategic doctrine had, in the past, rested upon the defensive theory of deterrence or Mutually Assured Destruction—i.e. threatening to hit enemy cities if one side was attacked first—counterforce involves the capacity to win wars and even a potentially offensive theory, of using the accuracy of missiles to launch the first strike that could hit the ICBMS, SLBMS and long-range bombers of the enemy force in one knock-out blow. In the words of one analysis: 'It would seem that both the purpose and effect of military technological efforts since 1945 have been to overcome the notions that nuclear weapons are unusable and that nuclear war is unthinkable. The 1970s in particular have produced technological solutions to many of the limitations which in past years have inhibited national leaders from using nuclear weapons as instruments of political coercion and military power.'[40] The initiative in this field lies with the USA, whose accuracy and detection capabilities far outstrip those of the USSR: the result is that the temptation of building up a new superiority has opened up, much of the 'modernisation' of the US strategic force being designed to make that possibility a reality in the 1980s.

3. *Changed International Context*: On their own, these two trends in the strategic balance would not necessarily have aroused great concern and those military personnel concerned to advance the 'modernisation' programmes might have encountered resistance from politicians and the public. But anxiety about the details of the strategic balance was accentuated by other developments in international affairs: for the US margin of superiority in nuclear weapons of the 1950s and 1960s was associated with an overall political superiority—over the USSR, over the third world, and over its capitalist allies in Europe and Japan. In all three dimensions US power lessened in the 1970s. What served to highlight the change in the quantitative balance, and to enhance the attractions of counterforce, was this change in the political climate. The conclusion drawn in Washington was that by restoring a US strategic nuclear superiority these

---

[40.] SIPRI Yearbook 1981, p. 19.

other problems could the more easily be resolved. Behind the debate on strictly military matters, relating to quantities and quality of weapons, lie political concerns part rational part emotional, but all intelligible, which provide the underlying dynamic of the arms race.

The argument here has been that the US military programmes of the Second Cold War period reflect the combination of three interrelated considerations: an attempt to lengthen once again the quantitative gap between US and Soviet capabilities; a desire to take advantage of the opportunities for greater superiority opened up by new technological developments to develop a war-winning capacity; and anxiety at the manner in which the erosion of the US military superiority had led to the emergence of challenges to US policy in the world at large.

Forceful as these concerns might be, however, they still leave open the elementary question of what superiority is, and in particular what sense such an advantage has in an era of overkill and mutually assured destruction. What can be said of the US vulnerability to a Soviet attempt at a preemptive first strike can also be said of Soviet vulnerability, even when the full range of US counterforce weapons is in place: that it is impossible to assume that such a strike could be so successful that the Soviet side would not retain some capacity for second strikes against the USA's cities. Massive retaliatory destruction would be possible. In that sense, the kind of 'absolute' superiority which the USA did enjoy in the 1950s may now be unattainable by either side. But even if this absolute superiority is now a chimera, the same cannot be said of what may be termed 'relative' or 'strategic' superiority, i.e. a margin which it is believed could serve to intimidate the other side into submission. No one knows how effective, diplomatically and militarily, such superiority might be in the event of a real crisis. What matters is that many people in the USA believe it to be important for the reasons given at the beginning of this chapter and it is this belief which serves to justify the current US drive for strategic 'modernisation'.

Two conclusions follow from this survey of the arms race, and of the debate concerning it, in the 1970s and early 1980s. The first is that for all its secrecy and technological momentum, the arms race is to a considerable extent determined by political concerns: i.e. the two fundamental components of international politics, the Great Contest and the nuclear arms race, intersect with each other. Of the four reasons suggested as being behind the current US drive for relative superiority, three—ideology, bargaining power and burdening the enemy—derive from the globalised social conflict. The second and related conclusion is that on its own the arms race would not have precipitated the Second Cold War: that developed only out of the combination of the shift in the military balance with other developments that compounded us alarm at the change in the military sphere. It is now time to analyse these in more detail.

4.
A New Period
of Third World Revolutions

Throughout the postwar epoch, the stability of the dividing line in Europe, and the increased prosperity of the populations living on both sides of it, have contrasted with the experience of the third world where war, social revolution and mass poverty have been widespread. If conflict has been 'cold', in the sense of bloodless, in the European theatre, it has cost millions of lives in Asia, Africa and Latin America. Here revolutionary movements, supported to a greater or lesser extent by the USSR, have been fighting the armies of the west and its allies. Further millions have died in the avoidable human misery brought on by the system of exploitation implanted and maintained by the metropolitan capitalist countries. And many more have been killed in wars between third world states, in which both social systems have been involved, and where the arms sold by the developed countries of both blocs have been used to an increasing degree.[1] In all twenty-five million people are believed to have died in third world conflicts since 1945.

Of these three sources of death and destruction in the third world—campaigns to reverse social revolution, mass poverty, inter-state wars—it is the first which forms the subject of this chapter, for it is the increased incidence of third world revolution in the 1970s which has provoked such alarm in the west. Despite the extent of mass poverty, and the plight of the 800 millions estimated to be living in absolute misery, it is not these, on their own, which provoke international crises. The dangers of third world inter-state wars have threatened to draw their

---

[1] Lucio Magri, 'The Peace Movement and Europe', in *Exterminism and Cold War*, pp. 117-34, especially pp. 129-32. In 1982 undernourishment affected 28% of the population of Asia, 25% of that of Africa, and 13% of that of Latin America. The level of infant mortality in the third world was comparable to that of Europe in 1570.

respective sponsors into direct confrontation. As will be discussed in Chapter Seven, they could ignite world war. But it is social revolution itself and the response to it which has, above all, triggered the counter-revolutionary drive that is so central to the Second Cold War, and which has taken the greatest toll.

The particular place of the third world in Cold War II is a product of both the increased level of revolutionary activity there, and of its changed position within international capitalism. Together these have combined to encourage the advanced capitalist countries to reassert control over the third world, by deploying a wide range of weapons for this: direct military intervention, increased support for right-wing regimes, destabilisation of post-revolutionary states, economic pressures. Both processes are also elided, in a policy of ideological simplification, to the Soviet threat: the changes in the third world are ascribed to Soviet intervention, the increased importance of some third world producers of raw materials is cited as added reason for strategic alarm, the rising power of third world industrial producers is another index of the pervasive 'loss of strength' most symbolised by the changes in the military balance. This chapter will consider the revolutionary changes in the third world which have contributed to the Second Cold War: the changes in the third world's place within the capitalist system will be considered in the context of inter-capitalist conflict discussed in Chapter Seven.

Waves of Upheaval

Cold War I was accompanied by the creation of post-capitalist regimes in both Europe and the Far East. This first wave of postwar revolutions was a result of the weakening of the existing states by the war itself, and of the role played in the fight against fascism by the Red Army and by communist parties. New post-capitalist states were erected in eight eastern European states, two as a result of indigenous nationalist and revolutionary movements (Yugoslavia, Albania) and six as a result of the imposition from above of communist rule in countries with varying degrees of communist influence (Germany, Hungary, Romania, Bulgaria, Poland, Czechoslovakia). In only one eastern European country, namely Greece, was such a change prevented by armed counter-revolution, despite the initially powerful position of the local communists.

This establishment of a bloc of 'people's democracies' in eastern Europe was accompanied by a wave of revolutions in the Far East—in

China, Korea and Indo-China. In none of these did the revolutionaries succeed in bringing all of their national territories under revolutionary control: Taiwan, South Korea and South Vietnam remained under capitalist rule. But post-revolutionary regimes were established on at least part of the national territories, and attempts to reverse these revolutions completely were defeated. Yet several other significant revolutionary movements in the Far East were repressed—in the Philippines, Malaya, Indonesia—and by the time of the Korean and Vietnamese ceasefires in 1953 and 1954 respectively the first wave of third world revolutions had spent itself. This process was accompanied elsewhere in the world by the defeat of radical peasant movements (India, Madagascar) and by the overthrow of left-wing nationalist regimes which had threatened to weaken US control—in Iran (overthrow of Mosadeq, 1953) and Guatemala (overthrow of Arbenz, 1954).

A period of stabilisation in the third world then occurred, comparable to that which marked the end of the then postwar revolutionary wave in Europe in the mid-1920s. In this context of apparent tranquillity in the third world the metropolitan countries undertook the process of decolonisation, whereby dozens of new states acquired independence from the mid-1950s onwards. In most cases this transition went ahead without major problems for the advanced capitalist countries, but a second wave of revolt began in the late 1950s and early 1960s, in Latin America, the Middle East and in Africa. The two most signal victories of this epoch were the Cuban revolution of 1959 and the independence of Algeria in 1962; but this period was one in which many other regions of the third world underwent significant upheavals. In the Middle East, the overthrow of the Hashemite monarch in Iraq in July 1958 removed the eponymous pillar of the Baghdad Pact, while the North Yemeni revolution of September 1962 brought Nasserite forces, political and military, to the frontiers of Saudi Arabia and British-ruled South Yemen. In Africa the Sharpeville shooting of 1960 opened a more combative period of resistance against the Pretoria regime, and a year later the first guerrilla actions began in the Portuguese colonies. Perhaps the most important event of all for sub-Saharan Africa was the independence of the then Belgian Congo, now Zaire, under the leadership of the militant nationalist, Patrice Lumumba, in June 1960. In Latin America, guerrilla movements inspired by Cuba developed in several countries, and in Indo-China, the Vietnamese communists decided to re-launch their campaign in the south. In the face of continued refusal by the Saigon government and its American backers to honour the 1954 Geneva Accords, the National Liberation Front of South Vietnam was established in December 1960. It was this second wave of third world revolutions which led to the famous appeals of Che Guevara and Lin Piao respectively: to create many Vietnams, to encircle the cities of the world.[2]

Yet this second wave was met by a vigorous response from the USA, where the Kennedy Administration was especially alarmed by the Cuban example. US advisers were sent to Vietnam in 1961. Under the cover of the Alliance for Progress, counter-insurgency campaigns were launched throughout the Latin American continent. Later, in 1965, the attempted left-wing seizure of power in the Dominican Republic was defeated by a US invasion. The elected socialist government of Chile was ousted in 1973. In Africa a similar process of containment was enacted: in 1961 Lumumba was slain, power transferred to the CIA-financed Desiré Mobutu and in 1964 Belgian paratroops, with US and British support, crushed the left-wing forces of Pierre Mulele in the east; the Portuguese held on, with NATO and South African support; a series of coups removed nationalist leaders in Ghana (1966) and Mali (1968); the Zanzibar revolution of 1963 collapsed, as had the analogous slave revolt of Haiti a century and a half before, into a malign despotism. In the Middle East the prospect of radicalisation held out by the 1967 Israeli defeat of Egypt proved illusory: only in South Yemen did a left-wing nationalist guerrilla movement come to power, replacing British colonial rule in 1967; the Palestinians were crushed by King Hussein's bedouin legion in 1970; Egypt moved even more rapidly to the right under Sadat who replaced Nasser in October 1970; the Dhofar guerrillas in Oman fought on, unheeded by the rest of the Arab world except South Yemen, until finally defeated by Anglo-Iranian forces in 1975. Despite the objectively favourable conditions and a flood of militant rhetoric, the Arab world therefore swung markedly rightwards in this period.

[2.] Göran Therborn, 'From Petrograd to Saigon', *New Left Review*, No. 48 March-April 1968, provides an excellent theorisation of this period. For all their differences of emphasis, Guevara and Lin Piao laid common stress on the primacy of guerrilla struggle in the third world as the means of overthrowing capitalism. Both underplayed the importance of two problems: the necessary contribution to be made by the more established and industrialised communist states to the third world movements, and the manner in which the third world movement would, beyond eliciting solidarity activity as such, be mediated into the social conflicts of the developed capitalist states.

In four Arab or African states, coups, all in 1969, brought to power
regimes more radical than those which had previously existed: in South
Yemen, Somalia, Libya and Congo-Brazzaville. But only one of these,
South Yemen, reflected a process of social revolution, and none had yet
attained a clear ideological orientation or major strategic impact. Further
east, guerrilla movements in India (the Naxalites) and Ceylon (the JVP)
were contained by confident post-colonial regimes, and in Indo-China the
three revolutionary movements fought on, inflicting immense political
damage on the USA, but seemingly unable to wrest final victory, despite
their great sacrifices.

The greatest defeat of all came in a country near Indo-China, namely
Indonesia, where a right-wing counter coup in 1965 opened the way for
a massacre of up to 300,000 people, many of them communists or sym-
pathisers. The gravity of this setback has often been understated, either
by those who perpetrated the killings, or by those, such as the Chinese
leadership, who bore some responsibility for the policies which led the
local communist party, the PKI, to defeat. But prior to the 1965 coup the
PKI had been the third largest communist party in the world, with an official membership of three millions, in a country of over one hundred
million people that straddled the waterways of south-east Asia. A communist victory or active presence there during the decade of Indo-
chinese conflict that followed 1965 could have dramatically altered the
balance of power in the whole of Asia: the defeat of the communist
forces, in the early stages of the US intervention in Vietnam, provided the
USA with a protected flank that was of immense, if undeclared, importance.[3]

The result was that for twelve years, from 1962 until 1974, there was
only one case of a revolutionary seizure of power anywhere in the third
world (South Yemen). The second wave of anti-imperialist revolutions
had been blocked: it appeared that a relatively successful, if costly,
holding operation had been executed. The consensus among western
strategists in the early 1970s was that, with the troublesome exception
of Indo-China, conflict in the third world could be contained. Considerable effort was to be devoted to resolving the problems of Indo-China

Lucien Rey, 'Dossier of the Indonesian Drama', *New Left Review*, No. 36; Flora
Lentealegre, 'Background Information on Indonesia, the Invasion of East Timor and US
Military Assistance', *Institute for Policy Studies Resource*, May 1982; Noam Chomsky,
Towards a New Cold War, London 1982.

in a satisfactory manner, but elsewhere the USA's position was more or less secure. The view from Washington certainly seemed to confirm this strategic complacency. The Cuban revolution appeared to be bottled up on its island, its followers on the Latin American mainland routed by severe repression and their own militarist mistakes. In Africa, the Portuguese were believed by Washington to be able to hold on, as was Ian Smith in Rhodesia. The defection westwards of Egypt, the rise of the Arab oil states and the growing power of the Shah confirmed the security of the Middle East. In a view summarising the Washington consensus of the mid-1970s a Congressional report was able to say: 'The United States faces a politically multipolar and economically interdependent world which, except for southern Africa, *has become remarkably stabilized.*'[4] This belief was, of course, one of the foundations of Detente. But in 1974, the dam had burst. The third wave of third world revolution had commenced. Within six years no less than fourteen states were taken over by revolutionary movements, and in three others significant radicalisations occurred. Conversely, whereas there had been many successful counter-revolutionary initiatives in the dozen years preceding, the years from 1974 to 1980 saw only a few minor reverses.

Revolutions of the 1970s

The first breach came in February 1974, with the onset of the revolution in Ethiopia, the third most populous state in Africa, and the recipient of two-thirds of US military aid to the Sub-Saharan region since 1946. Although the Ethiopian upsurge took time to evolve, it led in September 1974 to the deposition of Haile Selassie, and in 1977 to the severing military ties with the USA. This break in US-Ethiopian military ties was followed a few months later by the Somali invasion of Ethiopia, an act encouraged by some conservative Arab states and by the USA. As a result Cuban troops and Soviet arms were deployed in Ethiopia. The Soviet advance in Ethiopia was accompanied by the shift of Somalia towards

---

4. My italics. Congressional Research Service, *The Soviet Union and the Third World. Watershed in Great Power Policy?*, Report Submitted to House of Representatives Committee on International Relations, May 1977, p. 7. The assumption upon which US and British policy towards the white settler regime in Rhodesia rested was that the Portuguese in neighbouring Mozambique would be able to hold their position there indefinitely. The so-called 'Tar Baby Option' was rudely overtaken by the fall of Portuguese fascism in April 1974.

closer alliance with the west, one of the latter's few gains in this period, and a change that enabled US forces to sign an agreement on naval and air facilities there in August 1980. But the Ethiopian crisis, which reached its zenith in early 1978, was presented in the west as a case of Soviet violation of previous understandings: National Security Adviser Brzezinski stated that it had 'buried' Detente. Therefore, despite the fact that the Horn of Africa was an area of little intrinsic importance to the USA, it became an important constituent of the charge-sheet against Soviet policy.[5]

Two months after the beginning of the Ethiopian revolution, there occurred another event with major implications for Europe and the third world, when one of the weakest links in the metropolitan chain snapped in Lisbon. As will be discussed in Chapter Eight, the Portuguese revolution formed part of that advance of left-wing forces in southern Europe which alarmed NATO in the mid-1970s. But the third world consequences were as important and more enduring, for the fall of fascism in Lisbon opened the door to guerrilla triumphs in no less that six African countries (five Portuguese colonies and Zimbabwe) and ushered in the first major third world revolutionary crisis of the 1970s. In the five Portuguese colonies power was assumed by the guerrilla leaderships: in Angola, Mozambique, Guinea-Bissau, Cape Verde and São Tome. The first two states had great international import, both because of their demographic and geographical weight, and because each stimulated increased opposition in other states of southern Africa. The accession of FRELIMO to power in Mozambique was the forerunner and primary catalyst for the triumph of ZANU-ZAPU in neighbouring Zimbabwe in April 1980; although masked by the formalities of Commonwealth negotiations and by the initial caution of the Mugabe government, the Zimbabwean revolution was potentially as profound as those in the Portuguese colonies. On the south-western flank of Africa, the Angolan revolution led to an intensification of opposition in Namibia, and, in October 1975, to the intervention of thousands of Cuban troops. Their mission was to defend the MPLA against the attacks of CIA-, Zaire- and South African-backed opponents.[6]

---

5. Brzezinski in *International Herald Tribune*, 4 December 1980.
6. The chronology of the US and Soviet-Cuban involvements in Angola is laid out in John Stockwell, *In Search of Enemies*, Toronto 1978. The USSR had stopped supporting the MPLA guerrillas in 1973; the CIA began aiding their rivals, the FNLA, in August 1974.

88

The liberation of Mozambique therefore led to a revolutionary triumph in a neighbouring state whose impact was obscured by the rituals of decolonisation. No such immediate success was registered by Angola in its neighbour Namibia; but the much greater mineral importance of this region, plus the involvement of Cuban forces, meant that it was events in Luanda which most preoccupied the west. It was above all the consolidation of the Angolan revolution, with Cuban and Soviet help, which undermined the illusion of a 'manageable' third world upon which so many western strategies had relied in the wake of Vietnam. If it was Ethiopia which was to harden Brzezinski's cold war resolve in 1978, it was Angola which had by the end of 1975 had the same effect upon Secretary of State Kissinger.[7]

These seven successful revolutions were accompanied by other developments in Africa which confirmed the sense that the continent was no longer as peaceful as had been anticipated. In four additional states significant radicalisations took place:[8] in Benin, formerly Dahomey, the government of Lt-Col. Mathieu Kerekou, in power since 1972, proclaimed 'Marxism-Leninism' to be the country's official ideology in November 1974; in June 1975 the military regime on the island of Madagascar chose as its leader a naval officer, Didier Ratsiraka, who also declared Marxism-Leninism to be the official ideology of the regime; and in Liberia, in April 1980, there occurred a military coup by lower ranks of the army who claimed to be influenced by Ethiopia; in Libya the nationalist regime of Moammar Qaddafi veered erratically towards confrontation with the west. In the western Sahara, POLISARIO guerrillas supported by Algeria sustained a difficult campaign against Moroccan forces. Western-backed interventions had to be mobilised to contain the two attempts by rebels to take over the copper-producing

Soviet arms shipments to the MPLA began again in March 1975. The first Cuban troops, 700 in all, arrived in Angola in October 1975—well over a year after the CIA operations in Angola restarted. His account is confirmed by the then Director of the Bureau of African Affairs at the State Department, Nathaniel Davis. Davis argued for non-involvement by the USA and a compromise solution, involving the MPLA, but was overruled by Kissinger who, faced with defeat in Vietnam, was keen to make a show of US strength (Nathaniel Davis, 'The Angola Decision of 1975: A personal Memoir', *Foreign Affairs*, Fall 1978).
[7.] Kissinger was later to say that after the Cuban intervention in Angola he ceased using the word 'detente'.
[8.] For details see David and Marina Ottoway, *Afrocommunism*, London 1982.

region of Zaire in 1977 and 1978 (Belgian and Moroccan troops, with French and logistical support) and the attempted revolutionary coup in the Gambia in 1981 (Senegalese troops, with French and British support). All of these conflicts were, however, only preludes to what could be seen as potentially the most important third world conflict of the last years of the twentieth century, the conflict in South Africa itself. As their interventions over Namibia showed, the western states were now far more preoccupied with this region than had been the case half way through the 1970s.

In Asia there were revolutionary advances in two distinct regions: the Indo-Chinese peninsula and the central Asian plateau. The wars in Vietnam, Laos and Cambodia all came to a head in 1975 with the fall of pro-American regimes there after three decades of conflict. These three conflicts had formed a backdrop of insurgency throughout the late 1960s and early 1970s and the simultaneous collapse was by far the most dramatic setback for the metropolitan countries, coming as it did after the costly US intervention in the region. It marked the defeat of two alternative imperial strategies: direct intervention by US forces (1965–73) and the Nixon doctrine of delegating the front line role in Vietnam to local and other Asian troops (1973–5). It also signalled the failure of the Nixon-Kissinger attempt to offset military defeats in the third world by diplomatic agreements with Moscow and Peking and by sharpening the conflict between them: these initiatives had some success, but they were nonetheless unable to contain the Vietnamese revolutionaries.

Yet the immediate political impact of the Indo-Chinese events was muted on both right and left in the developed capitalist countries. For the Americans, the key date was 1973, when their own troops were withdrawn, not the final collapse of Thieu in 1975. The return of the US POWs was a symbolic end to the war, although it continued in an afterlife via the issue of the Missing In Action. The fall of Saigon two years later found the US temporarily dominated by a reluctance to engage in third world military ventures, the 'Vietnam Syndrome', and by the aftermath of the Watergate affair: the only immediate US response was the bathetic incident of the *Mayaguez* on 14 May 1975, when 41 US soldiers and an unknown number of Cambodians lost their lives in an American attempt to rescue the 39-member crew of a US ship, when the latter had already been released by their Cambodian captors. The very scale of the Indo-China failure, coupled with the face-saving nature of the US phased withdrawal, left the imperial consciousness numbed and defensive. There was, however, later to be a response to the defeat of Indo-China, a new vindication of the US role, first by Carter and then by Reagan.[9]

This disjuncture of event and response was also prominent in the US reaction to the upheavals of the Central Asian plateau, except that here the terms of the contrast were reversed. The US had intervened directly in Indo-China, but had temporarily repressed the ideological consequences of defeat. The US did not fight in Iran and Afghanistan but reacted vociferously to developments there, and in particular to two later consequences of the actual revolutions, the hostages crisis in Tehran and the Soviet intervention in Kabul. Afghanistan and Iran were very distinct countries, with none of even the relative homogeneity produced by French colonialism in the three Indo-Chinese states. One, Afghanistan, was an impoverished monarchy, which the USA had ceased to court in the 1950s and which was reliant on the USSR for most of its military and much of its economic aid. The other, Iran, was a rapidly developing oil state with a special place in US regional strategy.

The revolutions were equally diverse and individually paradoxical: a seizure of power in a left-wing military coup in the former under the control of a communist party, a mass insurrection from below in the latter under the leadership of ultra-conservative Islamic clergy. Although a Soviet hand was divined in each, no evidence of such involvement was ever produced. Both events were in fact the result of internal developments which matured into revolutionary crises: if there was an outside catalyst in Afghanistan, it was the Shah of Iran, whose own demise was prepared by the pattern of capitalist transformation he had been imposing on his country and by his sustained alliance with the USA.[10] However, both revolutions were seen in US public discourse as instances of a Soviet offensive against the west, and this perception was confirmed by what followed. In Afghanistan the mistaken attempt by the communist government to implement reforms from above in a precipitate manner, combined with the encouragement of counter-revolution from Pakistan, led to the crisis that produced the Soviet in-

[9] On the ideological counter-offensive after Vietnam and the removal of restraints upon US willingness to intervene in the third world see Chomsky, *Towards a New Cold War*, and Klare, *Beyond the 'Vietnam Syndrome'*.

[10] Selig Harrison, 'The Shah, Not Kremlin, touched off Afghan Coup', *Washington Post*, 13 May 1979.

tervention of December 1979, a holding operation with catastrophic international consequences. This development came on the heels of the seizure in the previous month of the US Embassy in Tehran by Islamic militants who held the US diplomats until January 1981.

More than any other events of this wave of third world defiance, these two disparate events in Central Asia were to become the supposed reasons for justifying a new assertion of US power in the third world. Although one occurred in a state where Soviet predominance had long been conceded, and the other, the hostage crisis, was, in any historical perspective, an incident of subaltern importance, they were invested with immense significance in the climate of impending Cold War. It was as if the pentup frustrations held over from the defeats in Indo-China and Angola were transferred, with the incremental force of repression, onto the figure of Babrak Karmal and the Students Following the Imam's Line. However spontaneous the reaction to the hostages crisis was it should not be abstracted from the Cold War atmosphere that already existed. When, in 1968, North Korea seized a US intelligence-gathering ship the *Pueblo* and held the 83-man crew for twelve months, there was no comparable outcry in the USA, even though one was killed and four wounded.

So far, four geographical foci of upheaval have been mentioned: the Horn of Africa, southern Africa, Indo-China and central Asia. There was, however, a fifth region where revolution broke out and which was to reopen one of the deepest vulnerabilities in US strategic thinking, one contained but not healed since the early 1960s, namely central America. Cuba had remained a source of irritation to the USA and the possibility of a new military assault on the island, to expunge the shame of Playa Giron, had remained a constituent of long-range imperial aspiration.[11] The Central American dimension had also been reintroduced into the US strategic debate by one of the potent prodromal symptoms of the Second Cold War, the issue of the Panama Canal Treaties which were debated in the USA from 1976 to 1978. Alarm over events in Central America was reinforced by the more important role which Latin America in general, and Mexico and the Caribbean in particular, had come to play in the

---

[11.] In an address to Congressional staffers in 1981, then Secretary of State Alexander Haig was quoted as saying that for many years he had gone to bed at night disturbed by the fact that Fidel Castro was still in power in Cuba. 'Now we are doing something about it,' he said.

global interests of US capitalism during the 1970s. The defeat of the guerrilla movements, the destruction of the Popular Unity government in Chile, and the role of Brazil as sub-continental power had earlier seemed to suggest that the Latin American flanks of the US domain were as secure as anywhere. Yet in 1979 two developments altered this perspective: the triumph of the Sandinista movement in Nicaragua in July 1979 preceded by the successful insurrection of the New Jewel Movement in Grenada in March of that year. Together they turned this into the fifth region of third world revolutionary upsurge during the late 1970s. Indeed, with the enhanced economic status of Mexico, and in a region adjacent to the USA where so much intervention had taken place in the past, Central America became an area of even greater activity than any other. It was here that Carter reversed his policy of third world caution by increasing aid to the military regime in El Salvador and the Reagan Administration was to make the whole region into a testing-ground for its new assertiveness. Central America was important both in its own right and for what action there might presage if US interests elsewhere, particularly in the Persian Gulf, were directly threatened.

Table Six
Revolutionary Upheavals in the Third World 1974–1980

Country	Event	Date
1. Ethiopia	Deposition Haile Selassie	12 September 1974
2. Cambodia	Khmers Rouges take Phnom Penh	17 April 1975
3. Vietnam	NLF take Saigon	30 April 1975
4. Laos	Pathet Lao take over state	9 May 1975
5. Guinea-Bissau	Independence from Portugal	9 September 1974
6. Mozambique	Independence from Portugal	25 June 1975
7. Cape Verde	Independence from Portugal	5 July 1975
8. São Tome	Independence from Portugal	12 July 1975
9. Angola	Independence from Portugal	11 November 1975
10. Afghanistan	PDPA military coup	27 April 1978
11. Iran	Khomeiny's government installed	11 February 1979
12. Grenada	New Jewel Movement to power	13 March 1979
13. Nicaragua	FSLN take Managua	19 July 1979
14. Zimbabwe	Independence from Britain	17 April 1980

The Diversity of Revolutions

These fourteen changes of regime had different political characters and involved very distinct political tendencies, societies, and levels of transformation; whilst their cumulative impact was certainly such as to provoke alarm in the advanced capitalist countries, their causes, and political character, and the manner in which these defeats were mediated into metropolitan response, require some more disaggregated analysis. Beyond their common characteristic of being upheavals in the third world in a single period, these fourteen instances varied greatly in the manner in which they were carried out. Eight were the product of relatively protracted rural guerrilla struggles against foreign-backed regimes (Vietnam, Laos, Cambodia, Angola, Guinea-Bissau, Mozambique, Nicaragua, Zimbabwe). One was the result of a massive urban protest movement that lasted for one year (Iran). Two were the results of popular mobilisation following the weakening of the colonial power through the crisis at the centre (São Tome, Cape Verde). One was the result of a sudden armed uprising against a weak state (Grenada). Two resulted from coups d'état in the context of protracted political crisis (Afghanistan, Ethiopia).

In four of these revolutions, communist parties played the leading role (Vietnam, Cambodia, Laos, Afghanistan). In one the organisations and ideology of right-wing religious populism were dominant (Iran). In the other nine various mixtures of radical nationalism and socialism combined, with the prospect that these would in the longer run adopt some affiliation to 'Marxism-Leninism'. While all claimed to have carried out 'revolutions', the ones in which revolutionary socialist parties won power and proceeded furthest to implement their programme were Vietnam, Laos, Cambodia, and Nicaragua. Elsewhere various degrees of social transformation accompanied and followed the upheavals; but these were not, at least initially, such as to justify the description that a socialist revolution was in progress. The most advanced radical nationalist forces were to be found in Angola, Mozambique and Ethiopia: here the rule of capital was being progressively weakened.

For all their differences, however, thirteen of these upheavals shared a common characteristic, one that limited their possible relevance for the future. This hallmark is that the forms of domination against which they were directed were becoming increasingly rare in the third world. Portuguese colonialism in Africa, and the white settler regime in Rhodesia were, with the exception of South Africa itself, the last of their kind on the continent. The governments of Afghanistan and Ethiopia were pre-capitalist monarchies that had survived, partly for reasons of geographic location, the onslaught of modern capitalism. The governments of Gairy in Grenada and Somoza in Nicaragua were more typical of other post-colonial states, but had narrow social bases at home and were dependent on outside support for that sustenance which they lacked because of their low level of internal implantation. The three Indo-Chinese revolutions were socially revolutionary, but they were continuations of anti-colonial struggles that had begun against French rule, and that had been invested with a second moment of anti-imperialist mobilisation by the intervention of the USA. In sum, this 'third wave' of upheavals in the colonial world came up against some of the last instances of the old colonial and pre-capitalist orders. For all the advanced character of the ideologies that inspired them, the majority took place in comparatively archaic conditions. Anti-colonial revolt and the overthrow of pre-capitalist monarchies would form the basis of relatively few upheavals in the future.[12]

The one exception was Iran, a revolution which took place in a quite different social context, of rapid capitalist transformation and substantial political independence. The novelty of the Iranian revolution resides in a central contradictory paradox: on the one hand, its leadership and ideology were resolutely retrogressive, the first ones in the history of modern revolution to be unequivocally religious, and so deeply hostile to ideas of progress; on the other hand, the social context in which the Iranian revolution took place, and the manner of its success, were far more 'modern' than that of any other comparable upheavals. Most importantly, this revolution took place exclusively in the cities, the first third world revolution to do so. Its means of struggle, the mass demonstration and the political general strike, were those normally associated with conflict in the developed capitalist countries. The country in which it occurred, over 50 per cent urbanised and with a per capita income of more than

---

[12.] Nepal remains the only substantial state where a pre-capitalist monarchy retains power, although the ruling dynasty in one other, more important, state uses pre-capitalist forms of recruitment and ideological control to maintain its hold on the country's riches—Saudi Arabia. The Saudi monarchy is not, however, a relic of some long-standing regime, but the creation of a modern movement of state formation that came to fruition in the 1920s. For a discussion of the dual character of some revolutions of the 1970s see Fred Halliday and Maxine Molyneux, *The Ethiopian Revolution*, London 1982, pp. 13-25.

$2,000, was in socio-economic terms far more 'developed' than Russia in 1917, or China in 1949. It was in the combination of these two characteristics, 'reactionary' and 'modern', that the originality of the Iranian revolution lay. And it was both of these dimensions that gave the Iranian revolution a different political character from the other upheavals of the third wave.[13]

These revolutions also varied considerably in importance. Four occurred in states with small populations and without major strategic implications: São Tome, Cape Verde, Guinea-Bissau, Grenada.[14] Of the major ten, the most important was that of Vietnam, for it was here that the USA suffered its greatest defeat and paid the highest price: the death of 50,000 men, the gigantic economic costs of an involvement that went on for more than a decade, the loss of prestige that followed the failure to deliver on such a commitment to counter-revolutionary victory. Within the USA Vietnam provoked a political crisis, a discrediting of the Presidency that it would take years to overcome and a revulsion against third world involvement that lasted into the 1980s. Internationally, it helped to weaken the USA vis-à-vis its major capitalist rivals, and to embolden revolutionary forces elsewhere in the third world.

The three other most strategically important defeats for the USA were Angola, Iran and Nicaragua. The importance of Angola lay in the fact that, in response to a covert US involvement and an overt South African and Zairean one, Cuban forces were transported, with Soviet protection, for action in support of revolutionary forces on the African continent. American strategists were right to see this as a significant new development, which gave the forces opposed to the USA some of the strategic mobility that had long been the monopoly of the west. It is doubtful if the Cubans would have taken the decision to go into Angola, and would have encountered no direct US opposition on the high seas and in the air, had the final defeat of Vietnam not taken its toll on US policy a few months before. The Iranian defeat had two parts: the fall of the Shah (January 1979) and the detention of the US hostages (November 1979). Both served, however, to underline the weakness of US policy in the

---

[13.] I have developed this further in 'Religious Populism and Uneven Development: The Case of Iran', *Journal of International Affairs*, Fall/Winter 1982-3.
[14.] The 1979 populations of these four states were São Tome, 82,000; Cape Verde, 328,000; Guinea-Bissau, 928,000; Grenada, 107,000.

region where so much had been invested in building up the Shah as a strong regional force and western ally. Nicaragua had once been chosen as the country through which the USA would build a second canal, to replace that which the traversed Panama, and Somoza had been one of Washington's closest allies in the third world. But Nicaragua was in itself a less momentous upheaval than these others, given the small size of the population involved. It nevertheless marked the first successful implantation on the Latin American mainland of the revolutionary movement till then restricted to Cuba. Moreover, located as it was in an increasingly menacing Central America, it brought the threat of third world revolution geographically much closer to the USA. The prospect of social upheaval in Central America was linked, in US political debate, to the issue of illegal immigration and demagogues of the right revived the spectre of the 1920s of left-wing agitators pouring into the Land of the Free.

The political effect of these revolutions upon the USA was not, however, always proportionate to their real importance. Thus the impact of Vietnam was felt during the war itself, but was then suppressed for some time after the 1973 withdrawal. It was only in 1982, nearly a decade after the US withdrawal, that a monument to the American dead was erected in Washington. The fall of the Ethiopian monarch in 1974, a long-standing US ally in Africa, provoked almost no immediate response: this came only with the 1977 Cuban intervention. The event which provoked the greatest political response at the public level in the USA was, in fact, a comparatively unimportant event, the seizure of the American hostages in November 1979. This, more than anything else, served to highlight what was seen as a loss of political will in the USA. Right-wing commentators had already begun to blame the fall of the Shah on a weakness of will in Washington, but the seizure of the hostages unleashed a tidal wave of popular chauvinism in the USA, which was only temporarily contained by the failure of a rescue mission in April 1980. The socially reactionary policies of the Khomeini regime and the repression and cruelty it inflicted on its own people also alienated many abroad.

One other country did, however, occupy a central place in the American vision of a threatening third world, namely Afghanistan. The impact of Afghanistan was not that of the communist seizure of power in April 1978: the USA had long conceded Afghanistan to be in the sphere of Soviet influence.[15] Afghanistan became an issue in December 1979, when tens of thousands of Soviet troops were despatched to shore up the Kabul regime. It was the issue of Soviet involvement, rather than that of political upheaval, which put this hitherto remote central Asian state at the front of US strategic concerns. For beyond their intrinsic effects upon the USA, these third world revolutions were also seen as the products of a concerted Soviet drive for third world influence.

Soviet Involvement: Myth and Fact

The common response of most western commentators was to attribute responsibility for the new wave of revolutions to the Soviet Union and to see in the incidence of third world upheaval a violation of detente on the part of the USSR. This charge, of Soviet adventurism and aggression in the third world, served both to explain the various upheavals that confronted US policy makers, and to provide a second part to the indictment whose other element was the charge that the USSR now had military superiority. Together these two issues formed the central themes of the call for renewed confrontation in Cold War II.[16]

In tandem with the theme of a Soviet drive for military superiority, there have therefore come three specific charges concerning the third world: (1) that the USSR has violated a particular agreed 'code of detente' by refusing to accept the status quo in the third world in return for SALT negotiations and trade; (2) that Soviet conduct in the third world has been criminal and expansionist, conduct that violates 'rules' to which the western states adhere; and (3) that Soviet policy in the third world changed during the 1970s, becoming more aggressive and expansionist as a result of the USSR's new military capabilities.

Against these, alternative arguments can be suggested. (1) The 'violation of detente' charge arises from the belief that the USSR should concede continued western domination of the third world, something Moscow

---

[15.] Leon Poullada, 'Afghanistan and the United States: The Crucial Years', *Middle East Journal*, Spring 1981: Poullada discusses the early 1950s. The western governments were quite willing to recognise the government that issued from the April 1978 communist coup: the USA, Britain and other NATO countries had diplomatic relations with the government of Nur Mohammed Taraki. Only when Soviet forces intervened did this policy change.

[16.] See my *Threat from the East? Soviet Policy from Afghanistan and Iran to the Horn of Africa*, Penguin Books, London 1982; also published in the USA as *Soviet Policy in the Arc of Crisis*, Institute for Policy Studies, Washington 1981.

never accepted even at the height of detente.[17] (2) The charge of criminal and expansionist behaviour comes strangely from states with a long record of military intervention, economic sabotage and assassination attempts in the third world. (3) The accusation that there has been a shift in Soviet policy during the 1970s is sometimes linked to internal trends that are supposed to motivate this shift: leadership strains, the thirst for oil, general economic difficulties. While, as we shall see, such endogenous explanations lack analytic force, the increased strategic power of the USSR, coupled with improved air and naval capabilities, has given the Soviet leadership the ability to play a more active role in the third world, to fulfill in practice the 'internationalist' commitment of which Soviet leaderships have long talked in theory.

The USSR did play a significant part in the new wave of upheaval in the third world, and the changed international balance of forces served to encourage and to guarantee movements that would otherwise have found themselves solitary in the face of western counter-attack. Some guerrilla forces were provided with military assistance; revolutionary states, once established, were given strategic protection by the USSR. It is unlikely that the Vietnamese could have triumphed without Soviet aid, or that the governments of Cuba, South Yemen, Ethiopia or Afghanistan would have survived without Soviet support. Yet the ability to play such a role has depended even more on something beyond the USSR's control, namely the evolution of the political situations in the particular countries concerned. The facts of internal Soviet political and economic life indicate a great measure of steadiness and consistency from the mid-1960s onwards: the sudden changes have been *within* the third world countries

---

[17.] Some American writers have argued that in 1972 the USSR and USA signed a code of conduct with regard to the third world, which the Russians subsequently violated. Details of this agreement, known as 'Basic Principles of US-Soviet Relations', are given in Henry Kissinger, *The White House Years*, Boston 1979, p. 1250. These included the need for mutual restraint, and the rejection of attempts to exploit tensions to gain unilateral advantage. These were not, as Kissinger points out, legally binding agreements, of the SALT kind, and neither side can be shown to have given them much respect in the following years. An illuminating sign of the US interpretation of this agreement came within a day of the departure of the US delegation from the USSR. Nixon flew from Moscow to Tehran, where he reached a secret agreement with the Shah of Iran on covert action, using Kurdish guerrillas, against the Soviet-supported government of neighbouring Iraq (Tad Szulc, *The Illusion of Peace*, New York 1978, pp. 582-7).

most prominent in the globalised social conflict, and in the response of the USA to these developments, not in Soviet policy.

All these three issues bring into focus the western refusal to accept anything like overall parity with the USSR. Just as the attainment of greater Soviet military strength is portrayed as a drive for superiority, so a measure of Soviet activity in the third world is depicted as a violation of Detente. In both instances, the call for a western response to redress Soviet 'superiority' is in reality a means of mobilising support for renewed western superiority, both in the field of the military balance, and in that of international influence. The west had, until 1970s, dominance in both the strategic nuclear field and in that of third world power projection, and both were eroded in that decade. The relationship established at the end of World War II between strategic nuclear and international political power appeared to have broken down. By presenting both problems in terms of a supposed Soviet threat, into which all problems facing the USA were merged, it became easier for western governments to offer an explanation and, it was hoped, a solution.

In three of these fourteen cases Soviet military influence did play a significant part: in the assistance given to Angola and Ethiopia by Soviet advisers, arms supplies and strategic guarantees, and in the direct intervention of Soviet forces to sustain the Afghanistan regime in December 1979. Yet the degree of Soviet influence was, even in these cases, exaggerated. In both Ethiopia and Afghanistan pro-Soviet regimes were already in place: the Soviet role was to prevent them from being overthrown, not to bring such regimes to power. In Angola, the Soviet intervention on behalf of the MPLA, in conjunction with the Cuban expeditionary corps, would not have been necessary had the MPLA not faced attack from South Africa and its allies in the south, and from Zaire, the CIA and their Angolan associates in the north. In none of these cases did the Soviet military role play a decisive part in initiating the revolutionary change.

Throughout the latter part of the 1970s the very real crises of Africa and Central America were accompanied by a series of fake crises, incidents in which Washington divined a Soviet or Cuban hand and which were seen in the context of some general Russian thrust into the third world. This was true for both of the uprisings in the Shaba province of Zaire in 1977 and 1978 when Cuba was held responsible for the actions of guerrillas who had entered the area from neighbouring Angola. It also applied in the case of the North Yemen crisis of February 1979 when the US government doctored reports from that country to justify a military response by the Carter Administration.[18] And the tendency for orchestrated alarmism reached its crescendo in September 1979 when the US Administration 'discovered' a brigade of 3,000 Soviet troops in Cuba, an issue used both to vilify the sixth summit of the Non-Aligned Movement, then taking place in Havana, and to torpedo the Senate debate on SALT-II.[19]

The emotional core of the 'Soviet Threat' charge lay, however, not in the Caribbean or Central Africa but in the Middle East, and in the combination of two crucial issues, Israel and oil. By the end of the 1970s US strategists were arguing that the focus of US efforts against the USSR should be the Gulf: 'Almost as certainly as did Europe in the 1940s, the Gulf provides *the* critical source of conflict between the United States and the Soviet Union. What in Europe resulted from war and defeat, in the Middle East has resulted from the withdrawal of the power that once controlled the region and the subsequent refusal of the United States to fill the vacuum.'[20] This stress upon the oil of the Gulf went together with a growing feeling that the USSR was responsible for the Arab successes against the Israelis. In particular, some writers alleged that the first blow against detente was the Arab attack of October 1973, and that the other incidents, from Ethiopia to Nicaragua, followed this pattern.[21] In fact,

---

[18.] On US media manipulation of the 1978 Zaire crisis see David Paletz and Robert Entman, *Media, Power, Politics*, London 1981, pp. 221 ff. On North Yemen see the testimony of the then US Military Attaché in North Yemen, Lt Col. Ruskiewicz, who told a Congressional audience that reports of fighting had been inflated but that he had been assured by his superiors: 'If Yemen had not happened at that particular time, it would have been invented.' He added: 'It seems to me we disastrously escalated our involvement in Vietnam as a result of an attack on an American warship in the Gulf of Tonkin which never occurred. I cannot help but view what happened in Yemen as a Middle East version of the Gulf of Tonkin incident' ('How the US Lost its Footing in the Shifting Sands of the Persian Gulf—A Case History in the Yemen Arab Republic', *Armed Forces Journal*, September 1980, p. 72).

[19.] In fact, the US government calculated that the level of Soviet troops in Cuba in 1979 was a tenth of the level of the early 1960s. Carter himself admitted that it 'is obviously not a threat to our country, not a violation of any Soviet commitment' Jimmy Carter, *Keeping Faith*, London 1982, p. 263.

[20.] Robert Tucker, 'American Power and the Persian Gulf', *Commentary*, November 1980.

[21.] E.g. Robert Tucker, 'The Purposes of American Power', *Foreign Affairs*, Winter 1980-1; Richard Lowenthal, 'The Shattered Balance', *Encounter*, November 1980.

this was a quite unfounded charge: there is no evidence whatsoever that the USSR instigated the Egyptian assault on Israel in October 1973, or that the Russians were even privy to Arab plans.[22] If anything, it was the continued refusal of the USA to take initiatives in the Middle East, despite appeals from Sadat to do so, that led the Egyptians to launch their attack. Yet the myth of a concerted Soviet assault upon US allies in the third world locates the first break in the dam here, on the shores of the Suez Canal, rather than in the paddy fields of Indo-China or the highlands of Ethiopia.

Despite these setbacks to US influence, the overall balance-sheet of third world politics remained favourable to the west. Comparisons of those states actively allied with the USSR in 1960 and in 1980 showed that, in GNP, population and strategic terms, the USSR was stronger in the earlier than in the later periods.[23] None of the gains of the latter half of the 1970s could make up for the breaking of the relationships with China, the most populous state in the world, and Egypt, the most important country in the Arab world. Of the one hundred or so third world states less than fifteen could be seen as committed allies of the USSR.[24] Most of these states were plagued with economic problems, to which the USSR could offer only small alleviation. Yet the combined impact of this wave of revolutions induced a crisis in US strategic thinking and confirmed the drift towards the Second Cold War already encouraged by other factors.

---

22. Karen Dawisha, *Soviet Policy Towards Egypt*, London 1979; William Quandt, 'Soviet Policy in the October Middle East War', *International Affairs*, July and October 1977.
23. In 1958 non-Soviet countries influenced by the USSR accounted for 31 per cent of the world's population and 9 per cent of its GNP. In 1979 the figures were 6 per cent and 5 per cent respectively ('Soviet Geopolitical Momentum: Myth of Menace?', *Defense Monitor*, Centre for Defense Information, January 1980). A survey of strategic power carried out by British Independent Television in 1981 yielded the following comparisons: the USSR had 11 significant allies outside Europe, the USA more than 50; the Soviet bloc had a population of 500 million, the US bloc 1,600 millions; the ratio of Soviet bloc to US bloc GNP was 1:7 (Jonathan Dimbleby, ITV, 7 September 1981).
24. An index of core support for the USSR is given by voting on certain issues at the UN. The lineup at the 20 November 1980 General Assembly vote on Afghanistan was 111 countries in favour of an immediate withdrawal of foreign troops, and 22 against. These 22 comprised: the USSR, Byelorussia, Ukraine, Czechoslovakia, Poland, Mongolia, Bulgaria, East Germany, Hungary, Cuba, Afghanistan, Angola, Ethiopia, Grenada, Laos, Madagascar, Mozambique, Sao Tome, Seychelles, Syria, Vietnam, South Yemen (*Kees-*

This mediation of third world revolutions into US and western policy has had several strategic consequences. First, as already noted, the third wave broke the link which successive US administrations had tried to make between the strategic nuclear and third world counter-revolutionary domains. As Kissinger explained, in the period up to the 1960s the USA had used its strategic superiority to limit the assistance given by the USSR and China to third world movements: the possibility of direct US nuclear attacks, as well as of conventional assaults backed by nuclear power, played their role in this. This was not a completely successful policy, but it registered several achievements—in containing the Korean and Vietnamese revolutions to name but two. The Cuban missile crisis of October 1962 was a classic instance of the use of nuclear superiority to face down the USSR in the third world, although even then the existence of a Soviet deterrent was a contributing factor in preventing the USA from exerting its full power to overthrow the Cuban government itself. In the 1970s, the US government tried to pursue a different policy, that of 'linkage', inducing the USSR and China to co-operate in restraining third world revolutions in return for concessions in the nuclear and economic fields. The 'third wave' of revolutions has shown that linkage will not succeed, for two reasons: one, the USSR is not willing to play according to these US rules; two, whilst Soviet assistance is an important factor it is not Moscow which generates or controls these third world upsurges. Faced with the collapse of 'linkage' initiatives, Washington is now proceeding to re-enforce the earlier policy, to acquire a margin of strategic superiority which, coupled with a new conventional interventionist capability, will make it easier to contain third world revolutions in the future.

This drive for a new counter-revolutionary order in the third world has involved a shift in US military policy itself. The Nixon doctrine of delegation, propounded on Guam in 1969, is no longer adequate. Cer-

---

ings Contemporary Archives, 22 May 1981. The funeral of CPSU leader Leonid Brezhnev in November 1982 provided another occasion at which to see, this time from the USSR's own point of view, what the constituents of its alliance are. Representatives from the core third world allies were divided into those that were from full members of the communist camp—Cuba, Mongolia, Vietnam, Laos, Cambodia, North Korea—and those that were from preferred members of the 20-odd group of 'socialist-oriented' states—South Yemen, Angola, Mozambique, Afghanistan, Nicaragua, Ethiopia (*Soviet News*, 17 November 1982).

tainly, it would be a mistake to see the Nixon Doctrine as having been an unequivocal failure. In all over 300,000 South Korean troops fought in Vietnam both before and after Nixon expounded his policy, and there were many other cases of interventions by US surrogates: the Iranian role in Oman, Pakistan and Iraq; the Indonesian role in Timor; the Moroccan role in Zaire; the Brazilian in Uruguay, Bolivia and Argentina; all are cases in which an element of delegation to US allies has been positive for Washington. The activities of such more developed allies as Britain, Belgium and France, confirm the benefits of spreading the load of counter-revolutionary activity widely. Most successfully, the two rogue states of the third world, South Africa and Israel, have ravaged their neighbours with impunity, and with the tacit support of Washington and its allies. But the fall of the Shah of Iran, and the challenges posed by the role of Cuban and Soviet forces in some third world states, have enabled the US military to call once again for direct US involvement in the third world, a policy epitomised in preparations for a Rapid Deployment Force. Such a change not only challenges the political and ideological impact of the Vietnam war, but also enables the US military to acquire budgetary appropriations far larger and far more immediately operable than those devoted to strategic nuclear spending. In a parallel development, the division between third world intervention capabilities and nuclear preparations has become less significant since one of the uses to which tactical nuclear weapons and neutron bombs could be put is for actions in the third world. The attainment of greater strategic nuclear superiority would make any such activities, whatever the mix of nuclear superiority and conventional force, all the easier.

This shift in military policy itself would not, however, have been possible without a third change, the modification in US public attitudes and more particularly Congressional opinion on matters of third world intervention that emerged in the late seventies. The shift in US opinion was not as complete as appearances suggested: it was not possible, for example, for either Carter or Reagan simply to reinstitute the draft. The new advocacy of intervention was also a delayed response to Vietnam, which had taken several years to work itself through. Yet the revival of interventionist sentiment as a result of the late 1970s enabled the unregenerate right, which had never accepted its defeats in China, Cuba or Indo-China, to fight back: to press for new legislation and new appropriations that would facilitate an imperial role. The rhetoric about a loss of US power and influence found one of its easiest victories in this change of the US political climate vis-à-vis the third world. And even where, as in the case of Central America, the US public remained opposed to a direct US involvement, the US state was able to take interventionist initiatives.

The third world has therefore a special place in the Second Cold War, both as a symbol and as a substantive cause. It has become one area where actual combat rages and lives are lost as a result of US policies and those of US allies: in El Salvador, Guatemala, Timor, Lebanon, Namibia and Angola, among others. Yet this revival of militarism towards the third world has been enhanced by other factors also present within the genesis of Cold War II. One is the disarray of the metropolitan left in the latter half of the 1970s, where doves and opponents of the US role in Vietnam on both sides of the Atlantic were stampeded into Cold War attitudes. Even within the peace movement there is a tendency to dissociate the problems of Europe from those of the third world, to see the struggles of third world peoples as an embarrassment, a destabilising factor, which complicates the debate on east-west relations in Europe itself. This reproduces precisely that separation of hostility to nuclear weapons and solidarity with third world peoples which marked the protests of the 1960s. The other factor facilitating the revival of militarism has been the new, i.e. increased, importance of certain third world countries within the overall reorganisation of international capitalism. Of greatest significance, however, has been the changed political climate in the USA where, in response to the multiple setbacks and tensions of the 1970s, domestic and international, a new militarist climate had come to predominate at the government level by the end of the 1970s. It is this component of the Second Cold War that can now be considered.

5.
Right-wing Offensive in the USA

Despite its relative loss of power in relation to the USSR and capitalist rivals alike, the USA remains indisputably the strongest country in the world, both militarily and economically. The dominance of the USA in the world economy began after World War I, but it was after 1945 that its real political eminence began, and it then sought to fashion a world order after its own image. This attempt failed, insofar as the post-capitalist section of the world remained beyond US influence. But the majority of the world's population and economies did fall within the US sphere, and the USA has remained the leader of the capitalist system that still covers most of the globe.

For this reason alone, changes within the USA have immense implications for the rest of the world, and this is particularly so because the domestic politics of that country are tied to its foreign policy in a way that is peculiar and especially unpredictable. The success of post-1945 US politics has lain in its ability to deploy domestic features of the American system for foreign policy ends. But there have been failures and sudden changes, in part because the way in which the domestic and the foreign have been linked has itself proved to be unstable and subject to upsets and reverses.

The 1980 Election

Two features of domestic American politics are particularly important in this respect. One lies within the political culture of the USA, namely the suspicious, fearful, and often primitive way in which foreign policy is viewed by many within the US polity. The existence of this trend has enabled Presidents to build a strong support for continued military expenditure and the pursuit of a hegemonic American role in the world, and it is this suspicion, rather than an overt militarism, which has underlain the hostility to the USSR. The other, institutional feature is the particular power of the President in matters of foreign policy and defense, and the uncertain role, obstructive but not capable of major initiative, which the Constitution gives to Congress. The conduct of a world-wide foreign policy, and the particular decisions associated with nuclear weapons, have greatly enhanced the power of the President in the postwar epoch.[1] The drafters of the US Constitution, who sought to avoid a repetition of what George III had inflicted upon them, might have been surprised to see the danger which post-1945 developments created—of a new George III, with nuclear weapons. But despite the tendencies to a monarchical Presidency, Congress has, under conditions favourable to it, been able to use its position to oppose and in some measure inflect the policy of the President.

From the late 1940s until the early 1970s there prevailed a bipartisan approach to foreign policy, a consensus between Congress and the Presidency, through which the latter was accorded considerable freedom to lead and to execute US foreign policy on an ongoing basis. This institutional settlement was itself backed by a wider consensus within US society, which harnessed and directed the primitivism of the political culture in matters of foreign policy. But this broad sharing of agreement had been undermined by the mid-1970s and, as a result, there emerged a much more polarised foreign policy debate in the USA than had been the case since the debates on involvement in the Second World War before Pearl Harbour. Many issues contributed to this erosion: the Vietnam war, the discrediting of the Presidency in that war and in the Watergate scandal, the increased economic difficulties of the USA, the issue of Israel. By the middle of the 1970s there was no longer a working consensus between President and Congress, nor between Democrats and Republicans, nor between political leadership and the country at large.

The culmination of this process was the November 1980 election, a moment central to Cold War II.[2] The First Cold War was accompanied

---

[1] Michael Mandelbaum, *The Nuclear Revolution*, London 1982, pp. 177-189.

[2] For analysis of the election see Thomas Ferguson and Joel Rogers, *The Hidden Election,* New York 1981; Alan Wolfe, *America's Impasse, The Rise and Fall of the Politics of Growth*, New York 1981; David Chagall, *The New Kingmakers,* New York 1981; Edmund Fawcett and Tony Thomas, *America, Americans,* London 1983, Chapters Four and Five.

by no such electoral break or deep shift in US domestic politics. Truman became President on the death of Roosevelt and the Cold War began soon afterwards. He continued to preside over US foreign policy until the beginning of 1953, i.e. through over six years of Cold War. The foreign policy change occurred as a result of the advent of a new President to power and the altered international circumstances following the end of the war, not as a result of a significant economic or political crisis within US society itself. The change to Cold War policies in the late 1970s involves a much closer look at the internal workings of the USA than did the switch from war-time co-operation in 1945.

To some extent Carter had begun, by early 1978, to move his policies in a Cold War direction. But even the policies he pursued at the end of his Administration were far short of the Cold War policies advocated and implemented by Reagan. Carter's defeat reflected significant tensions within the USA itself. With the Republican President's accession to office in January 1981 a marked break occurred in US foreign policy, and the Second Cold War entered a much more stormy, menacing phase. Whatever the limits of his electoral support—he won only 28% of registered votes—and however much part of his support came from those who opposed Carter rather then endorsed his Cold War, Reagan's election marks a turning-point in both US foreign and US domestic politics. His later inability to sustain the Cold War momentum of 1980 should not obscure the importance of Reagan's election in the Cold War.

Explanation of the election result as such must involve detailed analysis of processes internal to US politics: to explain how international events contributed to Reagan's election it has to be shown how these events took effect within the USA and how they influenced the election itself. On the other hand, it is mistaken to focus on the domestic determination of the election alone. This cannot explain the growth of Cold War politics in the USA; for, whatever the force of these domestic tensions, they could only acquire an international import by interacting with other processes external to the USA itself. The purpose of this chapter is not to provide a comprehensive analysis of the 1980 election but to identify those changes within US society and politics in the 1970s which contributed to the Second Cold War. The underlying domestic causes of Cold War II are to be found in the shifting socio-economic structure of the USA; but at least four other more strictly political developments confirmed this drive towards the Cold War.

Socio-Economic Changes in the 1970s

Three general trends within US society underlie the rise of a new and more militant conservative coalition in the latter 1970s. The first is the increased influence of the south and west, the 'sunbelt', an area of greater demographic importance than ever before and the home of a more right-wing capitalism than that normally associated with the east. Between 1970 and 1980 the population of the western states rose by 24%, that of the south by 21% and that of the north-east by only 1%. By 1980 the northeast-midwest sector of the USA, the 'frostbelt', contained under half—46 per cent—of the total population. The capitalists of the south and west tend to be more hostile to unions, more in favour of anti-communist rhetoric, more sympathetic to defence spending, and more hostile to state intervention. They are the protagonists of laissez-faire capitalism, and of an ideology of American promise and power that has become somewhat dented in the east. The backers of Ronald Reagan epitomise this outlook.[3]

It is often argued that this sector of US capitalism, and the populations associated with it, are less concerned with foreign affairs and much less informed about them. They are therefore more likely to favour policies that ignore the qualms of European and Japanese allies. Whereas the east coast is, it is said, associated with internationalist perspectives, the south and west are nationalist. Indeed they berate the east coast establishment which has traditionally controlled foreign affairs for its cosmopolitan and defeatist attitudes where US national interests are concerned. However, this contrast between an externally oriented east and a more internally oriented south and west is, on its own, insufficient, since these latter areas have specific foreign policy orientations of their own. They tend to favour higher military spending and the maintainance of clear military superiority over the USSR; while this reflects the interest of areas where much of the aerospace industry is located, it also illustrates the belief in nuclear superiority as a panacea, one that enables the USA to dispense with the irritations of diplomacy and allied consultation. The difference between the capitalists of east and sunbelt may also lie not so much in an internationalist/nationalist division, as in contrasting geographical em-

---

[3.] Ferguson and Rogers provide an analysis of the 1980 election which concentrates on the coalition of corporate interests that worked for a Reagan victory. Whilst their focus on such elite coalitions may be unduly monist, they are right to see Reagan as having won the support of a new grouping in US business.

phases of US concern. The east coast has historically always had closest ties to Europe, the region most suspected in south and west. The west has looked to Asia, and has been more concerned with the Far East and the projection of US power there. The USSR and China had divergent approaches to relations with the USA in the late 1950s because the one faced calm in Europe, and the other continued conflict in the Far East; in the same way the differing geographical orientations of US capital towards a tranquil Europe and an insurgent Far East may account for some of the policy differences between them.

For its part, the south is historically concerned with Latin America; the enhanced prominence of the Caribbean and Central America in the 1970s has brought this region and those associated with it greater influence within US politics. The one zone far removed from all of these areas is the Middle East, but for reasons of oil and arms sales this too became a concern of the sunbelt regions in the 1970s: as much as Asia, the Middle East is an area of economic and geopolitical concern to which the sunbelt attaches particular importance.[4]

The second major trend that underlay the 1980 election was the recession. The 1940s, 1950s and 1960s had been decades of greatly increasing prosperity in the USA; the domestic consensus behind US foreign policy had to a considerable extent rested upon the ability of successive US Presidents to stimulate growth in the economy. In the 1960s there had been high growth rates and low rates of inflation. In the 1970-81 period, the averages were 2.9 per cent for growth, 8.1 per cent for inflation, and 6.5 per cent for unemployment. Even this contrast of decades masks the much more abrupt rate of decline in the period closer to the 1980 election. In the 1977-9 period the US economy had undergone a period of relative expansion; but in 1980 the GNP growth rate was zero, inflation was over 9 per cent, and the rate of unemployment had risen to 7.5 per cent.[5] The average purchasing power of a US family was 8.5 per cent lower in 1980 than it was in 1976.[6] Those most hit were blue-collar workers and there was an 8.5 per cent swing to the Republicans

4. Franz Schurman, *The Logic of World Power,* New York 1974, provides a brilliant synoptic view of this tension within US politics. Schurman's stress on the Asian perspectives of the 'nationalist' bloc in contrast to the European orientation of the 'internationalists' is particularly important, especially as in the subsequent period the 'nationalist' bloc began to show greater interest in the Middle East.
5. Ferguson and Rogers, pp. 141-2.
6. David Chagall, p. 260.

among them on election day; of all the issues which comprise the impression of lost power, that of unemployment was apparently the most significant.

The recession produced a generalised shift in consciousness within the USA about the very importance of economics itself in national politics.[7] When prosperity reigns at home and a country is strong in world markets, there is comparatively little reason for economic issues to become a matter of national debate. Only when recession and loss of competitive edge begin to take effect does the situation change: it is not that, in better times, economic issues were not central to domestic and international politics; rather, there is less need to be explicit about what the economic assumptions of political power and political conflict are.[8] The British experienced precisely such an increase in the economic content of political debate as the industrial and commercial foundations of their empire were eroded, first in the gold standard crisis of 1931, and then in the chronic slide that followed World War II. A similar increase in concern about economic issues could be detected in the USA, from the payments deficits brought on by the Vietnam war in the early 1970s, through the slowing of growth and the rise of inflation and unemployment later in the decade.

While much of the rhetoric about a loss of American power focussed on the military balance with the USSR or on the humiliations of Iran, the greatest impression of weakness was conveyed in this economic sphere, changes in which telegraphed the decline of US influence to every home. Yet, whilst registered domestically, this economic deterioration had consequences for foreign policy: the difficulties of the US economy were blamed on the challenges of rival capitalist powers, especially Japan and OPEC, and the call for military superiority over the USSR, redolent as it was of a past era of US greatness, subsumed and displaced the frustrations brought on by the recession.

The onset of the recession coincided with another major change in US society, namely the breakup of pre-existing patterns of urban society, and strains attendant upon these. Some of this involved the emergence of

---

[7.] Walter Dean Burnham, 'The 1980 Earthquake', in Ferguson and Rogers, op. cit.; Douglas Hibbs, 'Political Parties and Macroeconomic Policy', *American Political Science Review*, vol. 71, 1977.

[8.] For the changing focus of political leaders in the USA on economic issues see pp. 185-6 below.

new movements of protest and assertion, by ethnic and sexual groups challenging the conformism of Middle America. The response on the part of those threatened by these movements was to support policies of ideological counter-attack, in education, welfare programmes and the law. A groundswell of conservatism was thereby gathering force in response to radical political challenges that had emerged in the late 1960s and early 1970s. But this sense of threat was overlain by the crisis of the inner cities and in particular by the enormous rise in urban crime, which while they threatened all sections of society affected the more vulnerable working class in particular. The appeals of patriarchy, religion, police gained new force in an atmosphere where traditional patterns of control and authority had given way to insecurity and decline.

Internal to the USA as these changes were, they nonetheless had implications for foreign policy. The capitalists of the south and west favoured greater military spending, and more attention to the Far East, Middle East and Latin America. The recession was to a considerable extent blamed on the oil price rises of OPEC and on Japanese imports. The positing of an external threat and of the need to organise against it was an important instrument for mobilising against laxity at home. The function of war scares in strengthening domestic authority is as self-evident as it is important. One of the central themes in the Reagan campaign was the call for increased military spending, and this was seen as of benefit to many individual sections of US industry, whatever its overall macroeconomic effect. The commitment to greater military spending to confront the USSR therefore seemed to provide a means of solving, or at least alleviating, these internal tensions that had been growing within US society during the 1970s. Reagan's campaign rhetoric summed this up: 'They say the United States has passed its zenith,' he declared. 'They tell you the American people no longer have the will to cope, that the future will be one of sacrifice and few opportunities. I utterly reject this view. I will not stand by and watch this country destroy itself under mediocre leadership that drifts from one crisis to the next, eroding our national will...Isn't it time to renew our compact of freedom, to pledge to each other all that is best in our lives, for the sake of this, our beloved and blessed land? Together, let us make a new beginning.'[9]

---

9. Chagall, p. 192.

These social and economic processes would not, in themselves, be sufficient to explain the domestic basis for the Second Cold War: rather they provided the stimulus for other changes in the realm of politics proper, which themselves created the domestic foundation for the Cold War climate of the early 1980s. In particular, four other changes within US politics accompanied this process: the rise of a militant right; the changed role of Congress; the pressure for increased military expenditure from the 'Iron Triangle'; the need to counter the recession.

The Rise of a Militant Right

The 1980 election did represent a significant change in US politics, with the election of Ronald Reagan in a crushing defeat of the incumbent Jimmy Carter, and the victory in Congressional election campaigns of candidates of the right who unseated 14 Senators and over 50 Representatives deemed to be too liberal. All of these newly elected candidates subscribed to a Cold War consensus—increased military expenditure, an emphasis on the Soviet threat, a commitment to reasserting American power. Their triumph coincided with a much wider adoption of Cold War attitudes in US politics, a change already evident under Carter but confirmed and developed by the November 1980 poll.

The militant right was itself a coalition, the divisions of which soon became evident once Reagan came into office. The most vociferous section was the New Right as such, which played a large role in the election and much less in the subsequent formation of policy. It has been described as 'more a climate of resentment and a money-raising system than a body of ideas.'[10] Other components included the traditional Cold War conservative bloc within the Republican Party, and the neo-conservation forces of the Democratic Party. But despite their differences in the 1980 elections themselves, and in the pressure for Cold War policies, the various trends of the coalition coincided.

As the most vocal exponents of the new belligerency the forces of the New Right have played a major catalytic role in altering opinion within the USA. The origins of this movement go back many decades in US

---

[10] Fawcett and Thomas, p. 177. On the New Right see Alan Wolfe, 'Sociology, Liberalism and the Radical Right', and Mike Davis, 'The New Right's Road to Power', *New Left Review* 128, July-August 1981; Alan Crawford, *Thunder on the Right,* New York 1980; and Ferguson and Rogers, and Wolfe, op. cit.

history. It revives primitivist themes familiar from much earlier times—hostility to the east coast, enmity towards Europe, a paranoid approach to internal dissent, a Know-Nothing attitude to foreign affairs, a macho patriotism redolent of the high school football field. If 1980 was the first time this movement contributed to an election victory, it was far from being the first time such a trend had emerged. The spread of Cold War attitudes in the USA has drawn on deep strands in American political culture which are supportive of such policies, the competitiveness, aggression and desire to be 'Number One' which Reagan has learnt well how to tap in an apparently effortless manner. Assertive and militaristic as it is, this culture has another side, equally supportive of the Cold War: a self-pitying, suspicious, vicious streak which has found its expression in the torrent of laments for America's lost power that burst forth in the late 1970s.

Many of those active in the New Right draw their inspiration from the heroes of the First Cold War: Richard Viguerie, the promoter of the Political Action Committees, claims as his heroes 'the two Macs'—Joseph McCarthy and Douglas MacArthur. Many of those now prominent in the New Right narrowly defined, and in the broader conservative community, were people who came to adulthood in the early 1950s—the time of the Korean war and of problem-free US power. But while it draws inspiration from the First Cold War, the New Right traces its organisational origins to the conflicts within the Republican Party in the early 1960s: to the opposition to Rockefeller as Nixon's vice-presidential running mate in the 1960 election, and to the first successful imposition of a western candidate on the party since before World War I, with the nomination of Barry Goldwater in 1964. Goldwater was of course defeated, and Johnson then mobilised patriotic sentiment around the Vietnam war. But with the onset of Detente in the early 1970s the right once again became more active, opposing the foreign policies of Nixon and Ford, pouring venom on such east coast 'liberals' as Kissinger and Rockefeller, and again mobilising in opposition to the appointment of Rockefeller, this time as Ford's vice-president in the 1974-6 period. The term New Right was first used in 1975, and in 1976 these forces tried and almost succeeded in having Reagan nominated for the Republican candidacy. Their initial victories came in the 1978 mid-term long recessional elections, when some Congressmen were unseated. 1980 represented the later victorious cascade.

A number of developments in the middle 1970s encouraged the New Right's expansion. Growing discontent within the Republican Party at Detente was one such factor. Another was the Federal Election Campaign Act of October 1974 whereby Congress limited campaign donations by individuals and so opened the door to the surrogate system of Political Action Committees, or PACs, self-appointed single-issue bodies which solicited funds by direct mail and then waged campaigns for particular candidates: these PACs spent $55 million in the 1980 election. The New Right and the PACs derived their greatest support from the growth of a range of single-issue campaigns which mobilised large numbers of people and copious funds behind conservative causes: against abortion, gun-control, bussing, gay and women's rights, and in favour of capital punishment, school prayer and Creationism (a theory opposed to that of evolution). The white working class was moving to the right; Catholics, Jews and Fundamentalists combined forces on relevant issues. By 1980 the electorate included 40 million born-again Christians.[11]

The institutions of the New Right were in place by the mid-1970s, i.e. long before the apparent onset of the Second Cold War. Young Americans for Freedom had been established to oppose the Rockefeller nomination in 1960. The Richard A. Viguerie Corporation, the core of the PAC system, was set up in 1964. Accuracy in Media, the right-wing press lobby, was established in 1969. In 1971 the Colorado beer magnate Joseph Coors began seeking a base in Washington, and in 1973 he established the Heritage Foundation, later to be a major source of right-wing policy research. In 1972 the campaign to secure an Equal Rights Amendment to the Constitution produced the STOP-ERA campaign of Phyllis Schlafly, and in 1973 the Catholic bishops began organising around abortion in opposition to the Supreme Court judgement in the case of *Roe vs. Wade* which gave women a constitutional right to an abortion for at least the first six months of pregnancy. In 1974 the traditional right began to organise in tandem: the Committee on the Present Danger, a group of 141 anti-detente Republicans and Democrats first established during the First Cold War, reassembled, and a parallel group, the Committee for a Free Congress came into being. It was this interlocking system of right-wing activist groups, some New Right, some more

---

[11.] Chagall, p. 236.

traditional, which mobilised support in the country as a whole and in Washington for the New Cold War policies of the later part of the decade.

In the field of foreign policy, the New Right represents a coalition of distinct ideological and organisational forces. Despite the formal emphasis on 'single issues', the unity of the different policies is quite patent: the mixture of reasserting traditional family and religious values at home with militarism abroad, both seen as a response to some dangerous menace.[12] Patriotism, warmongering and strategic paranoia combine easily with piety and domestic repression. Such themes as hostility to gun control, support for capital punishment and patriotism fuse the domestic single-issue approach with New Cold War belligerency, and in a resurgent white racism and hostility to women and homosexuals the right found convenient functional substitutes for the red scare. The movement was, as one critic said, 'pro-life and pro-gun'. Opposition to bussing in such areas as South Boston combined with a rejection of those who encouraged a more sympathetic attitude to third world peoples—Asians were bad enough after Vietnam, blacks were worse and Arabs the worst of all. Among Jews the sense of identification with Israel produced a new alarm about what was seen as growing Arab influence, whilst the issue of Jewish dissidents in the USSR locked these other trends into a New Cold War perspective. There was an 11 per cent swing by Jews to the Republicans in the 1980 Presidential election. In the figure of Andy Young, the black UN representative dismissed in 1979 by Carter for private discussions with a Palestinian representative, a perfect composite scape-goat was found.

The multiple and apparently distinct domestic issues therefore formed a single ideological torrent with direct foreign policy implications. Yet the unity of domestic and international issues was not just at this psychological and ideological level: what is striking is how far the political biographies of key members of the New Right are, despite their superficial obsession with domestic concerns, constituted by international issues. Richard Viguerie's descent from MacArthur and McCarthy has already been alluded to. He himself has written that for him the main issues are not the domestic ones, but the military: 'Our primary

---

[12.] This dimension of Cold War II is quite distinct from Cold War I which was marked by an anti-communist witch-hunt, but not by a religious revival and comparable reassertion of traditional values.

goal is military superiority,' he once declared. Phyllis Schlafly, the STOP-ERA campaigner, has co-authored five books on strategic doctrine in which she argues for an invulnerable first-strike capacity. According to Schlafly the US government had been taken over by a conspiracy of 'gravediggers', officials such as Kissinger who believed in unilateral US disarmament. Her own political provenance is illustrative: she began her career as an opponent of the wartime alliance with Russia against Nazi Germany.[13] Anita Bryant, the promoter of an anti-gay crusade in Dade County, Florida, in 1977, had her campaign managed by Mike Thompson, producer of a documentry film opposed to the SALT-II treaty. And Jerry Falwell, spokesman of the Moral Majority, has called for a speedy return to the McCarthy period. All communists should be registered, he told an audience in 1977: 'We should stamp it on their foreheads and send them back to Russia.' The link between Falwell's evangelism and the New Cold War mood is plain enough. As he puts it: 'Jesus was not a pacifist. He was not a sissy.'[14]

The coalescence of domestic single-issue campaigns with foreign policy comes about through the overlapping of different organisational dynamics that converge on the terrain of foreign policy. The New Right is opposed to what it sees as the elite, soft, east-coast, detente-prone group which dominated Republican policy in the earlier part of the 1970s: Kissinger has been one of its important targets. Yet the New Right has not so much dominated the discussion on foreign policy as opened the door for an alternative elite current to regain audiences and power. The New Right had only one representative in the Reagan cabinet, James Watt, the Secretary of the Interior. All the main foreign policy and defence positions were occupied by members of previous administrations or by Reagan appointees: Secretaries of State Haig and Shultz, Theatre Nuclear Weapons negotiator Nitze, Secretary of Defense Weinberger, head of disarmament policy Eugene Rostow, UN Representative Kirkpatrick, CIA chief Casey. For, parallel to the rise of the New Right, elite opinion-making bodies, notably the Committee on the Present Danger, were generating their own alternative in the middle 1970s, spreading the alarmism and New Cold war atmosphere that was later to

---

[13.] Frances Fitgerald, 'The Triumphs of the New Right', *New York Review of Books*, 19 November 1981.
[14.] Crawford, op. cit., pp. 159-60.

carry all before it. Kissinger himself was warning about the dangers of the Soviet threat from 1977 onwards. The group of bellicose advisers asked by Ford to prepare an alternative view of Soviet power—Team B—was working in 1976: though their views were rejected by Ford, they came to play an important role in the Reagan Administration.

A separate evolution was taking place among Democrats, including many who had been doveish during the Vietnam war. This process yielded the 'neo-conservative' group of Moynihan and Jackson, Podhoretz and Kirkpatrick. Ferociously hostile to the USSR from the early 1970s onwards, and reflecting the changing moods of white Democrats, this section of the right was particularly affected by the related questions of Soviet Jewry and the Middle East: despite the passage of the Jackson-Vanik Amendment of 1974, the fact that over a quarter of a million Jews were allowed to leave the USSR, and continued US support for an ever more powerful Israel, these Jewish issues combined to foster anti-Soviet sentiment amongst Democrats and to recruit a previously more restrained section of US opinion for the cold war consensus. The leading figure in this Democratic cold war fraction was Senator Henry Jackson, who, from 1972 onwards, was assailing the Republican Administration from the right for its dealings with the USSR. But this evolution amongst pro-Israeli sentiment was only a recent extension of what had long been a close involvement of much of the Democratic Party in cold war policy.

A central role in this had been played by the trades union federation, AFL-CIO, whose long-term President George Meany was a hawk on relations with the USSR. The AFL-CIO had opposed Eisenhower's invitation to Khrushchev to visit the USA in 1959, and had backed the Vietnam war and the 1965 invasion of the Dominican Republic; but it also helped on the ground by working with the CIA to set up pro-US trades union organisations, through its international affiliate, the American Institute for Free Labour Development.[15] When the Committee on the Present Danger was reconstituted in 1974 US labour leaders were prominent amongst its members, and Lane Kirkland, the AFL-CIO President, was appointed one of its co-chairmen. As Marcus Raskin has pointed out, this

---

[15] David Mobert in *In These Times*, 24-30 March 1962; a letter in the same issue reveal that the AFL-CIO received 90 per cent of the $20 million allocated to its international training programme from the State Department.

cold war orientation of the US labour movement reflects at least three factors which well predate Cold War II: the suppression of the left within the trades union movement which accompanied the First Cold War, an economic interest in maintaining employment levels through military programmes, and the deep-seated nationalism of the US working class.[16] When the time came to mobilise for Cold War II in the latter half of the 1970s US labour was not found wanting, and with the crisis in Poland which unfolded in 1980 and 1981 it found the perfect issue on which to present itself as the champion of a working-class anti-communism.

Belligerence on Capitol Hill

Three components of the conservative coalition of the late 1970s have been identified here: the militant New Right, espousing single issues and new forms of extra-party fund-raising and mobilisation; the traditional Republican right which, after the interruptions of Vietnam and Watergate, had re-formed in Washington by the mid-1970s; and the Democratic right, encompassing neo-conservatives and cold war Labour, which endorsed the policies of the other two, even as it tried to present its own party candidates as the representatives of the new conservative consensus. Ultimately, all such political forces operating in the USA sought to place a nominee embodying these principles in the White House, the site of the chief executive and since World War II the focus of a large foreign policy and defence bureaucracy. But it was not initially in the White House that the conservative forces took effect: rather, as a reflection of the breakdown of the postwar consensus between White House and Capitol Hill, it was in the US Congress and particularly in the Senate that the forces advocating the New Cold War began to make substantial advances in the period prior to Ronald Reagan's entry to the Presidential office.

The rise of the New Right and neo-conservative forces across the USA has been accompanied by substantive changes in the attitude and initiative shown by Congress towards foreign policy.[17] The conflict of Con-

---

16. In *Exterminism and Cold War,* pp. 217-19.

17. Joshua Muravchik, *The Senate and National Security: A New Mood,* Washington papers No. 80, London 1980; Godfrey Hodgson, *Congress and American Foreign Policy,* Chatham House, London 1980.

gress and Presidency in foreign policy had a long history prior to the 1940s consensus: the rejection of Woodrow Wilson's peace programme in 1920 was an outstanding case of such opposition on Capitol Hill, and it highlighted the most convenient means for Congress to oppose Presidential policy, namely on matters where it is given constitutional prerogatives—treaties and government appointments. However, for US domestic consumption the key debates concern another point where Congress plays a role, namely on annual defence budget appropriations. These come before Congress each spring in anticipation of the Financial Year that begins on 1 October. The military appropriations have long been the symbolic focus of the battle between Congress and Presidency and a litmus of both parties' orientations on east-west relations. One of the key indices of the Second Cold War has been the shift in Congressional posture on military spending—cutting back on Presidential requests in the early 1970s and increasing them in the later 1970s. Reagan's enormous initial increases in military appropriations, put through in 1981 with Congressional enthusiasm, reflected the triumph of a new unity in foreign policy, the first foreign policy consensus since Vietnam.

Congress's militancy has several causes. One was the breakdown of the earlier compact. During the First Cold War President Truman and the Republican Congressional leader Vandenberg established a foreign policy consensus. In the wake of the triumph of the Chinese Revolution McCarthy tried to challenge the Republican Party leadership; but McCarthy's hearings failed to secure him control of the Party and from then onwards, with colonial revolutions checked in Asia after 1954, Eisenhower was able successfully to chloroform the more militant right. What truly broke the consensus was the Vietnam war. Congressional criticism at first took the form of doveish opposition to Johnson's policies; but this move to the left was later offset by the emergence of hawkish factions in Congress, opposed to the Nixon-Kissinger approach to detente. This tendency was found not only amongst right-wing Republicans, but it also developed among Democrats: surveys of the forty northern Democratic senators who had dominated Congressional discussion of foreign policy show a marked shift to the right in the later 1970s—from McGovern's urging of a US invasion of Cambodia in 1978, to Church's cynical exploitation of the Soviet 'combat brigade' allegedly discovered in Cuba in 1979.

Organisational changes within Congress facilitated the emergence of greater dissent: the old committee system, based on consensus-inclined seniority, was abandoned in the 1970s and gave the opportunity to more discordant elements to have their say. Far more important, however, was the sharpening of conflict between President and Congress which began with Vietnam but reached its culmination during the Watergate crisis of 1973–4. This Congressional hostility to the White House was politically ambivalent: it initially took the form of a series of measures designed to check Presidential military actions abroad—the Cooper-Church Amendment of 1970, prohibiting US combat forces in Cambodia; the 1971 resolutions on US withdrawal from Vietnam; the 1973 resolution banning all US involvement in Indo-China from 15 August of that year; the Hughes-Ryan Amendment of 1974 limiting the powers of the CIA; the Clark Amendment of 1976 preventing CIA underground military activity in Angola. But this independence and assertiveness could easily be turned to the service of other policies and in the later part of Carter's Presidency it was being used to promote rearmament and greater activism abroad. In the words of one commentator: 'By 1979, the Senate was clearly the most hawkish body in the US government.'[18]

The three issues upon which this Cold War militancy was most evident were defence expenditure, SALT-II, and the Panama Canal Treaties debate. In the early 1970s, up to 1975, Congress was cutting back on requests for defence appropriations; from 1976 through 1978 there was relatively little Congressional debate on this matter. In 1979 and 1980, however, Congress took the lead in pressing for military appropriations above those requested by Carter: in September 1979, for FY 1980, it added $35 billions, a sum equal to the total amount deducted in the previous ten Financial Years; this was some months before either the Iranian hostage or Afghan crises erupted. Allocations for FY 1981 were 40 per cent higher in real terms than those for FY 1976. There was therefore a concerted drive for military expenditure increases well before Reagan came to office, a process in which Congress played a leading part.

The SALT-II treaty came before Congress in the summer of 1979 following upon the initialling of the agreement by Carter and Brezhnev in Vienna in June of that year. By general agreement the terms of SALT-II were more favourable to the USA than had been those of SALT-I: yet while SALT-I had passed through Congress without major debate, the reception

---

[18.] Muravchik, p. 7.

of SALT-II was so hostile that Carter withdrew the treaty rather than face possible defeat. Criticism of the treaty did not focus upon the actual terms so much as upon the more nebulous issues, of the supposed decline in US strength and the continued Soviet buildup. In other words, it was on the alarmist questions, dramatised by the PACs, the press and Congressmen coming up for re-election that the SALT-II treaty foundered. The fate of SALT-II bore out one of the underlying features of the foreign policy debate in the USA: whilst the discussion purported to be about details and facts, it was predominantly about a mood.

If the impeding of SALT-II was the most substantial of the foreign policy issues upon which Congress made its mark as a promoter of the Second Cold War, the trend towards right-wing revolt on the Hill had already been evident in the earlier debate, in the first half of 1978, upon the Panama Canal Treaties. Originally raised by Reagan in the Republican primaries for the 1976 election, this apparently minor issue was invested by its opponents with immense symbolic significance.[19] It was tailor-made for Congressional intervention, since it involved ratification of a treaty. It concerned an area where US susceptibilities had never been fully soothed since the Cuban revolution: General Omar Torrijos, the Panamanian leader, became a surrogate Fidel Castro. It embodied two components known to stir particular emotions in both British and French colonialism—canals, the finest precipitants of strategic anxiety, and kith-and-kin, in the shape of the 15,000 'Zonians', US pieds noirs who mobilised support within the USA.

In the end the Treaties passed Congress: but they had been tempered by new amendments, validating US intervention into the next century, and the Panama Canal issue had given the New Right forces a trial run for the 1980 election. Reagan himself expanded his reputation as a candidate by opposing the agreements, and the PACs and all other right-wing organisations of any significance organised direct-mail, TV and radio commercials, and press campaigns against the Treaties. Carter expended much of his Congressional credit getting agreement for the Treaties; the New Right and Reagan's associates realised the need for even greater efforts if they were to prevail in 1980. The erosion of Presidential power in the earlier half of the decade therefore prepared the way for Congress in

---

[19] Jimmy Carter reveals that some Republican leaders who backed him on the Panama Canal Treaties were not prepared to support him on SALT-II. Support on one difficult issue was enough—any more would have antagonised their backers (*Keeping Faith*, p. 224).

the later 1970s to anticipate the outcome of the 1980 election and act as an advance-guard for the Second Cold War.

The Iron Triangle

Cold War II was preceded by great pressure for increased military expenditure: this came both from political forces operating upon the US government and from specific forces with a material interest in the arms race. in other words, the arms race is the product of convergent forces in which specific institutions favouring such expansion—the arms manufacturers, the Pentagon—combine with the Congress and the Presidency. Analysis of the genesis and structure of US military expenditure is essential for unravelling the complex determination of Cold War II, for discerning those factors which have sought to increase international tension and so facilitate a new arms boom. The institutions favouring higher military expenditure prepare the ground for their success by a barrage of political propaganda: promoting the idea of Soviet superiority, of declining US capabilities, of gaps in missiles, civil defence or naval strength.

The linkage between different forces involved in this has been characterised as an 'iron triangle', binding Congress, the Pentagon and the arms industry together in an unchallenged process of military expansion.[20] Studies of the personnel involved in the three sectors show a high rate of switching from one to the other, sustained lobbying efforts in Washington by the major arms firms, and a network of social and professional links holding Pentagon, Congress and armourers together. The role of Congressmen in securing contracts for their home areas is well-known: under the rubric 'My district right or wrong', Congressmen from all regions of the USA have encouraged military expenditure which will benefit their constituents; and through the practice of mutual assistance known as log-rolling, groups of Congressmen have banded together to secure contracts for all their districts. Yet it is simplistic to attribute the arms buildup uniquely to the workings of such an interested coalition. In the same way, it is relevant, but misleading, to ascribe the arms buildup to a set of inertial processes within the Pentagon or the arms industry, as if the mere fact of new technical opportunities were suf-

---

[20] On the interlocking interests of the arms trade see Mary Kaldor, *The Baroque Arsenal,* London 1982; Anthony Sampson, *The Arms Bazaar,* London 1977; Russell Warren Howe, *Weapons,* London 1980. It has been said of the US military that their only peacetime victories are in procurement.

ficient to provide the funds and executive authorisation for major weapons outlays. The analysts of the arms race who point to these factors of bureaucratic inertia and technical imperative are correct to insist that these be included in any account of the causes of the race; but they tend, on occasion, to overstate their case by excluding those other factors, in the politics of the situation, which gain for the generals and arms manufacturers the legitimacy and support which they seek for their increased military appropriations.

The US military apparatus suffered a double blow as a result of Vietnam: to its prestige and self-image, and to the willingness of Congress to satisfy Presidential requests for financial appropriation. But by the time the Ford Administration had come to office, after Nixon's resignation in August 1974, the Pentagon had once again begun to press for higher spending rates, and found support in Congress and the Administration for such policies from Congressmen and cabinet officials specialising in these issues. By 1976, therefore, there already existed a reorganised programme of militarisation, drawing attention both to the need for increased conventional forces, for action in the third world, and for new nuclear forces, to meet supposed Soviet advances.

The proclamation of counter-force as a major practical US option in 1974 reflected a conscious move towards the use of tactical nuclear weapons in precisely those situations where large bodies of conventional forces, as in Vietnam, had shown themselves to be incapable of wresting victory. The planning for new interventionary forces in the third world, rapid and stripped-down in contrast to the half a million despatched to Vietnam, began at the same time. The groundwork for the decision to station Cruise and Pershing II missiles in Europe was laid in 1975-6 by a joint Pentagon-Congressional policy-forming group which prepared the way for the later Presidential decisions. One of the great myths of the Second Cold War offensive in the USA is that following the Vietnam defeat the USA simply slid into a state of greater and greater military weakness. In fact, no sooner was the defeat first registered, in 1968, than planning for a new generation of weapons, the third major such wave since World War II, got under way. Cruise, MX, Trident, the B-1 bomber were all conceived at this time. The strategic modernisation undertaken by Reagan was already prepared in 1972, and whilst military expenditure did dip immediately after the withdrawal from Vietnam, it began to rise again from 1977 onwards: far from having continued to 'dismantle' US defences as his critics allege, Carter presided over a steady increase in expenditure that covered his whole Administration and not just the period, from 1978 onwards, when he called for a real rise in military outlays.[21]

The Pentagon had other reasons, apart from Vietnam, for pressing for higher appropriations. One was the internal condition of the US armed forces. The transition to a volunteer army had been accompanied by what were presented as serious internal problems. Whereas 11 per cent of US adults have no high school diploma, this applied to 60 per cent of the army's recruits. Key maintenance personnel were lacking: in one test 98 per cent of the tank repairmen failed the test for proficiency, as did 91 per cent of the aviation maintenance men. Vital air combat personnel were being lured away by more lucrative pay and the promise of more flying time: 65 per cent of the pilots coming up for re-enlistment in 1980 left the service.[22] In the same year all 33 of the specialists in maintaining the F-15's 'black box' avionics left for civilian life, whilst the navy complained it was 20,000 petty officers short. Problems of morale were also significant: the US armed forces report a rate of 12,000 defections each year, but only 6 prosecutions.[23] 20 per cent of army personnel were said to be on hard drugs; 5 of 22 plane crashes in 1979 were believed to be because the pilots had hangovers. There is no need to accept the Pentagon's evaluation that such problems seriously undermined the USA's fighting ability; it is, however, evident that tendencies of this kind were used by the US armed forces as arguments for higher rates of military pay, the latter being a major part of the overall defence bill.

A third source of pressure for higher appropriations came from the inflationary dynamic built into the arms contract system, with rising costs for constant products, and a much greater level of technical complexity in new weapons systems. In November 1981 the Budget Director David Stockman attacked what he called the 'contracting idiocy' of the Pentagon. The navy chief Admiral Hyman Rickover told Congress in January 1982 of the system of 'sophisticated procurement fraud' that now operated as firms consistently raised their costs. The complicities of the iron triangle play an important part here, since as a result of the interchange of personnel and the defence contractors the same people can

---

[21.] SIPRI Yearbook 1981, p. 156.

[21.] *The Economist*, 7 February 1981.

[23.] BBC TV Panorama, 18 May 1981.

be both evaluators and producers of the product. Through the 'buy-in' system contractors secure agreement at artificially low prices. Only 30 per cent of military expenditure contracts in 1975 had any competition at all, and there is little check on the increase of costs once contracts have been agreed upon. Contractors can charge not only for increased costs on agreed items, but for 'gold-plating', the addition of sophisticated extras to what was initially a simpler weapon. Since the Pentagon also has an interest in acquiring a more complex weapon, there is again a shared source of benefit. The classic case is that of the F-18, which began in 1971 as a simple navy fighter plane, costing $5 million. By 1980 the cost had risen to $30 million apiece, to which were added an estimated $3.5 billion in aircraft carriers and escort ships designed to protect this aircraft. The US army's XM-1 tank, scheduled for production runs of between 4,000 and 7,000, costs $2.7 million apiece. The Trident submarine, the first of which came into service at the end of 1981, was $280 million or 40 per cent over budget. The B-1 bomber, originally scheduled to cost $50 million each, may now cost $200 or even $300 million. In June 1981 the Pentagon estimated that current cost estimates on 47 major weapons systems had more than doubled from original calculations.[24]

The three mechanisms promoting increased expenditure—the counter-attack after Vietnam, the demand for higher pay, and the inflation in contract costs—are only part of the complex pushing for increased confrontation with the USSR and promoting the New Cold War. They do however point to the fact that the forces behind the arms race are not particularly hidden, secretive or beyond human control: specific economic and administrative interests are at stake, and are promoted in conjunction with the wider political changes in Congress and the Presidency already discussed.

Behind the specific workings of the iron triangle lies the much wider pressure of the military community itself, which propounds a belief in the overall beneficial interests of military expenditure. Military firms are not the largest in the economy and even Reagan's 5-year expenditure of $1.6 trillion is only a small component of what is a $3 trillion per year

[24]. *The Costs and Consequences of Reagan's Military Buildup*, by R. De-Grasse and others, Council on Eonomic Priorities, New York 1982, p. 42. On cost overruns see Mary Kaldor, pp. 70 ff.; *Newsweek*, 8 June 1981.

US economy. But whatever the macroeconomic effects of military spending, there is no doubt that these arms firms do benefit from increased appropriations and their place within the US economy as a whole is pervasive. Three-quarters of all defence contracts go to one hundred large companies, but these all sub-contract so that more than three and a half million jobs in US industry are directly defence-related, and over three million other people are federal employees in some branch of defence, civilian or military. This has created a constituency in favour of military expenditure which, if military pensioners are included, covers a tenth of all the salary-earners and pensioners in the USA.[25] Although most defence contractors are located in the south-west, this military constituency is a nation-wide one, able to exert pressure through Congressmen at a much wider level than would be the case if the industry was bunched in the sunbelt.[26] The latter's influence is felt as much in the triumph of a Know-Nothing belligerency and the rejection of welfare expenditures as in a specifically greater pressure for military outlays against a more reticent or doveish north-east.

Countering the Recession

So far the pressures for increased expenditure under discussion have been from sections of US society which stand to gain from raised appropriations. There is, however, the much broader question of how far the arms boom is beneficial to the capitalist economies as a whole, and in particular how far the Second Cold War can be seen as a response to the recession of the US economy in the latter part of the 1970s. The theoretical issues involved have been widely debated. At one extreme stand the advocates of military Keynesianism or the permanent arms economy, who stress the way in which military expenditure can resolve the cyclical problems of capitalist production; at the other are those who see arms outlays as promoting recession and inflation by diverting funds from productive investment and using up spare skills and raw materials.

[25.] James Cypher, 'The Basic Economics of 'Rearming America',' *Monthly Review*, vol. 33, on. 6, November 1981.

[26.] The 18 older industrial states of the northeast and midwest comprising the 'frostbelt' account for 46 per cent of the US population, but receive only 41 per cent of the Pentagon's prime contract awards and only 18 per cent of its salary expenditures. Figures for Pentagon prime defence contracts awarded in 1980 show California in the lead with $13.9 billion, but several frostbelt states in prominent follow-up positions—New York $5.6 b. at number two; Connecticut with $3.9 b. at number four; and Massachusetts with $3.7 b. at number five (*New York Times*, 19 March 1981).

The evidence for the Cold War II period confirms neither of these polar interpretations.[27] A boom in military production will certainly benefit

Table Seven

The 30 leading industries in us defense business

Industry	Defence business (Billions of 1980 dollars)		Average annual growth in defense business (Percent)	Average annual growth in nondefense business (Percent)
Projections 1981-87	1981	1987	1981-87	1981-87
Radio, TV equipment	$12.1	$25.2	13.0%	4.1%
Petroleum products	7.8	12.3	8.0	0.9
Aircraft	7.8	16.4	13.2	5.0
Aircraft parts, equipment	6.8	13.5	12.0	3.9
Aircraft engines, parts	6.4	13.2	12.7	4.1
Guided missiles	6.2	12.8	12.9	-0.4
Shipbuilding, repairs	4.9	7.6	7.5	3.8
Misc. business services	4.8	9.1	11.3	4.8
Crude oil, natural gas	3.2	5.1	7.7	0.7
Steel	2.9	5.3	10.4	3.6
Truck transport	2.9	4.6	8.3	4.5
Electric power	2.8	5.0	10.1	2.7
Electronic components	2.6	6.0	14.9	8.2
Ammunition (excluding small arms)	2.3	5.3	15.0	6.7
Maintenance, repair	2.3	4.0	9.6	2.6
Professional services	2.3	4.7	12.2	4.3
Chemicals	2.1	4.0	11.3	4.4
Ordinance, accessories	1.8	3.7	12.6	6.7
Communications (excluding radio and TV)	1.7	3.3	11.6	5.3
Tanks, components	1.5	3.7	12.6	4.5
Water transport, related services	1.4	1.9	3.5	4.0
Air carriers, related services	1.4	2.4	9.4	4.2
Motor vehicle parts, accessories	1.3	2.6	12.7	5.3
Misc. machinery	1.3	2.4	11.6	4.2
Engineering, scientific instruments	1.3	2.1	9.0	5.6
Lodging services	1.2	1.9	8.9	3.7
Electronic computing equipment	1.2	3.0	16.4	11.8
Railroads, related services	1.1	1.9	9.8	4.4
Semiconductors	1.0	2.8	18.3	11.8
Aluminum fabrication	0.9	2.1	14.3	6.1

Source: Business Week, February 8 1982

---

27. For a general critique of military Keynesian theories see Ron Smith, 'Military Expenditure and Capitalism', *Cambridge Journal of Economics*, vol. 1 1977. See also

the arms manufacturers and those ailing sections of the ship-building and motor industries which can incorporate such output. As Table Seven show, arms contracts will assist a wide range of civilian producers for whom state purchases will act as a form of subsidy. When Carter made his statement on the US willingness to defend the Persian Gulf in January 1980 this led to a temporary rally on the New York Stock Exchange, where brokers expressed the belief that Khomeini and Brezhnev had 'postponed' the recession. A firm like Chrysler, nearing bankruptcy in 1979, will benefit greatly from receiving the contract for the XM-1 tank.

Employment will also be affected, though with the capital-intensive nature of weapons production this may not be on a scale comparable to that of earlier booms. The Pentagon has estimated that employment in military-related industries will rise by 350,000 to 2.86 million in 1984.[28] On the other hand, the arms boom must also have inflationary effects by drawing away skilled personnel. General Robert Marsh, chief of the airforce Systems Command, has stated the US forces do not have enough skilled engineers to fulfill existing demands, and will be in no position to meet the increased demands of the mid-1980s; only by drawing engineers from the civilian sector will the situation be alleviated. And such demand for skilled professionals will do little to lessen mass unemployment. Military expenditure is bound to go even beyond that level projected by Reagan; this will further unbalance the US Federal budget and thereby stimulate inflation. Even the estimates for 1981–7 military expenditure are based on the assumption that inflation will level out at around 5 per cent and that the level of increase in military costs will remain at 15 per cent. Neither of these premisses are at all certain. An unpublished Pentagon report reckons expenditure will be 50 per cent above the $1.5 trillion proposed.[30]

The rise in military spending may have other consequences which conflict with the overall Cold War aim of restoring US hegemony. The

---

Costs and Consequences, as note 24; Mary Kaldor, op. cit.; Seymour Melman, *The Permanent War Economy,* New York 1974; Ernest Mandel, 'The Permanent Arms Economy and Late Capitalism', in *Late Capitalism,* London 1975; Ken Trachte, 'Interventionism, Cold War Economics and the Capitalist Class', Paper presented to American Political Science Convention, 29 August 1980.

[28.] *International Herald Tribune,* 2 June 1982.

[29.] *Costs and Consequences,* pp. 26 ff.

[30.] *International Herald Tribune,* 9 March 1982.

strains upon civilian sectors in the USA will provide greater opportunity to capitalist rivals not so burdened; only a global reorganisation under US direction would resolve this problem. The US fear is that technical advances made for arms production will be used by civilian firms abroad. The standard example is the video-cassette, developed by the US military in the 1960s: by the late 1970s the world-wide civilian market in these was dominated by the Japanese. The American economic leadership remember how the Vietnam war benefited Japanese capitalism and weakened the dollar in the Far East and Europe. They are reluctant to see advantages accruing to their rivals under analogous circumstances.[31]

It is doubtful how far the arms boom is functional even for stimulating the US economy in its current plight. For the time lags involved are considerable, and far longer than those conventionally permitted in macroeconomic management. Although the annual figures for total obligational authority—TOA—may be high, real expenditures are much lower and it may be years before TOAS are spent. The highest TOA in the Reagan budget is for 1982, whilst the largest real rise will take place in 1985. Evaluations carried out in the aftermath of Reagan's MX and B-1 announcements of October 1981 reported that the effects on business were 'more psychological than anything else'.[32] Research and development on these programmes would last through 1984 and production begin only in 1985. Military Keynesianism, if such it was, could do little to meet the demands of the US economy in 1981, let alone prepare the way for a boom in the election years of 1982 and 1984.

The strategic nuclear buildup is therefore only remotely related to any programme for countering the overall onset of recession in the civilian sectors of the economy. Where there is a more palpable economic result is in the field of conventional military weapons expenditures: these are much more easily translated into operable contracts, i.e. have much more direct effects on the economy, and they account for a higher proportion of US military outlays than do strategic nuclear weapons. Under

---

[31.] See Kaldor and Melman for elaboration of this argument. Melman argues that the relevant basis for calculating the economic effect of military spending on the economy is not as a percentage of GNP, but as a percentage of total fixed capital formation. In 1977 the US military budget was 4.9 per cent of GNP, but 46 per cent of fixed capital formation. This was a far higher figure than that of other advanced capitalist countries—West Germany 18.9 and Japan 3.7 (*The Nation,* 9 May 1981).

[32.] *International Herald Tribune,* 10-11 October 1981.

10 per cent of the US military budget is devoted to strategic nuclear weapons, as compared to 25 per cent for third world intervention. Of the $33 billion in extra allocation sought for 1983 only $1 billion is for strategic weapons, against $10.5 billion for 'readiness' forces.[33] Since the major rationale for such increases in conventional expenditures is to prepare for US deployment in the south, to protect raw materials and sustain debtor governments, there is further confirmation of the economic function of such non-nuclear allocations. If nuclear weapons would, when used, destroy the economic fabric of contemporary capitalism as it is now known, the conventional weapons are designed to sustain and reinforce it both as products of that system and as guarantors of its interests. Much of the discussion on arms expenditure understates this significant asymmetry: that the destructive power of nuclear weapons is disproportionate to the amount of money invested in them and to their political potential; the social and administrative forces pushing for the arms race have a much greater interest in fostering the production of conventional weapons which, whilst inferior in destructive potential, do consume the greater part of the military budget.

While the arms boom is therefore related to the recession and to the overall political crisis of the capitalist economies, the nature of this relationship is more contradictory and multi-dimensional than is conventionally assumed. In an era of inflation and bottlenecks in industrial input such increases have far more ambiguous effects than was the case during the World Wars or the Korea War. During the Vietnam war the contradictory impact of arms expenditure was already evident. The logic of the Reagan spending is to be found as much in the political domain as in that of counter-cyclical expenditure and his Defense Secretary Weinberger has often stated that he is not arguing for an increasing arms expenditure on macroeconomic grounds.

The Second Cold War cannot, therefore, be seen as a means of overcoming the capitalist recession. Yet, whilst this traditional consideration does not hold, Cold War II has important domestic functions. The increases in expenditure have a general symbolic value, as a demonstration at home and abroad of a new hegemonic intent. In the words of one US commentator: 'Expenditures for military forces, whether well conceived or not, have become a banner to display national determination.'[34]

[33.] Michael Klare, *In These Times,* 20-26 May 1981.
[34.] *International Herald Tribune*, 12 January 1981.

Nowhere has the success of the new Cold Warriors been greater than in propagating the myth of US military inferiority and so legitimising greater outlays: a poll conducted in May 1981 showed 64 per cent of those asked approving of Reagan's defence spending increases, as against only 29 per cent who disapproved.[35] At the same time, the projection of a New Cold War atmosphere serves to legitimise a more diverse process of reimposing political and social controls, in the work-place, the school and the home. The intimate ideological and organisational relation between New Right single-issue campaigns and the drive for military superiority demonstrates this, encoded as this link is in the call to patriotism.

The arms drive also has a compensatory ideological effect at a time of recession: by propagating the idea of an external threat that has to be met by military increases, or, in the self-pitying double-talk of the US Department of Defense, by 're-arming' America, the Second Cold War serves to deflect criticism of a system that has put many millions out of work since the middle 1970s and has generalised double-digit inflation. Precisely because military expenditure no longer has the overall macroeconomic effects that it had in the 1940s, an increase in arms spending has different social effects than it had in previous periods. By redistributing money to what are now capital-intensive industries, military outlays confirm the shift in US income distribution which the introduction of Reaganomics has brought about. While it would be simplistic to see the Cold War as primarily motivated by the desire to intensify this process of income redistribution, from the poor to the rich, such a change is one of the consequences, and one the right welcomes, of the arms production boom.[36]

As indicated at the beginning of this chapter, such analysis of the domestic causes of the Second Cold War raises two problems. The first is that of establishing the relative weight to be given to these domestic as opposed to international factors. There are those who clearly allot primacy to the first. Thus Alan Wolfe writes of anti-Soviet sentiment in the USA: 'The real issue is not whether the Soviets become more aggressive, but whether the US decides to view them as more

---

[35] *Newsweek,* 8 June 1981.
[36] Frances Fox Piven and Richard Cloward, *The New Class War, Reagan's Attack on the Welfare State and Its Consequences,* New York, 1982, p. 8.

aggressive...Actions by the Soviet Union are of *only tangential impor-tance* in understanding the rise and fall of the Soviet threat.'[37] And Mary Kaldor writes of the expansion of the US arms industry through the pressure to follow on with new arms programmes: 'Since 1945 the arms industry has developed its own momentum, that increased the American rate of armament...Each jump occurred in an atmosphere of interna-tional tension, and, to some extent, economic insecurity, and the first two at least were associated with a shift in military strategy. Never-theless, the fact that the response to these external factors took the form that it did and occurred at the time that it did *is much more easily ex-plained* in terms of the logic of the follow-on than in terms of the logic of the world political and military situation.'[38]

It would be possible to take any of the factors identified in this chapter and stress its contribution to the growth of Cold War sentiment in the USA. But, for all their apparent cogency, such 'internalist' analyses pose difficulties: they tend to understate the degree to which even apparently domestic problems are themselves partly caused by international events—the Vietnam war and the OPEC price rises being cases in point; and they provide only some of the picture, since the processes discussed in Chapters Three and Four are not secondary in the constitution of Cold War II. The domestic dimension of the Cold War cannot be ignored, but neither can it be given an autonomy or a primacy irrespective of those changes in international politics with which it intersects.

The second analytic problem concerns the relative importance to be accorded to different constituents of the US domestic situation. The discussion so far has concentrated on changes in the economy, society and national politics of the USA in the latter part of the 1970s and has argued that these, accentuated by and in turn affecting foreign policy, provided the domestic foundations for the Second Cold War. What has been omitted, except in discussion of the Iron Triangle, are shifts within the US state apparatus itself. Yet many American commentators see the state as the primary locus for the generation of the Second Cold War and ascribe the change in political climate to processes within the state: either to the predominance of anti-democratic and military interests within it, the 'national security state' approach, or to the emergence

[37.] Alan Wolfe, *The Rise and Fall of the 'Soviet Threat'*, pp. 31-3. My italics.
[38.] Mary Kaldor, *The Baroque Arsenal*, pp. 82-3. My italics.

through bureaucratic in-fighting of a cold war faction that had been excluded from power in the period of detente. While serving to unmask the liberal pretensions of the US government, the concept of a 'national security state' is analytically a questionable one: first, on definitional grounds, since it obscures the fact that all states have national security as a prime concern, and that this is not a plausible definition of the specific character of the US state in the 1970s; secondly, on empirical grounds, because it is doubtful if the US state has become more internally repressive or internationally agressive in the 1970s than it was in earlier decades. The stress on conflicting bureaucracies is an important one, and such conflicts do provide part of the dynamic for Washington politics. But the bureaucracies are themselves subject to fluctuations in politics in the nation as a whole. Indeed, it was mobilisations outside state and even outside established party structures which provide the basis for the Cold War election of November 1980.

It is not, however, only the politics of the USA which provide an important component of the Second Cold War. Given its importance within international relations, the particularly volatile nature of its domestic politics, and the peculiar institutional manner in which its domestic and foreign policies intersect, it is certainly true that domestic developments within the USA play a more important role in determining world affairs than do those in any other country. But the domestic dimensions of other states have also made their contribution. Those of the Soviet Union and China have played a contributory role which, in conjunction with their foreign policies, will be examined in Chapter Six. Those in the advanced capitalist countries will be discussed in Chapter Seven. These contributions are, however, of a different weight and quality. The changes in US domestic politics have played an *instigatory* role in the development of Cold War II. Those of the USSR and China have played an *enabling* role. Those of the other advanced capitalist states have played a *supportive* one, reinforcing the trends in the dominant member of the capitalist world.

6
The Involution of
the Post-Revolutionary States

The three causes of Cold War II already identified concern the responsibility of the USA and its allies for the worsening of east-west relations: faced with a reduced military superiority, third world revolution, and tensions within the USA, Washington has resorted to this new phase of confrontation. But to identify these western options as the only causes of the Second Cold War is not sufficient, for it involves denying the contribution of the USSR. The role of the Soviet Union, and of the post-revolutionary states more generally, is to be differentiated from that of the capitalist world. It is nonetheless considerable.

A Distinct Role

Given the temptation felt by many analysts and peace activists to equate the contributions of the Soviet Union and the USA, it may be helpful to begin by re-examining the three causes so far identified and seeing if, suitably adjusted, they can be said to appy to the east. There are many in the west who would advance such an argument, reproducing, with application to the communist world, the three tendencies already identified as evident in the capitalist world. Those who advocate such a view would argue: (a) that the Soviet Union is pursuing military superiority over the USA and its allies; (b) that the Soviet Union is becoming more aggressive in the third world; and (c) that internal pressures—economic crisis, an increased influence of the military—have had their impact on Soviet policy.

The first of these claims, that the USSR has attained military superiority, cannot survive examination. As already analysed in Chapter Three, the USA retains superiority over the USSR in most areas of military strength and has been responsible throughout the postwar period for nearly all the escalations in military technology and the arms race. The Soviet role in the third world, the second putative element, has certainly become a more active one in the 1970s; but it is the very *fact* of a Soviet role where previously there was none, not any Soviet superiority in level of activity or military strength that has so alarmed the west. The third element, internal crisis, has given rise to even more confusion. The USSR certainly faces economic problems, as manifest in the declining growth rates of the late 1970s. But there is no evidence to suggest that these economic problems determine its foreign policy, by rendering it either more active or more cautious. The supposed Soviet need for Persian Gulf oil, a factor often adduced to explain the Afghanistan intervention, is baseless.[1] The allegations of a militarist takeover or of increased militarism within the USSR are exaggerated: despite the weight of the military institutions, decisions on military expenditure and policy are taken by the civilian party leadership based in the Politburo.[2] There is not the autonomous impact of arms manufacturers and military chiefs evident in the USA, no Soviet 'iron triangle'. If anything the 1960s and 1970s have involved even tighter party control. Nor is there any groundswell of bellicist public opinion in the USSR analogous to that which swept the USA in the latter part of the 1970s: such a tendency would be anathema to the Soviet population, whose memory of World War II has given it a sobriety in matters of war and peace quite different from the lightminded belligerence that appears in much US debate. In all the wars it experienced up to 1945 the USA lost a total of 1.2 million people. Russia lost 25 millions in the twentieth century alone. This contrast has produced a very different attitude to matters of war in the two countries.

Yet the USSR *has* helped to bring Cold War II about. The underlying contribution of the USSR to world conflicts is its systemic opposition to the USA, an opposition often muted by weakness and convenience, and taking different forms as the world situation alters. As outlined in Chapter One, this systemic opposition is not mere rhetoric nor is it simply the opposition of one great power to another. A long-term settlement of the issues

---

[1.] Marshall Goldman, *The Enigma of Soviet Petroleum*, London 1980; *Soviet Oil and Gas to 1990*, Economist Intelligence Unit, London, December 1980.

[2.] David Holloway, 'Decision-Making in Soviet Defence Policies', in *Prospects of Soviet Power in the 1980s*, Part II, International Institute for Strategic Studies, Adelphi Papers 152, 1979, and *The Soviet Union and the Arms Race*, London 1983, Chapter 9.

in dispute between the two rival social systems of capitalism and communism is not possible. Yet this conflict, precisely because it is general, cannot on its own explain the particular evolution of events in the 1960s and 1970s. Here there were other changes which translated this systemic opposition into particular policies. It was the latter that, in time, aroused the opposition of the USA and so helped to produce the Second Cold War.

Prime amongst these policies was the decision to pursue military parity with the USA. Yet the striking characteristic of these changes was that they occurred not in the late 1970s in the runup to Cold War II, but much earlier, in the first part of the 1960s, towards the end of the Khrushchev period and the beginnings of the Brezhnev era, i.e. well prior to the Detente of the early 1970s. They cannot therefore be sensibly cited as reasons for Detente's breakdown. In contrast to the sharp changes in US policy during the 1970s, Soviet policy in this period has been marked by a steady pursuit of established goals. These goals emerged in military strategy and domestic politics from a period of turmoil—the early 1960s; it was decisions taken at that time to which the capitalist states took exception in the late 1970s. Far from having contributed to the Second Cold War by betraying Detente through a shift of policy, the Soviet Union based its policies in both Detente and Cold War on similar principles. Yet, as perceived outside the communist bloc, and in conjunction with other developments in China and the newer revolutionary states, Soviet policies played a crucial role in enabling the west to launch Cold War II.

Taking the post-revolutionary states as a whole, it is possible to identify several major tendencies which played their part in bringing on the cold war. These include: The Entropy of the Brezhnev Period; the Soviet Acceptance of the Logic of the Arms Race; the Ambivalent Soviet Role in the Third World; the Record of the Newer Post-Revolutionary States; China's Negative Contributions. To these may be added the Retreat of Socialism in the Advanced Capitalist Countries. None of these played the kind of active, instigatory role which the major trends already identified within the capitalist world played. But they made it far easier for the west to launch the Cold War, and to convince much of the world that this was justified. One of the preconditions for the Second Cold War has been the political discrediting in which the USSR and the post-revolutionary states as a whole are held, a process which has enabled the USA and its allies to mobilise widespread support for their policies and in so doing to conceal other factors which have impelled them along this course. In sum this involution has made it easier for the west to blame the USSR for a process that the west has taken the lead in bringing about.

The Entropy of the Brezhnev Period

Two decades ago, as the USSR was proclaiming the theory of peaceful co-existence and renouncing the view that war with capitalism was inevitable, Nikita Khrushchev predicted that the Soviet Union would in time prevail over the capitalist countries by demonstrating its economic superiority. In Khrushchev's view, the evident pre-eminence of the 'socialist camp' over the capitalist world would be evident by the late 1970s and this, by mobilising working-class support for socialism, would provoke such a political crisis in the capitalist world that the need for a military confrontation would be avoided. The launching of Sputnik, the first satellite, in 1957, the photographing of the far side of the moon in 1959 and the sending of the first man into space in 1961 seemed to promise a Soviet surge in modern technology. Khrushchev's economic optimism formed part of a wider offensive by the post-Stalin Soviet leadership, in which it promised that the potential inherent in socialism and stifled by Stalin would gradually be realised. It was hoped by many that economic development would enable a relaxation of political controls. And in foreign policy Khrushchev made a concerted effort to present the USSR as the champion of peace in contrast to the warmongers of Washington.[3]

Even in his own period, Khrushchev's perspectives were open to question. He himself was responsible for many economic decisions, on agriculture and industry, that were later to prove disastrous. His erratic tolerance of critical writers fell far short of any maintenance of serious, and lasting, political debate. His pacific initiatives in foreign policy, culminating with the Nuclear Test Ban Treaty of 1963, were offset by acts of wilful bellicosity, such as the explosion of a 60 megaton bomb in 1961. Overestimating the USSR's strength, he led the USSR into foreign policy débâcles from which he had to retreat—over Berlin in 1959, the

---

[3.] Isaac Deutscher, *The Great Contest*, London 1960; Roy and Zhores Medvedev, *Khrushchev, The Years in Power*, London 1977; Fernando Claudin, *Eurocommunism and Socialism*, London 1978.

summit in 1960, and Cuba in 1962. Above all, by provoking the split with China that developed in the 1960–1963 period, Khrushchev gravely weakened the communist world: this dispute provided one of the key conditions of the Vietnam war, and produced an opportunity which the west was later to exploit to considerable advantage by forging ties to Peking. But in two important respects Khrushchev's vision was vindicated. He himself was able in an imaginative way to present the Soviet Union as a peaceful country, inferior to the USA in military strength, and cautious in a way that the Chinese, apparently indifferent to the effects of nuclear war, were not. Secondly he to some extent revived hope in the moral possibilities of communism, by promising a new society at once prosperous and liberalised, yet still combative against capitalism.

Khrushchev's optimism rested upon the expectation of a continued real improvement in Soviet economic performance that had been under way since the early 1950s. Between 1950 and 1970 real GNP in the Comecon countries as a whole doubled. This was a slightly slower rate than in the advanced capitalist countries but was none the less impressive.[4] In the same period, Soviet food consumption per head doubled,

Table Eight

Selected Measures of Output and Productivity Growth in the US, UK, FRG, Japan and USSR, 1950–1978

(% per annum)

	GDP	GDP per employed civilian		Manufacturing output/person-hour	
	1973–78	1950–73	1973–78	1950–73	1973–78
United States	2.5	2.1	0.1	2.7	2.8
United Kingdom	2.0	2.5	0.5	3.1	1.0
West Germany	2.7	5.0	3.1	5.8	3.9
Japan	3.7	7.8	3.3	9.7	4.0
Soviet Union	3.5	4.0 (GNP)	1.6 (GNP)	5.2	3.2

Source: Philip Hanson, 'Economic Constraints on Soviet Policy', *International Affairs*, winter 1980/81, p. 25

---

4. *The Economist*, 22 August 1981.

disposable income quadrupled, and purchases of consumer durables rose twelve times.[5] In the mid-1970s Soviet GDP growth per annum out-

Table Nine

Soviet Living Standards 1965-78

	1965	1978
Monthly wage	96.5 rubles	159.9 rubles
Number of doctors	554,000	929,000
Families with TV sets	24 per cent	82 per cent
Families with refrigerators	11 per cent	78 per cent
Living space per person: urban areas	10 sq. metres	12.7 sq. metres
Consumption of meat and meat products per person	41 kilograms	57 kilograms
Consumption of vegetables per person	72 kilograms	90 kilograms
Consumption of potatoes per person	142 kilograms	120 kilograms
Consumption of bread and grain per person	156 kilograms	140 kilograms

Source: *The Guardian*, 17 August 1981.

Table Ten

Annual Production Soviet Industry 1965-81
in millions of metric tons except where noted

	1965	1981
Electricity (millions of kilowatt-hours)	507	1,325
Crude oil	243	609
Natural gas (billions of cubic metres)	127.7	465
Iron ore	153.4	242
Steel	91	149
Grain	121.1	160(est.)
Milk	72.6	88.5
Meat	9.9	15.2
Passenger cars (thousands)	201.2	1,324

Source: *Time*, 22 November 1982.

---

[5] Hedrick Smith, *The Russians*, London 1976, p. 80, quoting the US economist Gertrude Schroeder.

stripped US growth by 3.5 per cent to 2.5 per cent.[6] So, not only were rates of expansion considerable, but they were for some of this period greater than in certain major capitalist economies.

This improvement in economic conditions went together with a considerable lessening of political repression. The total number of those imprisoned at any one time for political offences in the Brezhnev period was estimated at between two and ten thousand, a far cry from the millions incarcerated under Stalin.[7] Execution for political offences ceased. Contact with foreign visitors became possible. This process was one which Khrushchev began, but which Brezhnev largerly sustained. Since 1969 some emigration has been permitted for dissident writers, Jews and ethnic Germans. Since 1972 the system of internal passports, designed to limit mobility of peasants within the country, has been ended. The one area of net regression under Brezhnev was the use of psychiatric imprisonment for political offences.

Whilst verification is impossible, the evidence suggests that the Soviet regime enjoys the support of the mass of its population. Its legitimacy derives from three separate factors: the revolution, the Second World War and the recent improvement in living standards. Despite its symbolic primacy, the first is possibly the least important in popular thinking: rather, patriotism and the memory of how economic conditions have recently improved constitute the bases for a grudging acceptance of the system. Those who have studied Soviet life at first hand consider the mass of Soviet citizens to be apolitical, but fundamentally loyal to their regime. In the words of one observer, 'Soviets privately grouse about their living conditions, complain about corruption, mock the pretences of their ideology, and privately joke about their leaders, but they accept the system as fundamentally sound, as paradoxical as that may seem. It never seems to strike more than a mere handful of dissidents and perhaps

---

[6.] *Business Week*, 19 October 1981.

[7.] Zhores Medvedev, 'Russia Under Brezhnev', *New Left Review*, 117, p. 20. The CIA puts the figure of political prisoners at 10,000 (*International Herald Tribune* 8 November 1982). In a report published in 1981, Amnesty International said that more than four hundred people had been jailed or otherwise punished for political activities since the Helsinki Agreement of 1975. Of these over one hundred were known to have been confined to psychiatric hospitals.

some hidden loyal oppositionists within the establishment that anything major is on the wrong track.'[8]

Despite these achievements, the years since the early 1960s have witnessed the entropy of Khrushchevite optimism. The dour style of the Brezhnev regime struck few responsive chords in the west: there were few bold proposals, no *coups de théâtre*, to break the mould of debate. Inside the USSR the level of economic development has not been as great as expected and consumer shortages, in particular failings in agriculture, have sapped popular enthusiasm and given encouragement to enemies abroad. Whilst the economic crisis of the advanced capitalist countries was in the late 1970s relatively more acute than that in the east —measured by levels of inflation, unemployment and decline in rates of growth—the competition in perceived economic conditions between east and west continued to run in the latter's favour. Indebtedness to the west by Soviet bloc countries rose to $80.7 billions in 1981. Above all, the persistence of consumer shortages which accompanied the substantial expansion of the 1950–1975 period became more noticeable as growth rates declined in the later years of the decade. By the early 1980s certain foods especially meat were absolutely less available in the major cities than in earlier years, with the result that consumer standards were judged as inferior not only to those of the capitalist west, but also to the immediately preceding levels experienced by Soviet society.

The aim of visibly overtaking the west has not been achieved. Despite the growth in Soviet GNP, per capita levels of income in the USSR and Eastern Europe remain substantially below those in Western Europe and the USA. The underlying reality of this inequality is compounded by the relative weakness of the eastern bloc countries in the most visible indices of prosperity—consumer goods and food. The prevalence of shortages, low quality and queuing in the east is well known to the population of both blocs, and is not offset in general perception by the dole queues and poor social services in the west. The opening of more economic contacts between east and west in the 1970s, whilst objectively assisting economic growth in the east, has only underlined the apparent superiority of the west: the need for western credits, western technology and even western food, on top of the popular desire for western consumer goods, has served in some measure to discredit the planned economies and

---

8. Hedrick Smith, op. cit., p. 452.

validate the capitalist ones, although this is at a time when the latter have, on their own internal record, entered a period of recession. The slowing down in Soviet growth rates and shortages of food in the latter part of the 1970s have then compounded this unfavourable comparison.

This popular perception of economic conditions is itself reinforced by less quantifiable but none the less evident scientific and cultural phenomena. In some branches of theoretical science, the USSR is the world's leader. But the practical application and diffusion of science is far less than in the west. Culture can be used in both restricted and looser senses. In the former sense of literature, art and music the very high standards of training and professional support in the east are offset by the evidently much greater creativity in the west. In the domain of popular culture, and of music in particular, the east is wholly derivative of the west: gone are the days when it was even claimed that jazz was invented by the Soviet musician Leon Utesov. It is probably music which provides one of the chief attractions of western radio stations in the east. Press, TV and radio remain censored and dull. On top of this, there is the very character of everyday life in the east—the drabness, the lack of forms of spontaneous entertainment, the boredom which many face. Hanging over all of these is the most evident restriction of all, that on travel. How many in the east would like to leave permanently is debatable: but that many would like to visit the west is indisputable. The limits on travel in most east bloc states (though not Hungary), combined with the petty harassment of those who do leave and a partial blockade of information and other contacts, compound the attraction of the unobtainable.

As in all such comparisons, there are two levels of disparity: the real and the perceived. The former is far less favourable to the west than the latter: it is significant how many of those who have emigrated from the east to the west have found the latter more heartless and difficult to survive in. The 20 per cent of the population in the USA and Western Europe who live below the poverty line might have a thing or two to tell the discontented of the east. But, for all the exaggerations of the perceived, there remains a real disparity which is recognised in east and west and which has contributed to the virtual end of the Soviet model as a pole of attraction in the advanced capitalist countries.

The determinant factor is, however, the one most visible in and most central to the Second Cold War, namely politics. Over the past two decades, while repression has declined and terror ended, there has been no significant increase in the level of substantive political liberty within the USSR: the party leadership retains centralised control. The perception of this political stasis has been accentuated internationally by the rise of the dissident movement in the early 1960s and the post-Khrushchev repression. The overtly dissident movement has no great popular support in the USSR; estimates of those involved suggest a thousand. Its very existence is in one sense an index of the lowered levels of repression now enforced, compared to earlier periods, when no such opposition would have been tolerated. Yet the projection of the dissident movement in the west has been damaging to the USSR's political image especially in countries where strong communist movements once propagated utopian images of the USSR. The limited space opened by Khrushchev began to close soon after his fall. The debate on economic liberalism, with its promise of decentralisation, was ended in 1965, within a year of Khrushchev's removal. The first trial of dissident writers, that of Sinyavsky and Daniel, occurred in 1966. In 1968 there were arrests of those protesting at the intervention in Czechoslovakia. But until the end of the 1960s considerable discussion amongst intellectuals remained possible. In 1970 the influential patron of critical literature, Alexander Tvardovsky, was dismissed from the editorship of the journal *Novyi Mir*. In 1971–2 the sociology department of Moscow University, a centre of critical work, was purged. In 1973 the opposition journal *Chronicle of Current Events* was closed down, and the campaign against Andrei Sakharov began. In 1974 Solzhenitsyn was exiled. Dozens of other less well known writers were also despatched to Western Europe and the USA.

This harassment of dissident writers would have been damaging enough in itself but it was accompanied by conflict over the separate issue of the right of Jews to emigrate, and by the impression, widespread in the west, of official anti-semitism in the USSR. In fact, emigration for Jews became possible in 1969, a privilege granted to only one other ethnic group, the Germans. Over a quarter of a million Jews left in the 1970s, 35,000 in 1973 alone, as did around 150,000 Germans. But those leaving were subject to harassment and delay; a small percentage employed in sensitive jobs were refused permission to leave; and trials of Jewish dissidents continued. That of Anatoly Shcharansky, in particular, convicted in July 1978 of being a CIA agent, after passing information on Jewish activists to an American journalist, aroused storms of criticism in the US Congress and western press. The political expectations of the post-Stalin 'thaw' have therefore been disappointed. Economic growth has not led to substantial political change. The denial of democracy associated with Stalin's rule has been shown to be a feature rooted in the system, not the imposition of one man and his associates. Continued control by a secretive and self-appointed bureaucracy has been maintained, although this has been accompanied by economic growth and the ending of terror and mass incarceration.

This involution in the USSR has gone together with a comparable diminution in optimism on the left internationally. In Eastern Europe, this has involved the continued maintenance of Soviet strategic control and of rule by party bureaucracies. States hostile to the USSR, Albania and, intermittently, Romania, have not exhibited any inclinations towards political democracy. Above all, the Soviet intervention in Czechoslovakia in 1968 dispersed the hopes of liberalisation far more thoroughly than had the intervention in Hungary in 1956. Few doubted that the leadership of the Czech reform movement remained socialist in intention, and the Soviet invasion destroyed the hope that the USSR might feel more able, as a result of increased strategic confidence, to permit greater freedom in Eastern Europe. If Khrushchev had dealt a blow to communist unity in the east, by pushing the Chinese to a full break, Brezhnev dealt a comparable blow in the west by occupying Prague and stimulating the Eurocommunist breach. In both cases the initial damage of the split was to be compounded by the alliance of these former Soviet allies with the west—whether China's ties to Washington, or the Italian Communist Party's acceptance of NATO. At the same time, both the Chinese and the Eurocommunists proceeded to assail their former allies by spreading theories of Soviet 'imperialism' that were, in substance, parallel to those of the western governments. Events in Poland in 1980 and 1981 have not led Eurocommunist critics and these of similar persuasion to reverse this judgement and have not brought the USSR any political benefits. Soviet reluctance to use armed force in Poland is seen as a reflection of objective limits on its action—the difficulties of managing an occupied Poland, the international repercussions—not as a political evolution in Soviet thinking itself. Indeed, given the persistent reports in the west about an imminent Soviet intervention and the critique of the party's political and social policies developed by Solidarity, the Polish crisis has compounded the political problems of the Soviet leadership. It has continued that discrediting of the post-revolutionary regimes characteristic of the whole Brezhnev era.

Such a discrediting has most effect upon those political forces in the west who might resist the onset of a new Cold War. But the conflicts in the Soviet bloc have also had an effect on less well-disposed sectors, namely those in the west who have an interest in launching the current Cold War. They see the stresses within the USSR and Eastern Europe as providing the context for a western offensive against the opposed camp, one designed to accentuate these weaknesses and provoke greater difficulties. Launching a new arms race is a direct means of provoking further economic problems, since it will force the USSR to divert resources from civilian to military uses. However great or small the stimulative effects of an arms boom may be to the US economy, the different organisation of the Soviet economy means that increased military expenditure marks a net subtraction from the output of the rest of the economy and so encourages consumer discontent. The offensive in the third world is designed to press home certain advantages enjoyed by the west: in powers of military intervention, but also in disposable economic resources of both a financial and commodity kind. The political tensions in the eastern bloc, whether the advance of Solidarity or the fate of Soviet dissidents, provide a good occasion for sustained political propaganda against the east, while the rise of nationalism in both Eastern Europe and the USSR has led many western strategists to evolve policies designed precisely to exploit these nationalisms and so weaken the cohesion of the USSR and its allies. The future alone will tell how far these policies have succeeded: what is beyond doubt is that the expectation of provoking such problems has been a significant factor in the launching of the Second Cold War. The problems of the Brezhnev era have therefore demoralised those who aspire to a socialist alternative and have emboldened those who want to roll back the revolutions of this century by advocating a capitalist restoration in the east.

The Logic of the Arms Race Accepted

Throughout the postwar period the Soviet Union has lagged behind the United States in most main areas of military production and technology.[9] But the Soviet attitude to this lag has not been a constant one, and varia-

---

[9.] In the words of two former US officials: 'There have only been two brief periods—1946-7 and during the 1957-9 "missile gap"—when the Soviet Union has enjoyed temporary military advantages. In the first period, she made major gains; the second proved to be less politically exploitable. But for most of her 61 years, while political gains varied, she has operated from a position of relative military weakness' (Helmut Sonnenfeldt and William Hyland, *Soviet Perspectives on Security*, International Institute for Strategic Studies, Adelphi Paper 150, 1979). Or as Jimmy Carter has put it: 'The United States

tions in this attitude have in turn affected the image which the Soviet Union presents of itself in international affairs. As already suggested, the Khrushchev period was one in which the Soviet Union presented itself as a country aggressively competing with the capitalist world but pursuing peace. The USSR visibly sought not to imitate the west in levels of military equipment. Whilst this policy assured the Soviet Union the ability to respond to a western attack, what can be called a deterrent capability, it clearly distinguished the Soviet Union from its NATO rivals who sought overall superiority. But such a policy was not long sustained, and, in a series of revisions, the USSR has brought its military policy more and more into line with that of the USA. This alteration of policy has been one of the facilitating conditions of the Second Cold War.

The clearest statements of the Khrushchevite approach to defence policy came at the Twenty-First Congress of the CPSU in 1959 and at the Fourth Session of the Supreme Soviet in 1960.[10] Khrushchev had already made his mark as a critic of the military when in October 1957 he dismissed Marshal Zhukov from the Ministry of Defence and enhanced the role of the Main Political Administration, the body through which the party exerts control over the armed forces. In the pronouncements of the 1959–1960 period Khruschev announced a wide-ranging shift in Soviet military policy. His great belief, boosted by the *Sputnik* success, was in long-range missiles and after the establishment of the Strategic Rocket Forces as the prime wing of the armed forces, he proceeded to downgrade the conventional forces. Theoretically, this involved promoting the belief that nuclear war would be brief and that the first encounters would be decisive. There was therefore less need for large conventional forces. Practically, he planned to cut the armed forces by 1.2 million men, to 2.4 millions, and laid the stress on the quality of the military personnel rather than on the overall quantitative levels.

This 'Revolution in Military Affairs', as it was known, involved tighter political control over the armed forces, combined with the stress on higher technical training to implement the new reliance on strategic

---

has more often been in the forefront of technical advances. We were first with atomic explosives, long-range missiles, submarine-launched missiles, multiple warheads on the same launcher and miniaturized circuitry permitting greater destruction with smaller weapons' (*Keeping Faith*, p. 214).

[10.] For a general discussion see Roman Kolkowicz, *The Soviet Military and the Communist Party*, Princeton 1967, and Holloway, op. cit.

missiles.[11] But it went together with a pacific emphasis, an awareness of the dangers of nuclear war, and a belief that the west would not launch such a war, if it knew the Soviet Union could retaliate. Although it was never expressed in these terms, Khrushchev's policy was one of what in the west is known as 'minimum deterrence'. He did not think that the western leaders were prepared to sustain the heavy losses involved in a nuclear exchange, and he concluded that they would therefore be deterred from using their nuclear forces if they felt that the Soviet Union was capable of a destructive response. It was not therefore necessary for the USSR to match every US missile and warhead, only to maintain a force sufficiently powerful and invulnerable to retaliate against the USA if the latter launched a first strike. Whilst not pacifist or unilaterally disarming, such a policy was also one that rejected the competitive logic of the arms race.

Such a position, in contrast to that of the Chinese who believed in the inevitability of war and seemed negligent about its consequences, was tied to Khrushchev's vision of building the USSR up economically. Provided war could be avoided, and if sufficient resources could be diverted from military to civilian investment, then the communist system would prevail over the capitalist.[12] Khrushchev openly voiced his dislike of military matters: he once said he felt ill while watching tank manoeuvres, because he knew they would all be incinerated before they ever got to the front line. On another occasion he attacked the organisers of military production as 'metal eaters' who weakened the civilian economy. As he put it: 'Comrades! Our country has all the requisites for moving still more confidently and rapidly along the road to communism. For this we need only one thing—peace, an opportunity to labour undisturbed, to build our big bright house.'[13]

Powerful as this vision was, it could not withstand countervailing pressures, from within the USSR and from the course of world events. As early as the middle of 1961, the guidelines of the Twenty-First Congress were being overthrown. The central reason for this reversal appears to have been not opposition from the military, who had been successfully

---

[11.] Christopher Jones, 'The "Revolution in Military Affairs" and Party Military Relations 1965-70', *Survey*, Winter 1974.
[12.] Kolkowicz, op. cit., pp. 292; Mary Kaldor, *The Baroque Arsenal*, Chapter 4, London 1982; Holloway, Chapter Five.
[13.] As quoted in Kolkowicz, p. 285.

subjected, but the fear which the Kennedy Administration's expansion in strategic weapons, Polaris and ICBMs produced.[14] The result was that Soviet ICBM production expanded from 50 to 200 a year by the mid-60s. More missile-carrying submarines were commissioned. The surface fleet began preparing to compete with US forces on the oceans. A new civil defence programme was started under the Ministry of Defence. Soviet missiles were also changed: from the large megaton bombs of the counter-city policy, designed as deterrents, Soviet planners began to shift to the smaller megaton SS-11s designed for hitting military targets. The shift away from minimum deterrence was encouraged even more by the great débâcle of the Cuba missile crisis in October 1962: this occurred because Khrushchev had tried to offset the Soviet lag in strategic weapons by stationing intermediate range rockets in Cuba. The failure of this Cuban initiative encouraged those pressing for allout rivalry with the USA. The hope that western leaders would not risk nuclear war was contradicted by Kennedy's willingness to go to the brink over Cuba. Khrushchev managed to get the Nuclear Test Ban Treaty passed in 1963 but when he fell in 1964 his successors undid much of what he had proposed: 'minimum deterrence' was completely abandoned and the doctrine of fighting a protracted nuclear war to win came into fashion; the budget was expanded, rising 5 per cent in 1966 over that for 1965. Marshal M. Zakharov, Chief of General Staff dismissed after the Cuba crisis, was brought back. The theorist of winning nuclear war, Colonel Rybkin, was once again influential.[15]

Under Brezhnev, further changes in Soviet policy on nuclear weapons could be detected, this time in the field of disarmament policy. This shift in Soviet military policy led to a move away from earlier positions on deterrence and disarmament.[16] Until after the Twenty-Fourth Congress of the CPSU in 1971 the USSR based its policy on three proposals: (a) the simultaneous dissolution of NATO and the WTO; (b) a treaty banning all nuclear weapons; (c) the removal of all foreign bases. These were policies that went a long way towards meeting the aspirations of the anti-nuclear-

---

14. Michael MccGwire, 'Soviet Military Doctrine: Contingency Planning and the Reality of World War', *Survival*, May/June 1980.
15. Kolkowicz, p. 304.
16. Central Committee, Japanese Communist Party, *Bulletin*, Information for Abroad, no. 468, September 1981, pp. 15-22, contains a good summary and criticism of this shift in Soviet policy.

weapon movement in the west, and they marked the policies of the USSR off from those of the USA. This was particularly so as the USA rejected these proposals at a time when it had a clear superiority in nuclear weapons and a virtual monopoly on foreign bases. When it convened in 1975 the Twenty-Fifth Congress of the CPSU did not repeat these demands: Soviet policy became instead a call for equilibrium, for a stop to further escalation and for mutual and balanced reductions in nuclear and conventional forces. The call for a complete ban on nuclear weapons was relegated.[17] This does not reflect an increased militarism *within* the USSR. Indeed, the history of party-military relations in the Brezhnev period is one of apparent harmony as far as strategic matters are concerned, and the personnel allocated in a mid-1970s reshuffle to the highest places have been Brezhnev appointees. Brezhnev himself had a background in sophisticated weapons production. Marshal Ustinov, who became Minister of Defence in 1976, was a specialist in military production, without major combat experience. Marshal Ogarkov, who became Chief of General Staff, was one of the Soviet negotiators in the SALT talks, and an apparent supporter of Detente. Marshal Kulikov, appointed Commander in Chief of Warsaw Pact forces, is a highly qualified commanding officer with a long record of loyalty to the party authorities.[18]

The shift in Soviet policies during the early 1960s appears to have been a reaction to events in the outside world, more than to changes in factional balance or popular mood wihtin the USSR itself. In particular, the initial militancy of the Kennedy Administration when it came to office in 1961, followed by the Cuban missile crisis, seem to have undermined those within the USSR who sought a more restrained approach. The breach with China in 1963 must have confirmed this sense of the Soviet Union's international vulnerability. The consensual view, that the USSR should seek parity, was therefore one adopted by the top party leadership, and was not forced upon them by a recalcitrant military.

---

[17]. The programme of the 24th Congress is summarised in *Keesings Contemporary Archives*, 12 June 1971; that of the 25th Congress in ibid., 21 May 1976. See also Sam Russell, 'Goodbye to Detente?, *Marxism Today*, June 1981 for discussion of changes in Soviet policy.

[18]. Dimitri Simes, *Detente and Conflict, Soviet Foreign Policy 1972-1977*, Center for Strategic and International Studies, Georgetown University, The Washington Papers 44, Washington 1977, pp. 51-2.

The result of these alterations in defence and disarmament policy was that by the late 1970s the distinction between the Soviet and US military policies was to a considerable extent eroded. The USSR was committed to parity and appeared to many to have achieved it. The pacific stress of the early 1960s had been replaced by a dogged attempt to reduce the lead of the USA. This is true of strategic missiles, where the USSR has built up its ICBM forces to a superior level, in order to offset the US lead in SLBMs. But the option with the greater political effect has been in intermediate range missiles. Despite the reality of continued Soviet inferiority, the decision to begin deployment of new missiles, the SS-20s, in 1977 has provided NATO with an ideal opportunity to falsify the situation and portray the Soviet Union as acquiring superiority and as being the source of escalation. Thereby NATO can legitimate its own escalation, via the stationing of Cruise and Pershing in Europe. The strength of a Khrushchevite policy of minimum deterrence lay in the fact that, while it did not abandon the use of nuclear weapons, it did reject the competitive logic of the arms race, and such a rejection provided the USSR with a considerable political advantage. A relatively small but invulnerable set of warheads and delivery systems would serve to deter the USA as much as the many thousands which the USSR now possesses; but for reasons of technical inferiority on the Soviet side, and political support for the newer policy within the party and military, the Soviet leadership has maintained the other option of seeking parity. In this way it has become possible to portray the USSR as a militaristic power on a par with the USA, or even as one that is more belligerent.

The Soviet acceptance of 'maximum deterrence' might be justified on the grounds of improvements in the accuracy of US techniques, which made any Soviet 'minimum deterrent' vulnerable to a first-strike attack. The pursuit of a maximum or numerically equal deterrent could therefore be said to be necessary even to preserve a second-strike capability of the most reduced kind. Soviet military leaders like to imply this when they say they have done the minimum to guarantee defence. Such an argument is, however, dubious, since the US forces themselves have shown that a secure second-strike capability lies not so much in the realm of numbers, but in the qualitative dimension of invulnerability. This is the logic of the French and British deterrents. A relatively small but undetectable set of warheads and delivery systems would serve as well. It is not known how far technical deficiencies, and how far political choice, led to the Soviet choice of strategy; but the negative political consequences of this option in enabling assimilation of Soviet and US policies have been considerable.

The Ambivalent Soviet Role in the Third World

The increasingly military profile of the USSR resulting from these shifts in Soviet strategic doctrine was compounded by increased Soviet military and political activity in the most visible of spheres, namely the third world. The period of Khrushchev's tenure of power in the Soviet Union was one in which policy towards the third world was also substantially revised. Stalin's policy had been to discourage communist parties from attempting to take power, as in China and Korea, and to treat nationalist forces, as in Iran, India and Egypt, with disdain. Khrushchev was little more sympathetic to communist advances—the Vietnamese relaunched their campaign in the south in 1960 against Russian advice—but he did see the possibilities of allying with the new nationalist states of the third world, especially Egypt, and he aided the Cubans after initial hesitation. His successors continued this policy, and, in their time, became more sympathetic to radical nationalist and communist forces. This was evident in Cuba, Vietnam, Afghanistan, Ethiopia, and the former Portuguese colonies of Africa. The Brezhnev period was therefore marked by a more forward Soviet policy in the third world than was the case under Stalin or Khrushchev. Yet this forward policy has been a profoundly ambivalent one: whilst not following the 'imperial' or 'expansionist' pattern attributed to it by western and Chinese commentators, Soviet policy has nonetheless had both supportive and negative characteristics. It is both in the very fact of increased Soviet influence and in the ambivalent nature of this influence that Russia's opponents have found their justification for mounting the Second Cold War.

Soviet military involvement in the third world has taken two forms. One has been the provision of arms and training to guerrillas fighting against foreign rule or local dictatorships. The most outstanding case of this was in Vietnam, but arms were also sent to guerrillas in the Portuguese colonies of Africa and to the PLO, to give but some examples. Yet it is not this kind of support that has provoked the greatest outrage. These guerrillas have been fighting against forces, often those of outside powers, that are visibly much stronger than them. The victories of the guerrillas, when they occurred, were as much the result of political divisions in the enemy camp as of military triumph itself. Far more controversial have been the cases in which the USSR has defended *states* against attack by counter-revolutionary forces or against threats of such attack. It is aid to already established left-wing governments—in Cuba, Angola, Ethiopia, South Yemen and Afghanistan—which has most provoked criticism and which has most alarmed the west. For many observers, the Soviet military role in these cases appeared to be no different from that of the USA.

Several factors, of differing political provenance, combined to foster this perception of the Soviet role in the third world. First, the western response was to portray all Soviet policies as expansionist and illegal, whatever form they took. It is axiomatic that any advance by revolutionary movements and any support to them by the USSR will provoke a response of this kind. Thus even assistance to defend Nicaragua or Angola against foreign attack is portrayed as part of some Soviet expansionist logic. Secondly, the spread of Maoist ideas, coupled with a lack of political realism about the military facts of third world conflict, have led on the part of the metropolitan left to a perception of all Soviet military supplies as uniquely the tools of Soviet state power. The rhetoric of self-reliance and the heroism of popular struggles, as in Vietnam, have encouraged the illusion that the populations of the third world can, with their bare hands and spirit of combat alone, prevail over well-armed metropolitan forces and their allies. The reality was that without Soviet military aid the fate of these states and movements would have been very different.

These two factors are not, on their own, sufficient to explain why the increased Soviet role in the third world has been perceived in so hostile a light in the developed capitalist states. To explain this perception other factors have to be adduced—the manner in which Soviet military and economic aid was accompanied by negative political changes and a number of incidents in which the Soviet role could not be explained by the principle of solidarity with third world liberation at all. In many countries allied to Moscow, the provision of military and economic aid was accompanied by the imposition of controls on emigration and internal movement, the establishment of Soviet party structures, the spread of Soviet theories of what constitutes Marxism and Leninism, Soviet policies on the nationalities, and the diffusion of a paralysed press: in other words, an export model of the Brezhnevite political order differing from the home variety in that it was not claimed that these were already 'socialist' countries. Hence the undoubted increase in national independence and revolutionary change was counterbalanced by the erection of bureaucratic political structures within these states.

This process was not just the result of Soviet influence. Rather it reflected a malign marriage of exported Soviet bureaucratic and authoritarian political practices with ones already present in the political cultures and social structures of the countries concerned. Ethiopia, Afghanistan, South Yemen, even Cuba were instances of this. It was not that Russian political influence destroyed an already existing democratic potential, but rather that the indigenous trends towards authoritarian political consolidation were assisted and channelled by Soviet political models and advice. On some occasions the Russians did attempt to modify what they saw as inadvisable political and economic practices: they opposed the reigns of terror in Afghanistan and Ethiopia, and they often warned against rash economic policies for which the local countries were ill prepared. Cuba's attempt to introduce a non-monetary economy was a case in point. But, given the overall pattern of bureaucratic consolidation in these states for which they were blamed, the Russians won little credit for such attempts at moderation. Indeed, in the third world Soviet attempts to exert restraining influence upon local allies internally or externally were often construed, perversely, as yet another instance of imperialism.

This reproduction of the Soviet model was compounded by the considerable number of incidents in which the Soviet Union established substantial economic ties with, or provided military equipment to, regimes that were of a markedly right-wing character: to the Shah of Iran, Idi Amin of Uganda, Macias Nguema of Equatorial Guinea, General Videla of Argentina. No arguments about revolutionary solidarity could justify such actions. More important were those specific cases in which Soviet military assistance was used in apparent violation of the very principles that justified Soviet aid in the first place, namely national self-determination. This happened in the outstanding instances of Ethiopia, Cambodia and Afghanistan.

Soviet policy in Ethiopia raises three distinct questions: the Soviet evaluation of the 1974 revolution itself, Soviet support for the Ethiopians in their border conflict with Somalia that broke out in 1977, and the Soviet role in the military campaign that was launched in 1978 to suppress the independence movement in the province of Eritrea. The general Soviet position, that a profound social upheaval has occurred in Ethiopia following the ousting of the emperor in 1974, is a persuasive one, albeit a view to which the Russians were rather late in coming. Soviet support for the Ethiopian border against Somalia's claims is equally reasonable, and is a position also held officially by the USA. The USSR had previously armed Somalia and the Russians tried to avert the 1977 border war between Somalia and Ethiopia: they only sent arms in significant quantities to Ethiopia when the Somalis refused Soviet attempts to mediate between the two states and launched an invasion of Ethiopia.

The most questionable part of the Soviet role is its support for the Addis Ababa government against the Eritreans. The Soviet position on Eritrea was identical to that of the Americans during their alliance with Ethiopia: support for the territorial integrity of Ethiopia. Unjustifiable as this assistance was, it was not a sign of a new direction in Soviet policy. It was consistent with the longstanding Soviet policy of supporting the resolution of ethnic and regional problems within the confines of existing multinational states, rather than favouring secession. Contrary to general belief, the USSR had held this view prior to the fall of Haile Selassie. The USSR had also pursued a similar policy in Burma, Iraq and Nigeria—the one exception being its backing for the secession of Bangladesh in 1971.

In Cambodia, it was not Soviet policy but that of its ally, Vietnam, which raised opposition. Vietnamese forces invaded and imposed a new regime in December 1978. But while the Russians gave general support to this invasion, it was not a product of some new Soviet militancy. Much of the Vietnamese weaponry was captured from the Americans in 1975 and this followed months of border attacks by the Khmer Rouge along the Cambodian-Vietnamese border. It also came after both China and the USA had increased pressure upon Vietnam and so forced Hanoi to make a choice it had till then refused, namely to ally itself clearly with Moscow. Only when Vietnam had been pushed by Washington and Peking into alignment with the USSR and after all attempts to find a compromise with Cambodia had failed, did the invasion take place.[19] Inva-

---

[19.] On Vietnamese restraint in the face of Cambodia's early provocations see Derek Davies in *Far Eastern Economic Review*, 25 December 1981.

sion it certainly was, but the result was one which by all independent accounts the people of Cambodia welcomed, for it rid them of a tyrannical and murderous government. Instead, it established a state more humane and popular than that which it had replaced, and one that restored to the country some of the prosperity which over a decade of war had deprived it of.

The most contentious of these cases was Afghanistan. Long reliant on the USSR for most of its military aid, and for much of its trade and economic assistance, Afghanistan had remained a poor and largely undeveloped country until in April 1978 the local communist party, the PDPA, took power in a military coup. There is no evidence of Soviet encouragement for this coup—it was not like communist actions in eastern Europe after the war—and it appears that it was the PDPA who decided to act when faced with the choice of suppression by the then government or taking power itself. Once established, the PDPA government was recognised by both east and west. In other words, the presence of a pro-Soviet regime in Kabul was internationally accepted.

What altered the situation was the increase in rural opposition to the regime, an opposition born of the arbitrary manner in which the PDPA imposed its reforms, but also encouraged from outside, by Pakistan and China. The Soviet Union did not seek to intervene in Afghanistan but, faced with the prospect of its Afghan ally being overthrown completely, it decided, in late 1979, to send combat troops to Afghanistan. At the same time, embroiled in the factional disputes within the PDPA, it replaced the existing head of state, Hafizullah Amin, by someone more pliant to Soviet policies, Babrak Karmal. It was this action, not the advent of the PDPA to power, which provoked such a strong international reaction.

The negative image of the Soviet role has been compounded by the manner in which the Russians themselves have explained their actions: by lies about the way in which they intervened, by contradictory arguments about who invited them in, and by a spurious analysis of the reasons for the spread of counter-revolution in the country.[20] These false arguments have strengthened the image of the USSR as an expansionist

---

20. The Russians argue that they are helping the Afghan government fight aggression from abroad. The rebels are supported from Pakistan and, to a lesser extent, Iran, but the roots of the rebellion lie within Afghan society itself and in the reaction of the rural population to the imposition of reforms from the centre. The specific account given by the Russians of how they were invited to intervene in December 1979 is also preposterous:

state and have obscured the real issue lying behind the Afghan crisis and which predated the Soviet intervention, namely the battle between a small party of Afghan communists and a widespread counter-revolutionary movement. As a result of its timing, Afghanistan has become an apparently tailor-made justification of western arguments about Soviet 'imperialism'. Yet the Second Cold War had begun before the Soviet forces intervened in Afghanistan in December 1979 and that intervention represented not a new 'expansionist' phase of Soviet policy, but implementation of the policy already seen in Eastern Europe of supporting ruling communist parties against attempts to overthrow them (Hungary 1956, Czechoslovakia 1968). The Russians did not intervene in April 1978 when a communist coup took place, but only a year and a half later when the regime was in danger.

An element of historical proportion also shows that the Afghan intervention, in strategic and local terms, represented a continuation of Soviet policies long pursued in Asia. Whilst the 1979 intervention was the first such action since Yalta, i.e. since the end of the Second World War, it was not the first move of this kind in Soviet history. For in the 1920s and 1930s the Soviet Union faced a situation of opportunity and threat along its Far Eastern frontiers, comparable to that which it has recently faced along its southern frontier with the Middle East, and had responded then with military action. In Outer Mongolia Soviet forces intervened in 1921 to support and consolidate an indigenous revolutionary regime which has remained there ever since, and in 1939, prior to the outbreak of hostilities in Europe, Soviet forces defeated invading Japanese forces at the battle of Khalkhin Gol. In the Chinese province of Sinkiang, where the USSR was already supporting the regime of a reforming warlord, General Sheng Shih-t'sai, several thousand troops were sent in January 1934 to defeat Muslim rebels: this Soviet corps, backed by economic aid and political commissars in a manner similar to that in Afghanistan, remained there until 1944.[21] If Afghanistan is an index of Soviet intentions and practices, these are intentions which long predate the late 1970s. In strategic terms, the Soviet concern about its southern

---

although they were invited by Hafizullah Amin, he was the President they deposed and so they are not able to say that he invited them. Babrak Karmal, the leader whom they subsequently claim issued the invitation, was in fact installed by them after their troops had intervened.

[21.] Allen Whiting and Sheng Shih-t'sai, *Sinkiang: Pawn or Pivot?*, East Lansing 1956.

flank in the late 1970s was analogous to that on its Far Eastern frontiers in the 1920s and 1930s: the place of Japan in the earlier conflict was now taken by China. Its response was a similar one of moving forward to pre-empt hostile control of disputed regions.

The emphasis upon Soviet activity has involved a general exaggeration of the Soviet role by the west. The purpose of this has been to suggest that all changes in the third world have been the result of Soviet initiatives, and so to justify a new western interventionism in response. In a famous observation, Ronald Reagan once remarked that all the problems of the third world were the result of Soviet action.[22] In reality, the upheavals in the third world have been the result not of Soviet instigation but of the maturing of crises within the countries themselves; even in Afghanistan, the communist seizure of power was not the consequence of any Soviet initiative. This 'Soviet instigation' argument not only obscures the internal reasons for third world revolution, but also denies the role which the west has on occasion played in supporting repressive regimes that provoke popular resistance—Iran and Ethiopia being cases in point.

Above all, however, the attack on Soviet 'activism' in the third world obscures the many instances in which the Soviet Union has been passive and has not provided assistance to revolutionary states and movements. For example, in Cambodia it recognised the Lon Nol government when it came to power in 1970 and fought the Khmer Rouge. In Zimbabwe, the Russians long had poor relations with Robert Mugabe's ZANU. In southern Africa as a whole the USSR has done far less than it could do to provide military protection to Angola and Mozambique against conventional attacks by South Africa. On several occasions since 1977, a show of force by the Soviet navy and air force would have helped to restrain attacks by the Pretoria regime. In economic relations, the USSR has proved to be a less forthcoming ally than was initially hoped in many third world states, and it has proved no match for the west in the quantity of aid made available. Where third world countries have needed susbstantial economic assistance to compensate for a loss of support from the west, this has often not been available—as illustrated by the case of Chile, where a blockade was imposed by US banks against the Popular Unity government between 1970 and 1973 and where the USSR offered only a

---

22. See Chapter One, Note 11, p. 00.

158

meagre amount of aid as an alternative. It is here in its strategic and economic limits, as much as in cases of actual Soviet intervention, that criticism of the USSR's third world policy could be focussed.[23]

The Record of the Newer Post-Revolutionary States

The loss of optimism with regard to the advanced post-capitalist states during the 1960s and 1970s has been matched by an apparently parallel process in respect of the post-revolutionary states of the third world. This loss of hope by left-wing forces in the capitalist world has been particularly intense because of the marked enthusiasm which existed in the 1960s for these states and for third world liberation movements. This enthusiasm was often too negligent of the material constraints and attendant political limitations which characterise third world revolutions. It was sometimes utopian, but it was one partly encouraged by that very scepticism about the Soviet model of post-revolutionary society already discussed: it was hoped the third world would show another way. The great anti-imperialist mobilisations of the 1960s, in support of Cuba and Algeria early in the decade and of Vietnam later on, played their part in this, as did a widespread belief in the positive and innovative achievements of the Chinese model. Despite the success of a wide range of revolutionary movements in the third world, events of the 1970s have to a considerable extent eroded this enthusiasm.

One factor in this has been the incidence of terror in third world revolutionary states, one that has recalled earlier periods of Soviet history and has blunted the evident differences between capitalist and post-capitalist regimes. The massacres by the Khmer Rouge in Cambodia (1975–8), the red terror in Ethiopia (1977–8), and the executions of many thousands in Amin's Afghanistan (1978–9) have been horrendous instances of this and have done much to discredit the goals of socialism and the expectations of revolution, just as the earlier Russian terror did. This return of terror in post-revolutionary states has been compounded by the occurrence of something quite unexpected in post-revolutionary regimes, namely interstate military confrontations: between Russia and China (1969), Vietnam and Cambodia (1978), Viet-

---

[23.] For further elaboration see my *Threat from The East?* Penguin 1982, also published as *Soviet Policy in the Arc of Crisis*, Institute for Policy Studies, Washington 1981.

nam and China (1979). If relations between post-revolutionary states could have been expected to exhibit any dominating feature, it might have been non-belligerency. Stalin had by contrast refrained from engaging in war with Yugoslavia in 1948.

In addition to these striking developments, there was a further range of problems associated with the rigours of the transition period in these states, and the evident dissatisfaction provoked by a combination of economic transformation, sabotage from without and policy mistakes by the regimes in question. In many of the third world post-revolutionary states cults of the personality of a more or less grotesque character could be detected, North Korea being the most extreme instance of this. Given their starting points, and the pressure to which they were subjected, the achievements of these states in economic and social development were considerable and in some cases impressive, but these countries could not simply transcend the material constraints under which they operated and achieve a generalised prosperity. These problems produced shortages of consumer goods in the cities and exoduses of population as a result of both political and economic factors. The most spectacular case of such an exodus was that of the 'boat people', who left Vietnam; but the influx of Chinese to Hong Kong, of Cambodians into Thailand, of Afghans into Pakistan, of Eritreans to Sudan, of Ogaden nomads from Ethiopia to Somalia, of South Yemenis to the oil states and of Cubans to Miami all served to confirm an image of the negative character of socialist transformation, just as had the flight of Germans from east to west before 1961. The bad, often catastrophic economic records of other left-wing third world states—Tanzania, Guinea, Benin—reinforced this impression. None of these instances could be explained without reference to the particular problems of the country concerned; in the case of some countries that had experienced revolutions, this involved intervention by counter-revolutionary forces designed to disrupt life in the post-revolutionary state (e.g., Cuba, South Yemen, Afghanistan) as well as problems accumulated from years of revolutionary conflict and the resulting socio-economic dislocations. Yet the large numbers of refugees, the causes of whose flight were obscured by western propaganda, turned the very issue of displaced persons into a political weapon that was used against the post-revolutionary states.

However, the impact of these difficulties in the third world post-revolutionary states would not have been so great had it had not associated with what were seen as the problems of the more advanced post-revolutionary regimes: the absence of democracy, the denial of political rights, the consumer shortages. The limits of the USSR also took their toll in a more practical respect, through the inability of the more advanced states to provide sufficient quantities of economic aid to meet the demands of the newly created ones. This was true both in the field of investment funds needed to promote economic growth, and in that of consumer goods which the urban populations of the third world states were encouraged to seek by the example of the industrialised capitalist countries. The real ability of the USSR to provide effective military aid to third world allies contrasted with its very limited economic resources, except in exceptional cases such as Cuba and Vietnam which could not form the basis for a generalised economic assistance programme. In these ways, the economic and political problems of the post-revolutionary states of the third world therefore reproduced and were compounded by the pre-existing failings of the USSR itself.

Promptings from Peking

Nowhere was the decreased appeal of socialism more evident than in the largest post-revolutionary state of all, China, and China's foreign policy, its dispute with the USSR and its later accommodation with right-wing regimes in the third world, played a major role in laying the ground work for the Second Cold War. This process came about through a reversal of the issues upon which the original Sino-Soviet dispute had been based, and the development of an alliance between China and the west founded on hostility to the USSR that lasted well into the Second Cold War.

The origins of the Sino-Soviet dispute go back at least as early as the Stalin period: yet it was not the lukewarm Soviet support for the Chinese revolution after 1945, nor the difficulties between Mao and Stalin after 1949, which led to the breach. What appears to have caused the break, beyond historical and personal antagonisms, was Khrushchev's desire in the late 1950s to alter China's foreign policy in line with the accommodations which the USSR itself was seeking with Washington and the Soviet criticism, openly made to western listeners, of China's economic policy at that time, in the Great Leap Forward. The Russians were particularly intent on denying China the ability to produce nuclear weapons. When the conflict erupted in 1960, the USSR withdrew all its technicians, with their plans and funds, from China and in so doing provoked enormous economic difficulties for the Chinese. But the rupture with the USSR also left China dangerously exposed on its military flank, at a time when it was in conflict with the USA over the offshore islands of Quemoy and Matsu still held by the Kuomintang. Indeed, the military issue may have played a much greater part in the breach and the subsequent Chinese resentments than was evident at the time; the issue of nuclear war was a central one in the Sino-Soviet dispute—in the prominence occupied by the question of atomic weapons in the public polemics between the two parties, and in the Soviet refusal to honour a 1957 agreement promising China the data with which it could manufacture its own nuclear weapons.[24]

In the late 1950s and early 1960s it was the Russians who were primarily responsible for provoking the break, but who were seen as the less belligerent in the west. By the early 1970s the terms of the original Sino-Soviet dispute had been reversed: now it was the Chinese who bore most of the responsibility for the dispute, since they refused Soviet offers, repeatedly made since 1965, to negotiate and carry out joint support for Vietnam. It was Peking which cast Moscow as the militaristic and aggressive power, a policy which aligned China with the west. Indeed throughout much of the 1970s China was berating the USA and the European states for not being hostile enough to the USSR, i.e. for not doing more to hasten Cold War II.

The persistence of the Sino-Soviet dispute through the 1960s and early 1970s had immense benefits for the USA even though Peking remained at that time implacably hostile to it. One reason was that the division between China and the Soviet Union posed a grave problem for the Vietnamese, whose arms supplies were interrupted by quarrels between their two major allies and whose diplomacy was constantly hampered by their dispute. The Sino-Soviet rift constituted one gigantic permissive condition of the US intervention on Vietnam's north, matched by a comparable enabling factor, the simultaneous elimination of Indonesia as a diplomatic opponent of Washington's after the 1965 counter-coup, on the south. But by the early 1970s, when Chinese policy began to switch to one of collaboration with the USA, the Sino-Soviet split began to have

---

[24.] John Gittings, *The World and China, 1922-1972*, London 1974, pp. 307-10.

other consequences. First, China altered its critique of Soviet policy from being one of opposition from the left, critical of what was seen as undue Soviet tolerance of the west, to a right critique, in which the Soviet Union was portrayed as expansionist and imperialist. China began calling the USSR 'capitalist' in the mid-sixties, and added 'imperialist' or 'social-imperialist' after the 1969 border clash. This shift to the right dates from the Ninth Party Congress of 1969 and it opened the door to the Nixon visit of 1972 and the establishment of a Peking-Washington alliance. The purpose of Nixon's trip was to influence China by supporting it against the USSR and so recruit Chinese support for dampening the revolutionary movement throughout the third world, and in particular in Indochina.

While the particular aim of defeating the Vietnamese was not successful, Nixon's opening to China put great strains on Hanoi and US policy did succeed in encouraging the overall rightward shift in Chinese policy throughout the third world. The result was that China supported a diverse group of right-wing leaders across the world. The Shah of Iran, Emperor Haile Selassie of Ethiopia, and the Sultan of Oman had, in the 1960s, been objects of attack by opposition forces that enjoyed the support of Peking. By the early 1970s these groups had been abandoned by Peking, and these monarchs were being courted by the Chinese authorities. Even more striking were cases when China went out of its way to support third world leaders on the occasion of their suppression of popular movements—Mrs Bandaranaike of Sri Lanka and General Nimeiry of Sudan in 1971, and General Pinochet of Chile in 1973 were recipients of such endorsement. So too were General Mobutu of Zaire and President Sadat of Egypt whose hostility to the Soviet Union won them high marks in Peking. So far did Peking go in its pursuit of an international anti-Soviet line that it exempted only South Korea, South Africa and Israel from its diplomatic embrace. The culmination of this policy came in 1979 when China attacked Vietnam in a symbolic 'punishment' of Washington's tenacious foe. During the latter part of the 1970s, the Sino-Soviet dispute therefore came to represent a great source of strength to the proponents of a Second Cold War: China exposed the USSR on its eastern flank, gave the USA a potent ally in east Asia, and provided it with covert military facilities. Had the USA faced even a low key Peking-Moscow alliance, Washington would have felt much less confident about launching the Second Cold War than it did.

China's contribution to the Cold War came also through its political influence, the diffusion of those very ideas of Soviet 'imperialism' which echoed the themes of the cold warriors in the west. The concrete political effects of this Chinese viewpoint may not have been great outside east Asia, but China did continue to exert a considerable hold over sections of the left elsewhere in the third world as well as in the metropolitan countries. As a result, a set of supposedly 'left' positions were available, which were used by the gathering forces of the Second Cold War; under the impact of these ideas much of the left, in Europe, North America and elsewhere, stampeded into simplistic and polemical evaluations of the Soviet Union that were no more measured than the uncritical apologies of former times. China's influence therefore played a significant part in that erosion of an independent socialist analysis of world affairs which has come to be one of the hallmarks, and one of the contributing elements, of Cold War II. Vulgar, superficial, and enticing in its righteousness, this sinophilic view of the Soviet Union has come to be orthodoxy on much of the left in Europe and the USA.

Finally, the very internal evolution of the People's Republic played its part in that diminution of optimism about socialism which resulted from the Brezhnevite period in the USSR and the record of some of the newer post-revolutionary states in the third world. During the 1960s, in both the advanced capitalist and third world countries, China had enjoyed considerable sympathy, not to say indulgence, as an alternative model of socialist development and post-revolutionary democracy. The combination of an intransigent international stand with apparently superior political practices formed the bases for a widespread expectation that China could form an alternative to the USSR. This optimism about China was to be doubly confounded. First of all, it became evident that the Cultural Revolution, far from being an occasion for political experimentation and increased democracy, had in practice led to mass terror and repression on a scale comparable only to Stalin's purges in the 1930s. It differed from the Soviet purges in that the role of the Soviet secret police was here played not just by the *Gong 'Anju*, the Public Security or Chinese secret police, but also by the army and armed factions that arose during the Cultural Revolution. But as the purges did, the Cultural Revolution used a frenzied rhetoric of class struggle and combatting 'counter-revolutionary' tendencies to eliminate many of those who had built up the party and the state in previous years.

The overall toll of both events is hard to calculate. In the USSR around half a million people were executed in the purge years of 1936-1938, and up to three million of those sent to labour camps in the same period also died. In China, up to one million people were killed in the violence attendant upon the Cultural Revolution, but many millions more were terrorised or persecuted in other ways. Twelve million young people were forcibly sent to the countryside: their education was disrupted and they became a lost or 'wounded' generation in Chinese life. Many millions more were dismissed from their jobs, harassed, and humiliated. The later official figure, of thirty million persecuted, and one hundred million 'negatively affected', may reflect exaggeration, but there can be no doubt that the Cultural Revolution, far from having been a release of creative political energy, was a terrifying setback for the people of China.[25]

A somewhat indulgent attitude to China still persists in the west, in the publications of both the left and the right. Far less attention is paid to the actions of the *Gong 'Anju* than to those of the KGB, far less is heard of the millions in the Chinese Gulag than of those in the Soviet camps. Few in the west protest at Chinese restrictions on freedom of emigration, not least because the Peking government, concerned at a population of over one billion, would be only too happy to release millions of their own people upon the outside world. Yet the Cultural Revolution is no longer seen in the favourable light in which it once was, and this revision of opinion on the 1960s has been encouraged by another development, the reversal of official policy that supervened in the 1970s. For even those who sought to defend the Cultural Revolution could not now defend the tergiversations that passed for policy in the 1970s. The new economic policies of the Chinese leadership may well have had some justification in terms of realism about the country's potential and the greater popular support they enjoyed: but whatever their validity they ceased to provide a model of socialist transition alternative to the Soviet one and eroded any

---

[25.] Roy Medvedev, *Let History Judge*, Nottingham 1971, p. 239 gives a figure of half a million executed in the terror of the 1930s. Figures for the number of camp deaths as high as 12 million have been given, but more recent scholarship has suggested much lower figures, of 3 million or less (communication to the author from S.G. Wheatcroft Centre for Russian and East European Studies, Birmingham. For Wheatcroft's critique of conventional estimates of camp inmates during the terror see this article in *Soviet Studies* no. 2, April 1981). The toll of the cultural revolution is given in Philip Short, *The Dragon and The Bear*, London 1982, pp. 152 ff.

superiority that might have been detected between the organisation of Chinese society and that of the USSR. Faithful to Mao only in his right-wing foreign policy, the Great Helmsman's successors dismantled virtually everything that was distinctive about the Chinese model internally, and in so doing locked their economic future into the international capitalist system.

The importance of China's role in world affairs is often exaggerated, by Peking and its foes. Despite its demographic and geographical weight, China is not a world power. It is influential in east and south-east Asia, and is in this sense a regional power. But it lacks the economic or military strength to influence events further afield, in a manner comparable to the influence of the USSR or USA. Nonetheless, it played an immense role in the onset of what was a global phenomenon, namely the Second Cold War. Its break with Russia radically altered the strategic configuration in which the Soviet Union found itself, and reopened that two-front exposure which Stalin had faced in the 1930s, with Germany in the west and Japan in the east. Its role in Indochina was of considerable assistance to the USA, both negatively in the 1960s and positively in the 1970s. But beyond these contributions, confined to the east and south-east Asian theatres, China's policy did serve to demoralise many who had aspired to an alternative model of socialism and it provided a new source of ill-informed and defective analysis of the USSR that was to erode the obstacles within the west to the onset of Cold War II. Of all the five trends within the involution of the post-revolutionary states this was probably the second most important, after the entropy of the Soviet model which accompanied the Brezhnev era. From the image of a confident, unified and expanding communist bloc envisaged by Khrushchev in 1959, the picture was now of a tiring and divided communist system, one which held out little promise and seemed increasingly atrophied from within.

The Retreat of Socialism in the Advanced Capitalist Countries

If the prime responsibility for this involution of the communist movement lay with those parties that already held state power, the latter were nonetheless supported by the course of the left in the advanced capitalist countries over the 1960s and 1970s. The late 1960s and early 1970s had seen significant social conflicts in western Europe and the USA, but one factor singularly absent from the middle and late 1970s, the years leading up to Cold War II, was a sharpened conflict between the left within the advanced capitalist states and the governments of these countries that were laying the groundwork for the new confrontation. Whilst these governments certainly used Cold War II to press their advantage against the trade unions and working class parties, it could not be said that the Cold War was prompted by the threat which the left posed. The challenges of the French 68 and the Italian 69 had already been contained. Rather, it was the very weakness of the left parties, and of forces allied to them, which provided an additional enabling factor for those states that were themselves pursuing cold war policies.

In the most general terms, it is possible to distinguish between three different constituent elements of this left, in the advanced capitalist states. These three elements are: the communist parties, the socialist parties, and the non-party left forces. The communist parties had played a leading role in opposing Cold War I and fear of a revival in their fortunes in Europe during the mid-1970s undoubtedly prompted alarm in Washington. This apparent revival proved, however, to be illusory: there was no reversal in that decline in both the political power and combativity of the left which had been in progress from the mid-1950s. The Sino-Soviet dispute had had relatively little effect on the communist parties of Europe and the USA—the 'Marxist-Leninist' fragments that emerged under Chinese influence tended to be drawn from student or unrepresentative working class circles. Only in Japan did it make its mark, where the Communist Party adopted a stance of critical distance from both Moscow and Peking in 1966. But the dispute did destroy the constitutive aspiration of a world-wide and united communist movement, something that would, in however attenuated a form, continue that collaboration which had underlain the Comintern, dissolved in 1943, and the Cominform, established in 1947 and dissolved in 1954. The moral blow to the residual unity of the communist parties came with the Soviet invasion of Czechoslovakia in 1968. Subsequent Soviet attempts to co-ordinate the communist parties, at the world conference of parties in Moscow in June 1969 and at the conference of European parties in Berlin in June 1976, had little lasting effect.[26]

Accompanying this disintegration of communism as a unified international force came a generalised standstill or even reversal in the fate of individual communist parties. Of the four communist parties with substan-

---

26. Fernando Claudin, *Eurocommunism and Socialism*, passim.

tial influence in major capitalist countries—the Italian, French, Spanish and Japanese—only one, the Italian, won major electoral support by gaining over 30 per cent of the vote. But it failed to achieve political power and appeared trapped by the loss of its critical dynamic on the left and continued obstruction of an otherwise fragmented centre and right. The French party did take office with the election of Mitterand in 1981, but its four ministers, far from being able to use their positions to advance the party, were in effect political prisoners, hostages to the rightward drift of the socialist government. In Spain and Japan the two parties continued to play a significant part in political life, but they did not register major gains and the Spanish party lost much of its following. Elsewhere, in countries of less significance, the Portuguese and Greek parties emerged from the decades of suppression to find themselves confined after initial optimistic expectations to limited sections of the electorate. In one other European country where a communist party commanded massive electoral support it was unable, for reasons of ethnic and strategic delicacy, to translate this into political victory—namely Cyprus.[27]

The fact that most of these parties were now critical of the Soviet Union and refused to accept the dictates of the CPSU's International Department in the manner of former years was, potentially, a positive development. It could have opened up a free debate within the communist movement on state power in the east and strategy in the west that had been stifled since Bolshevisation of the western parties in the 1920s. It could also have broken that link between socialist opposition in the west and bureaucratic centralism in the east which so discredited the left in Europe and the USA. And it could have permitted a democratisation within these parties themselves. But the opportunity for such an opening was lost in favour of an increasingly rightward slippage by the Eurocommunist parties, which abandoned their loyalty to Moscow in order increasingly to align themselves with the capitalist west. Thus of the three main parties the Italian communist party was prepared to remain inside NATO, the French party, for all its remaining pro-Soviet sentiments, supported the militaristic foreign policies of the Elysée, and the Spanish par-

27. The Italian party won 30.4 per cent of the vote in the 1979 general elections, as against 34.4 per cent in 1976. The French party won 15.4 per cent in the first round of the 1981 Presidential elections, as against 21.3 per cent in the equivalent round of the 1978 parliamentary elections. The Spanish party won 3.9 per cent of the vote in the 1982 elections, compared with 10.7 per cent in 1979. The Japanese party won 9.8 per

ty encouraged ill-informed critiques of the Soviet Union which were scarcely distinguishable from those of the conservative right.

At the same time, for all their newfound enthusiasm for the policies of their capitalist rivals, these parties refused to learn properly the one lesson which their bourgeois counterparts might have taught them, namely the practice of substantive inner-party democracy. It was evident that those parties still predominantly loyal to Moscow—in France, Portugal, West Germany—would maintain the centralised models of political control. But the inner evolution of the Italian and Spanish parties, for all their emollience on foreign policy, did little to confirm the belief in the ability of constituent members of the communist movement to permit a democratic life within their organisations. While some debate was permitted, expulsions and centralist control persisted.

Much of the inspiration for the break with the CPSU came from revulsion at the policies pursued by Moscow at home and in Eastern Europe. Yet even this source of political independence was turned to disadvantage. Instead of opening up informed debate, from a socialist perspective, on the failings of the Russian model, this greater independence led to a flood of distortion of what was occurring in the USSR, one often accompanied by indulgence towards the supposedly magnificent achievements of the cultural revolution in China. The mindset of dogmatic loyalty to the Soviet Union was too easily replaced by that of ignorant abuse. Only in France did the Communist Party resist such an option: it adhered to the stereotypes of the 1950s. But the effect of this constancy was to polarise French intellectual life, so that those opposed to the PCF became themselves the perpetrators of an often vulgar anti-Russian propaganda. The truth about repression in the Soviet Union, both the slaughter of the 1930s and the sustained monolithism of the post-Stalin period, had long been public knowledge, documented by the Trotskyist and libertarian lefts as well as by the anti-communist right.[28] Yet in a climate where unstinting loyalty to the USSR had previously been the norm, the 'discovery' of the Gulag was treated as a novel and world-shattering revelation. The widespread adoption by the French intelligentsia of this unoriginal critique of the Soviet Union in the late 1970s was the most

---

cent in the 1980 elections, 9.6 per cent in 1977. AKEL, the Greek Cypriot party, won 33 per cent in the 1981 general elections.

[28]. Trotsky's *The Revolution Betrayed* was published in 1937, Victor Serge's *From Lenin to Stalin* and *Russia Twenty Years After* in the same year.

extreme case of the consequences of the communist movement's general failure to initiate a serious and balanced discussion of the Bolshevik experience to date.

The social democratic parties of Europe were, in one respect, better placed than the communist parties to break with the mould of cold war politics: they were not associated with the USSR and constrained by this association. They also were able in a variety of countries to assume state power. In practice, however, they compounded rather than resisted that linkage to Atlanticism which had been forged in the aftermath of World War II, and that tolerance of capitalism which dated from the rupture with Bolshevism in the years after World War I.

In Britain, the Labour Party made but the most minimal gesture of independence from Washington: the government of 1964–70 supported the US role in Vietnam, whilst remaining a staunch member of NATO. At the same time, the contraction of British colonialism across the third world was offset by the establishment of new ties of economic and military collaboration with the governments of formerly dominated regions in asociation with the USA. Four regions in particular were marked by such ties: south-east Asia, the Persian Gulf, South Africa, and the Caribbean. Although a reduced military power, Britain still played an important role as trainer and adviser, as well as arms supplier, and its economic links with Singapore and Pretoria, Kuwait and the Cayman Islands prospered to a degree unseen in the days of former colonialism. In the Falklands war of 1982 it showed it could be as vicious an imperialist power as any other. In Germany, the initial vigour of the Brandt period gave way to the pro-NATO enthusiasms of Helmut Schmidt. In France, the French socialist and communist parties vied with the Gaullists for control of the tricolour. In sum, the foreign policies of these governments were, at best, tepid modifications of the policies inherited from their conservative, Christian Democrat and Gaullist opponents. Instead of striking a new note, that would have contrasted with both Moscow and Washington, these parties nestled beneath the wings of the bald-headed eagle.

The emergence in the late 1960s and early 1970s of new political forces bound neither to the communist nor to the socialist parties constituted another development which had innovative possibilities. Whether in the new forms of worker militancy, or in the women's, gay and immigrant movements, the 'new social forces', as they were generically called, developed forms of protest and criticism that had hitherto been neglected by the traditional and organised left. As has been seen, new 'non-class' forces made particular progress in the USA, where despite the virulence of right-wing organisations and ideas the looser character of New World politics enabled these movements to advance. It was in Italy that the most powerful new working class movements emerged. Yet the opportunities opened up by these movements were not consolidated. Too often they were generational or geographically restricted affairs. The rejection of traditional forms of political power sometimes elided into a short-sighted neglect of the problem of state power itself. This was because the new and positive emphasis on the individual dimensions of power was allowed to obscure the endurance of larger institutions of domination. The impatience of spontaneity in certain cases degenerated into the horrors of terrorism. And, despite the less forceful nature of the threat, these movements also generated countermovements whose force and determination were underestimated. The US New Right fed on fear and prejudice against these social movements. The French May was followed by the French June—the triumphant electoral confirmation of Gaullism. In Germany the *Berufsverbot* symbolised an authoritarian turning. In Britain the latter part of the 1970s coincided with the advance of a newly invigorated conservative ideology epitomised in the person of Margaret Thatcher. From the renewed stress on family values and hard work, through to the patriotic carnage of the Falklands war, Thatcherism demonstrated that traditional values could find an organised form and a voice able to repel those who had, some years before, been gaining public ground.

The overall rightward shift in the advanced capitalist countries during the latter part of the 1970s was not, therefore, a response to an increased challenge from the left, organised or 'autonomous', but was rather facilitated by the manner in which this left had already to a considerable degree been blocked. Had this not occurred the left could have resisted the pressure for Cold War II both by greater organised opposition to it, and by challenging the bipolar mould of world politics through a pursuit of independent policies at home and abroad. Yet whilst this halting of the Left's forces strengthened that involution of the communist states, the latter also contributed to the halting of the left's advance. The shift in policies on peace and disarmament by the Soviet Union in particular, and the overall involution of the communist world as a possible alternative form of democratic social organisation, helped to diminish the appeals of

those within the advanced capitalist countries who sought to pose a cle
anti-capitalist alternative.

Of all these trends, the most important was, however, the involution of the USSR itself. This was not only because of the position of the Soviet Union as the prime military opponent of the west, but also because the very division of the communist world focussed attention more upon one state, Russia, than had been the case in Cold War I. China's aberrations and the trials of the third world would have counted for less had the Soviet Union pursued a different path. Within the realm of its own policies, even the economic failings of the USSR were probably of secondary importance: neither communism nor capitalism was performing well by the late 1970s when the Second Cold War began. The crucial areas were political—the absence of any trend towards democratisation, and the pursuit of military parity. These confirmed the western picture of the USSR as a 'totalitarian' power, repressive at home and aggressive abroad. Had the USSR been developing forms of socialist democracy at home and adhering to a clearly distinct military policy internationally, it could have blunted the western counter-offensive and rallied much greater sympathy for itself. But, in pursuit of an internal security based on their monopoly of power and of an international one founded on mimesis of the US military programme, the Soviet leaders ended by encouraging precisely that confrontation which they had tried, through Detente, to avoid.

ctions
ational Capitalism

The 1970s were a decade of increasing conflict within the capitalist world, between rich and poor nations, and within the groups of rich and poor themselves. It was also a decade of growing recession, as the postwar boom came to an end. The first half of the decade witnessed the challenge of the OPEC states, which multiplied their oil revenues, and at the same time widened the gap between themselves and the poorer non-oil producers of the third world. Later in the decade, the third world yielded a different 'threat', in the form of the new industrialising countries. Yet these rich-poor or north-south conflicts were overshadowed by the growing conflicts between the advanced capitalist countries themselves which produced intense disputes over trade, foreign policy and interest rates by the beginning of the 1980s. Nor were conflicts confined to economic matters. Wars between third world capitalist states were far more frequent in the 1970s, and in 1982 there was the first war in modern times between an advanced capitalist country and an anti-communist third world state, the Anglo-Argentinian conflict over the Falkland Islands. The onset of the Second Cold War between the west and the USSR therefore coincided with an overt sharpening of intra-west relations, and with a recession in the major capitalist economies.

Yet inter-capitalist rivalry certainly played a significant role in the First Cold War, far more so than contemporary accounts of the period tend to suggest. From the early months of World War II the US foreign policy establishment had begun to plan for a postwar order, dominated by the USA. It was determined to devise means for manipulating the war itself and the subsequent settlements to gain advantage over Europe and its colonial empires. Whilst the First Cold War was primarily caused by the US-Soviet conflicts, there is no doubt that the USA saw in the Cold War a context for advancing its plans for a global order controlling all capitalist states and that it was in part the drive to impose this order at the expense of capitalist competitors which brought the Cold War into being.[1] The world had changed to a great extent by the time of the Second Cold War: US hegemony over other capitalist states had been eroded, the number of sovereign states had increased by over fifty. The world was a far more complex place in 1979 than in 1947. Cold War I coincided with a boom, Cold War II with a recession. The questions which arise with regard to Cold War II nonetheless replicate those of Cold War I: what is the relation between these inter-capitalist conflicts, west-west and north-south disputes, and the east-west one? How far did inter-capitalist conflicts cause Cold War II?

Three answers, suggesting competing theories, can be given to this question. The first, already discussed in Chapter One, is that the west-west conflict is *the* fundamental conflict in world affairs. According to this view, the Cold War, an apparently overriding one between east and west, is in fact one artificially promoted to further the USA's interest in the west-west dispute.[2] A second, more cautious, linking of these two dimensions of conflict could argue that the Cold War, already promoted by other causes, is none the less aggravated by these inter-capitalist conflicts, and by the US pursuit of a re-established hegemony. A third theory would reverse the causation, suggesting that inter-capitalist conflict is itself in some measure a result of the Cold War—of the desire of the USA to force its policies on an unwilling alliance system that does not accept the necessity of such a forceful confrontation with the USSR.

The first of these theories, as already noted in Chapter Two, can only be sustained by downplaying the two major constitutents of world politics, namely inter-bloc conflict and the strategic arms race. While the relation of inter-capitalist conflict to the east-west conflict is certainly understated by western leaders in Cold War II as it was in Cold War I, it is not possible to argue that the east-west conflict and the cold war phases of it are simply displacements or diversions from this other west-west

---

[1.] Gabriel Kolko, *The Politics of War*, London 1969; Noam Chomsky, 'Strategic Arms, and the Cold War and the Third World', *in Exterminism and Cold War*, pp. 223-36.

[2.] See Chapter Two, pp. 27-9, for details of the arguments on the primacy of the west-west conflict. In a similar vein two American business consultants begin their work: 'If there is a single great fact of our era, it is not the continuing rivalry between Russia and the West. Instead, it is the emergence of the first truly international industrial marketplace and the struggle between the leading nations and blocs...' (Hunter Lewis and Donald Allison, *The Real World War*, New York 1982, p. 1).

dimension. It is, by contrast, more plausible to argue that the relationship between east-west and west-west conflict is determined by shifting patterns of reinforcement and collision. In the late 1970s inter-capitalist conflict in some measure aggravated the Cold War and helped bring it on. Later, the two were more contradictory. The Cold War itself has made inter-capitalist conflict more intense, as over the Soviet gas pipeline, and US-European divisions have served in some measure to restrain the USA.

The aggravation of inter-capitalist relations by the Cold War was especially evident in the period after the Reagan Administration came into office. The emphasis upon an overall economic embargo of the USSR met with little response from Europe. In particular, the pursuit by Washington of a blockage of the Soviet-European gas pipeline sharply strained Atlantic relations, producing a crisis comparable to the 1956 Suez affair and the Gaullist defiance of NATO in 1966. The call by both Reagan and his predecessor Carter for increased military expenditure on the part of the European NATO states and Japan also met with considerable resistance. Neither economic disparity between Europe and the USA nor European acceptance of the reality of the 'Soviet Threat' was as it had been during Cold War I. On these issues, the causative dynamic appeared to go from the Cold War to the crisis of inter-capitalist relations and to impede Washington's initatives. What concerns us here is, however, the earlier dynamic, of how these inter-capitalist conflicts shaped the Cold War in its formative period. This pertains neither to the theory of Cold War as displacement of west-west conflict, nor to that of Cold War as cause of west-west dispute, but to how, in its autonomous development, the realm of inter-capitalist conflict contributed to the increased confrontation with the USSR in the latter part of the 1970s.

Four dimensions of this relationship would appear to have been of particular importance: Conflict Between the Advanced Capitalist States; The Rise of Third World Capitalist Economies; The Strategic Resources Scare; The Increased Frequency of Inter-capitalist Wars.

Conflict Between the Advanced Capitalist States

Inter-imperialist conflict lay at the origins of both the First and Second World Wars, and despite its displacement from the primacy which, until 1941, it occupied in world politics, and despite US predominance, it has continued to fuel major international tensions in the postwar epoch.

After two decades of relative harmony, emphasis on the increased level of conflict between major capitalist states began to be noticeable from the late 1960s onwards, as the rivalry between the USA on one side, and Europe and Japan on the other, gathered force. It was an emphasis found in the analyses of both left and right. In his study of international finance, the Italian Marxist Riccardo Parboni has written: 'It is not inappropriate to define the 1970s as an extended period of economic warfare between the United States and the other capitalist powers.'[3] In a survey of US-European relations published in early 1982, *The Economist* stated: 'The trading relationship between America and western Europe is passing through its rockiest patch for 30 years.'[4]

The geographical terrain of this warfare is the entire international capitalist economy, as well as the capitalist world's trade and banking relations with the non-capitalist countries. Yet, whilst the *fact* of greater rivalry between the developed capitalist states in the 1970s is not in dispute, there is considerable room for argument as to the intensity of this trend. The term 'economic warfare' used by Parboni has two meanings: it can mean using economic pressures as a means of weakening the society of an enemy, often but not necessarilly coinciding with military conflict; or it can mean economic conflict, or competition, between states that are not, in the earlier sense, at war or likely to be so. Within capitalism economic competition is normal, and it can enter phases of greater intensity where the term warfare applies. States can move from one level of economic warfare to the other, as happened in 1914, but the distinction nonetheless holds.

In terms of these definitions, the USA has been waging economic warfare of the first kind against the USSR and its allies intermittently since 1917, and Cold War II has seen a revival of such warfare over Afghanistan and Poland. Economic pressure is a way to weaken and defeat the Soviet Union. But the USA has also been engaged in warfare of the second kind with its advanced capitalist allies, i.e. it has been involved in more acrimonious inter-capitalist competition than was the case in 1950s and 1960s. The disputes of the 1970s and early 1980s on currency, tariffs, oil prices and export subsidies have introduced a greater

---

[3.] Riccardo Parboni, *The Dollar and Its Rivals*, London 1981, p. 98. See also Martin Mayer, *The Fate of the Dollar*, New York 1980.
[4.] *The Economist*, 27 February 1982.

element of rancour and suspicion into the relations between the USA, Europe and Japan at a time of general recession in the capitalist world.

The degree of such economic warfare and of the decline of US power should not, however, be overstated. First of all, the very internationalisation of capitalist relations through the growth of multinational corporations, international currency markets and forms of international adjustment mean that some institutional forces that operate against inter-state rivalry have been established. The *prime* interest of the capitalist world and of the states and institutions comprising it lies in encouraging a generalised and shared prosperity within which competition can profitably be conducted. There has been increased competition in trade, but in the previously central realm of inter-capitalist competition, finance, the rivalry of former years has been largely reduced: far from the finance capitals of rival states competing to dominate the world, the process since 1945 has increasingly been one of international banking consortia combining in major operations to lend to firms and states. Indeed, the rise of the Eurodollar market since the late 1960s has created a money market somewhat independent of the controls of any single state. Secondly, the tension in currency and trade has at no point threatened, as it did in the past, to develop into full-scale conflict between the states in question. For all the difficulties posed by Gaullist France or industrial Japan, these states have not in the postwar epoch broken diplomatic, political or economic ties to the USA in the way that Yugoslavia and later China severed their links with the USSR. Even more importantly, it is not the conflict between capitalist states that fuels the nuclear arms race or threatens to bring a nuclear catastrophe into being. The intensity of conflict on certain economic issues should not, therefore, mask these elements of continued inter-capitalist collaboration at the political and strategic levels.

Similar reservations can apply to the picture of a declining US hegemony. Overall, such a decline has taken place, and the dimensions of it will be examined in the following paragraphs. However, there are respects in which US hegemony has not declined and may indeed have strengthened during the 1970s. The US lead in space technology and exploration has been maintained. The Anglo-French lead in supersonic civilian aircraft, embodied in *Concorde*, turned out to be a commercial burden. In the military sphere, the USA's advantage over its major capitalist allies in terms of strategic nuclear strength has expanded: the

British and French have retained their small nuclear deterrents, but have in no qualitative or quantitive sense kept pace, even in their own terms, with the USA. In conventional weapons, the initiative in terms of technical development has swung even more to the USA, and the balance of arms sales across the Atlantic has run at 10 to 1 in the USA's favour in recent years. Even if, as the USA hopes, the NATO allies and Japan increase their defence spending, this will not give them new nuclear potentials, and it will increase the market for US arms in these states. Although Europe and Japan spend more on defence than in the past, the USA still lays out 53 per cent of the total for the advanced capitalist countries.[5]

In the economic sphere, the record is also more differentiated than might appear. The USA has had a deficit in trade with Japan for some time, rising from $7 billion in 1980 to $13.4 billion in 1981. But it has not had one with Europe in the latter part of the 1970s: indeed the 1981 figures showed a surplus of $11 billion in the USA's favour. Part of this surplus, and an increasingly important component of the US export drive, has been in the realm of agricultural exports: in 1980 the USA had agricultural exports of $41.3 billion and an agricultural trade surplus of $23 billion; 1981 sales to the EEC were $9 billion, to Japan $7 billion. European livestock rearing depends for its survival on US animal feeds. US farmers produced 80 per cent of the corn, 70 per cent of the soya beans and 50 per cent of the wheat traded on international markets in 1980.[6]

The 'decline' of the dollar should also be placed in a comparative context. Although weakened as a reserve currency in the late 1960s and early 1970s, the dollar remained the dominant international currency. It was, first of all, the currency of a country that depended far less on trade than its major rivals and was therefore less liable to weakening as a result of the world recession: trade accounted for 10 per cent of US GNP in 1980 compared to 29 per cent for West Germany. Secondly, the dollar remained *the* international currency, as sterling had been in an earlier epoch: three quarters of world trade was invoiced in dollars, and it accounted for

---

[5.] *International Herald Tribune*, 3 August 1982. The same report states that the USA provides 66 per cent of total allied naval tonnage, 45 per cent of the tactical air power, 39 per cent of the ground forces and 41 per cent of those on active military duty. 'Allied' here includes Japan.

[6.] Lewis and Allison, pp. 26, 129. Susan George, *How the Other Half Dies*, London 1976, Chapter Eight, analyses the rise of US food domination.

three quarters of all international reserves, official and commercial.[7] Through the privileges of 'seigniorage' the USA continued to derive benefits from the role of the dollar as the main international currency.[8] And the continued power of the dollar was manifested in the way in which the high interest rates introduced by the Federal Reserve in 1979 forced rates up across the world. In another realm, US dominance of the sale of communications *equipment* was gradually lost to the Japanese, but US dominance of the *content* of international communications remained unchallenged, and the new technologies, of satellite transmission and television reception, gave the USA new opportunities for cultural predominance over the rest of the world in the 1980s. Sony transmitted *Dallas*.

The picture of sharpened inter-capitalist conflicts also involves the world recession which, by limiting opportunities, helped to increase competition and hostility between major economies in the 1970s. The facts of this recession are evident enough: from 1960 to 1973 industrial output in the OECD states rose by 6 per cent a year; between 1973 and 1980 it rose by 2 per cent a year. Unemployment in the OECD countries in 1982 was estimated at 30 millions. Yet the recession was not spread evenly across the capitalist world, and indeed the increased conflict between the constituent economies was in part a result of this unevenness. For during the 1970s capitalism, for all its problems, made considerable advances, particularly in the Far East, in Japan and the major New Industrialising Countries—Taiwan, South Korea, Hong Kong and Singapore.[9] World trade continued to expand, rising from $150 billion in 1965 to $1.5 trillion in 1980. Between 1974 and 1980 alone it more than doubled, although in the 1980–82 period it stagnated. Great technological advances were made as the third industrial revolution, that of the semiconductors and computers, spread rapidly. Capitalism had entered a period of comparative stagnation in output compared to the 1950s and 1960s, but it was by no means moribund: it was the strains produced by this uneven slump, rather than an unmitigated standstill, which characterised the crisis in inter-capitalist relations of the late 1970s.

[7.] *The Economist*, 22 May 1982; *The Economist*, 27 February 1982.

[8.] Parboni, pp. 40-49.

[9.] Jon Halliday, 'Capitalism and Socialism in East Asia', *New Left Review* 124 November-December 1980.

These three limitations are therefore important constraints upon the picture of untrammelled capitalist economic warfare: major areas of close collaboration remained, such that the axis of international and strategic conflict remained the east-west rather than the west-west one; US hegemony, although eroded, was by no means at an end, and the US counter-offensive was made possible precisely by the resources which Washington could still command; although the capitalist economies entered a recession in the 1970s, some economies remained far more vital than others and continued to innovate and expand, whilst challenging previously secure competitors; certain sectors of recessionary economies—arms, communication—continued to boom. The response of the USA to its economic problems, and the linkage made by Washington between this response and the Second Cold War, can be seen in this light, as a decisive and by no means desperate attempt to restore an eroded leadership by a combination of political and economic measures.

In both Cold Wars the USA has sought to use its leadership in the conflict with the Soviet Union as a means of consolidating or increasing its advantages over the other major capitalist states. In doing this it has acted both as a state, pursuing its rival political and strategic interests, and as the representative and manager of US capitalists in their international relations. This managerial role involves an aggressive function, of helping to break down barriers abroad to the state's own capitalists, and a defensive one, of maintaining monopolistic positions at home.[10] If the shifts in the US–Soviet relationship during the 1970s have provided an opportunity for an assertion of greater US power, the declining position of the USA in relation to its other major competitors has been a direct incentive to the US government to implement such a policy of counter-attack.

The postwar settlements and the onset of the Cold War provided the context for the establishment of the instruments of an alliance dominated by the USA: the Bretton Woods Agreement of 1944 codified the dominance of the dollar; the establishment of NATO in 1949 established a unified military structure. Under the cover of wartime and postwar collaboration, the USA gradually pushed back the barriers imposed by the

---

[10.] Robin Murray, 'Capital and the Nation State', *New Left Review* 67, May-June 1971; see also Jeff Freiden, 'International Finance and the Nation State in Advanced Capitalist and Less Developed Countries', paper presented to the 1981 Annual Meeting of the American Political Science Association.

European states: the Middle East was a major zone of competition, as shown in the US breakthrough to Greece and Turkey in 1947; Washington used the 1953 coup in Iran to break into that previously British-controlled country; it responded to the Suez crisis of 1956 by denouncing Britain and France and propounding the Eisenhower Doctrine, which gave the USA a direct strategic role in Arabia. The fear of the USSR was used as a means of validating US advances and of ensuring European compliance. Yet US hegemony also enabled a long period of expansion in the advanced capitalist countries initiated by Marshall Aid and under the dominance of the dollar: an increasingly unified world market coincided for some time with the interests of US capital, a combination that was to last until, beginning in the mid-1960s, the rise of rival capitalist powers, products of the very success of the postwar boom, was to place that dominance in peril.[11]

If in the First Cold War the USA used conflict with the USSR to establish an overall hegemony in the capitalist world, the Second Cold War is an attempt to strengthen that hegemony at a time when it has been weakened. The components of the weakening aré well-known and need only the briefest restatement here. In 1950 US GNP accounted for about 40 per cent of the world total, and by 1980 this had declined to around 20 per cent. The US economy remained the strongest in the world, but US per capita income fell below several of the other capitalist states by the end of the 1970s.[12] Growth rates also lagged behind those of several capitalist competitors: US output rose 2.9 per cent per year in the period 1970-81, compared to 4.7 per cent in Japan. In the same period, productivity in US industry declined by comparison with the other major capitalist states: until 1965 it rose by almost 3 per cent per annum, but from 1973 it rose by under 1 per cent a year.[13] As a result, the US share of world manufacturing trade declined substantially, from 25.5 per cent in 1956 to 17.3 per cent in 1976. The US share of world trade as a whole went from 17.2 per cent in 1964 to 11.8 per cent in 1980. And the US economy itself became far more dependent on imports than had previously been the

---

[11.] Ernest Mandel, *Europe versus America?*, London 1970.

[12.] 1979 per capita income figures were Switzerland $13,920, Sweden $11,930, Denmark $11,900, West Germany $11,730, Belgium $10,920, Norway $10,700 and the USA $10,630 (World Bank, *World Development Report 1981*, p. 135).

[13.] Samuel Bowles, David Gordon and Thomas Weisskopf, 'At the Heart of the Economic Decline', *The Nation*, 10-17 July 1982.

case, these rising from 7 per cent of GNP in the 1950s to around 14 per cent in 1977.

During the late 1960s the Bretton Woods system upon which the postwar system had relied came under considerable pressure. The USA had run a deficit on capital account through the 1950s and 1960s: this was a result of Marshall Aid, and foreign investment by US corporations in search of cheaper wage rates, and then because of military spending, including, in the latter half of the 1960s, the Vietnam war. But this outflow had been partly compensated by a balance of trade surplus, and foreign holders of dollar were willing to keep US currency for their own transactions: it was a solid currency, backed by gold and a strong economy, and the dollar was the main medium of international trade, as sterling had been before World War II.

The rise in foreign dollar holdings led, from the early 1960s onwards, to the growth of the Eurodollar market, a system of trading and speculation in US currency beyond the direct control of the US state itself, albeit still subject to US influence.[14] By 1971, however, the understandings upon which this system rested had broken down. The USA ran the first balance of trade deficit since before the civil war and the rest of the world was clearly no longer willing to accept dollars in the quantity that the US economy was exporting them. In a series of defensive actions in August 1971 Nixon devalued the dollar against gold, imposed a 10 per cent surcharge on all imports into the USA, and established wage and price controls in the US itself. In March 1973 the convertibility of the dollar into gold was suspended, and the Bretton Woods system thereby abolished. This was not as dramatic a shift as the ending of sterling convertibility in 1931, but it did mark the end of an era, and it opened a much more acute period of conflict between the USA and its allies, the 'extended warfare' decade to which Parboni alludes.

These disturbances in the international financial system had their impact on political relations, both inter-state and national. The instability of the dollar, coupled with US inflationary pressures, led to a growing hostility to US monetary and trade policy on the part of European and Japanese bankers: central bankers formed a closely connected and rapidly communicating group which reacted more immediately and with more visible effect than foreign ministers or chiefs of staff. Throughout the middle

14. See Parboni and Mayer for details.

1970s, the USA was also criticised for its energy policy—for the profligacy with which it used energy and in so doing pushed up the world price. Nixon's nationalistic solution did have some success in reversing the trends of the late 1960s, especially as it was accompanied by an end to Vietnam expenditure. But under Carter, as the world went further into recession, the US position declined again: the trade deficit rose from $31 billion in 1977 to $34 billion in 1978, and despite the flow of money into the USA the current account was nearly $16 billion in deficit in the latter year.

The Carter Administration hoped to get support for reflation from the Europeans, by promoting growth in the two stronger economies, the USA and Germany—the 'Locomotive Theory'. But this did not succeed and in 1978 the US Federal Reserve Bank was forced to intervene to support a dollar that was slipping again on international markets. Carter then began an aggressive campaign, presaging that of Reagan, to force open the markets of other countries as a means of boosting US exports. Ironically for a country that led the world in industrial output, the US export drive rested as much on the promotion of primary product sales as it did on the sale of manufactured goods: competition with the EEC involved clashes over Common Market restrictions on the import of wheat, soya beans, and fibres, the latter allegedly subsidised by cheaper US energy costs, whilst in 1980 Carter imposed price restrictions on the import of European steel, itself allegedly subsidised by what were presented in the USA as the 'socialist' policies, i.e. the state subsidies, of the EEC. In June 1982 the steel dispute took an even sharper turn, as the US administration directly limited the quantities of European steel imports to the USA.

The greatest conflict was, however, with Japan, whose surplus in trade with the USA rose from $7 billion in 1980 to $13.4 billion in 1981. By 1981 Japan had won 23 per cent of the US car market, 25 per cent of the television market, and 50 per cent of those for radios and recording equipment. 25 per cent of all Japan's exports went to the USA in 1981. This led to pressure inside the USA against the import of Japanese cars, combined with attempts to force the Japanese market wider open, under the rubric of 'reciprocity'. US irritation at the Japanese was increased by accusations that the Japanese were spending less than 1 per cent of their GNP on defence, a charge that Japan was reluctant to rebut since, because it wished to preserve the fiction of not having an army, it deliberately understated its military outlays. Even relations with the USA's northern neighbour, Canada, were complicated by a new desire on the latter's part to exert greater control over its own energy sector.

The domestic consequences of this decline were evident within the USA itself.[15] Oil dependency grew from imports of $4.3 billion in 1972 to $74 billion in 1980: if the expenditures of the Vietnam war had been eased, their place was more than filled by the demands of OPEC. Yet such were the conflicts within the US state that it proved impossible for Carter to put through his energy bill which would have introduced an increase in the gasoline and crude oil taxes. The economic front was, said Carter, 'the moral equivalent of war': but the version of an energy bill finally passed by Congress in October 1978 was almost worthless. At the same time, the flow of foreign capital into the USA increased, a result of political stability there as much as of high rates of return. In 1980 28 per cent of all West German foreign investment was placed in the USA and 23 per cent of Japanese. Total British investment in the USA came to $9.4 billion (1979), total Japanese to $7.4 billion and total German to $6.8 billion. Over two hundred branches of foreign banks had opened in the 1970s; the result was that by 1980 $38 billion out of a total of $154 billion of loans made in the USA were by foreign banks.[16]

The ideologically charged issue of Arab investment led to Congressional restrictions on foreign purchases of US equity: in fact most of the $70 billion held by OPEC states in 1981 were in Treasury Bonds and short-term loans, the more important investors being the other major capitalist states. OPEC states made up only 1 per cent of direct foreign investment in US corporations. Nevertherless, the myths and the realities combined to reduce that sense of supreme confidence and autarky upon which the USA had relied in the 1950s and 1960s. At home millions were unemployed because of what they saw as the declining economic power of the USA vis-à-vis its rivals: this sentiment was an important component in the pressure to cut back on steel imports, where by mid-1982 45% of the workforce—200,000 people—were unemployed and units were operating at only 42 per cent capacity. Abroad US tourists suffered from the decline of the dollar. At the end of the 1970s, in a sym-

---

[15.] Lester Thurow, 'The Moral Equivalent of Defeat', *Foreign Policy*, no. 32, Spring 1981; Robert Keohane, 'US Foreign Economic Policy Toward Other Advanced Capitalist States', in Oye, Rothchild, Lieber (eds), *Eagle Entangled*, New York 1979.
[16.] *International Herald Tribune*, 22 May 1981.

bolic inversion of that city's earlier role in the confrontation of east and west, GIS in West Berlin were organising special bus trips to buy provisions in the supermarkets of East Berlin.

No one-to-one relation exists between the decline of US hegemony and the Second Cold War: rather US leaders have sought to manage both contradictions, that with the USSR which is dominant, and that with the major capitalist states which is subordinate, in order to derive maximum advantage from each. By resuming the discussion so far certain connections can, however, be outlined.[17] (a) The pervasive US sense of a lost power, and of the need for reassertion and renewal, the ideological undercurrent of the Second Cold War, owed much to the economic impact of this declining position: the sense of vulnerability was, however, displaced from that of economic relations with Europe and Japan to the military realms of conflict with the USSR by the mobilisation of patriotic sentiment, and contributed in this manner to the promotion of a militaristic cold war atmosphere in the USA. (b) The increased challenge of the other major capitalist powers found expression in competition over the old terrain of the First Cold War, the third world, and particularly the Middle East markets. (c) The USA also sought to impose its policy of confrontation with the USSR on its European and Japanese allies, in such a way that much greater conflict was created within the whole alliance. The USA stood to lose much less by pressure on the economies of the Soviet bloc: its total exports to Comecon in 1980 ran at $4 billion (80 per cent of it food), compared to $23 billion for the European states. But this attempt to lessen economic ties with the east also reflected the special ideological importance of boycotts in US foreign policy.[18] (d) The relative loss of the previous US economic supremacy led to a reluctance by the USA to continue its previous level of defence expenditures: the European share of NATO expenditures rose from 22.7 per cent in 1969 to 41.6 per cent in 1979, but the USA was still spending over 5 per cent of its GNP on arms as compared to a European average of around 3.5 per cent. Japan on the other hand was said by US sources to be spending only 0.9 per cent of its GNP on military expenditures, one-sixth the level in the USA: the real

---

[17.] A comprehensive if somewhat indulgent analysis of the relationship between east-west and west-west conflict is given in *Western Security: What has changed? What should be done?*, Karl Kaiser, Winston Lord, Thierry de Montbrial, David Watt, London, Royal Institute of International Affairs, 1981. See also 'The Decline of US Power', *Business Week*, 12 March 1979.

[18.] 'East-West Trade: An end to business as usual', *The Economist*, 22 May 1982.

figure was probably nearer 2 per cent of GNP but this was still well below other states. The Japanese reluctance to rearm had been accepted by previous US administrations but had by the late 1970s come under considerable attack in retribution for Japanese inroads into US markets. (e) Beyond encouraging burden-sharing in the realm of defence, the Second Cold War served to inject an element of tutelage into all inter capitalist relations, an unquantifiable but definite sense that the state which has ultimate military responsibility should be accorded economic and other political concessions. For despite the increased financial contribution of the European states to NATO, the USA's military preponderance within the alliance has, as already noted, if anything increased: this is true both in the realm of strategic nuclear weapons, and in that of third world intervention capability. The growing emphasis upon a US military presence in the Middle East is expected in part to serve to remind the Europeans of what state ultimately guarantees their interests; even where the Europeans are encouraged to play a role, in the RDF or the Sinai peace-keeping force, this is in a position subordinate to the USA and as a guarantee that these Europeans will not take advantage of US failures to reap benefits for themselves. (f) The erosion of US power in the 1970s has produced a new awareness of the link between military and economic strength. The planners of the postwar settlement were conscious of the importance of economic policy and saw it as a means of weakening British influence. During the later 1950s and 1960s there was an assumption that US policy rested upon a secure economic foundation: Kennedy once said that he was more worried about the decline of the dollar than about nuclear war. But at that time US superiority in both spheres was unchallenged and throughout the subsequent years US foreign policy makers devoted little attention to economic matters. The two were institutionally separated: when Nixon announced the devaluation of August 1971 the decision was taken without anyone from the State Department or the National Security Adviser Kissinger being present. Indeed Kissinger was so ignorant of the issues involved that he went for after-hours instruction to the British ambassador, Lord Cromer, a former governor of the Bank of England.[19] The very divorce of economic and military power paved the way later in the 1970s for the idealistic nostalgia in which US strategists tended to indulge, whereby all problems

---

19. Mayer, p. 175.

of global order could be solved by an assertion of military strength alone. But despite the militaristic note struck by the Reagan Administration, a much sharper understanding of the need for economic strength could be detected in both its policies and those of the Carter Administration. Indeed Reagan spokesmen stressed that economic recovery was an even more important condition for renewed US strength than military expansion. The conclusion could, however, only be that if such an economic revival was so essential it would be necessary to prosecute the US case vis-à-vis its rivals even more vigorously, as a means of contributing to the buildup of US power. If inter-imperialist contradictions were in part responsible for generating Cold War II, the latter for its part served to sharpen these conflicts.

Strong as they might be, these inter-imperialist contradictions have remained within certain bounds. As already noted, there is little prospect of any major capitalist state so breaking with the USA that it forms an alliance with the USSR of the kind that China formed with the west in the 1970s. The era of major inter-imperialist wars, i.e. wars between advanced capitalist states, ended in 1945, when the conflict between the capitalist and post-capitalist states became the primary contradiction in world politics. The one inter-capitalist war involving an advanced capitalist country—the Falklands war of April-June 1982—was an anomaly, which rallied the suport of all major capitalist powers to the side of their colleague, Britain, and demonstrated the relative unity of these states in matters geopolitical. For all the rhetoric on trade and currency rivalry, this economic inter-imperialist conflict finds relatively little reflection in politics and strategy. So, while the international tensions between capitalist states had an important ideological and economic role in the generation of the Second Cold War, they cannot on their own explain it.

Rise of the Third World Capitalist Economies

The challenge of third world capitalism has taken two distinct forms —OPEC, with its financial power, and the growth of the Newly Industrialising Countries, or NICs, with their productive power. Whilst both developments represent a considerable strengthening of the world capitalist system as a whole, the tensions produced by the relative advance of these states vis-à-vis more traditionally established producers have provoked a drive to reassert the hegemony of the latter.

OPEC was founded in 1960 as a group of producing states intent on halting the decline in the price of oil. For a decade it was powerless; but in 1971, at the instigation of Libya, it began to raise the price per barrel very slightly, from $1.41 to 1.79. The first great advance, Oil Shock I, came in 1973, coincident with the Arab-Israeli war of October; the price rose from an August 1973 figure of $2.55 to a January 1974 level of $8.32. Over the next five years it rose only slowly, keeping pace with inflation to reach $13.34 in January 1979. But the Iranian revolution, which subtracted Iran's output from the world supply, followed by the Iran-Iraq war of September 1980, opened the way for a much greater rise, Oil Shock II. This brought the price to a January 1981 figure of $32, and to spot market rates of up to $40 a barrel in some weeks.

The challenge of OPEC was in the first instance to the oil companies, as determinants of the price; but this loss of oil company power at the point of production was compensated for by a great increase in profitability, resulting form the higher prices and the fact that other sources, in Europe and North America, were now made profitable for the first time. Between 1972 and 1979 the profits of the five major US oil companies rose by an average of 200 per cent. BP's net profit rose almost nine times between 1975 and 1980.[20] The companies were able to use profits from the oil sector to diversify into other energy activities: 40 per cent of US coal output and 55 per cent of US uranium reserves are controlled by oil companies. If the major oil companies suffered at all through the OPEC increases, it was rather because of the rise of other 'independent' oil producing enterprises who used the boom to prize open markets for their supplies. The more important consequencs of OPEC lay elsewhere, however: in the higher oil prices as experienced by consumers, i.e. in the political effect at the popular level in the advanced capitalist countries, and in the demonstration of financial power by a group of third world raw material producers, i.e. in the impact of the rises on strategic planners in the advanced capitalist states.

The claim that OPEC was uniquely responsible for the inflation and recession of the 1970s is without foundation: consumer price inflation had already affected the major industrialised economies by 1971 as a

---

[20.] *The Economist*, 26 December 1981.

result in part of the generalised commodity boom of this period, and the decline in productive investment which underlay the recession had begun in the late 1960s. OPEC rises certainly contributed to the inflation of the later years, but it is evident that they played a far less important part than myth would have it: the difference between Germany, which imported all its oil and had a low inflation rate, and Britian, which imported little but had high inflation, suggests that other international factors as well as factors internal to the economic structures of the country concerned were dominant: their respective annual inflation rates in the period 1970–81 were 5.2 per cent and 13.5 per cent.[21] The political effect of the OPEC rises coming together with a recession was however to fuel populist hostility to the producer states, to 'Arabs', 'sheikhs' and so forth. Indeed the ideological response was a nationalistic and often racist one, of blaming these alien scapegoats for the recession in the advanced countries and for the economic problems of the third world. If the most palpable index of the crisis of capitalist hegemony in the late 1970s was inflation, and if oil was blamed for the crisis, then it was above all through this means, through the price of energy at the garage pump and through the domestic heating bill, that the mobilisation of a new hostility to the third world was generated. It was far easier to hate rich people than poor ones, and especially easy to hate Arabs. The purchases of property and investment in the USA by Arab interests were treated in a spectacular nationalist manner. The OPEC states' pricing policies had nothing to do with Moscow, yet their action seemed part of a wider conspiracy. When the US hostages were seized in Tehran in 1979 it appeared as if the composite third world demon had at last materialised in full view.

The response at government and corporate levels to OPEC was less overt but more practical. US administrations and their European allies urged moderation on OPEC and encouraged the Saudis in particular to hold down the price of oil. But at the same time, through such coordinating bodies as NATO and the OECD, other less amicable measures were also taken. US politicians began to remind their audiences of the military power of the USA and of its ability, if necessary, to intervene in the Gulf. *The Economist* told its readers that in a world of lions and gazelles the Gulf states were gazelles: 'The growl that the lion might emit to the gazelle could at first be a suggestion that protection might be

---

[21.]*Sunday Times,* 30 May 1982.

withdrawn; then it might be elevated into a hint that coups might be supported on a different side (especially as nominally left-wing Arab politicians are often most especially venal) long before anybody would talk of another Suez operation 1956-style (although, in a western world that was really starved of oil, a Suez operation could be immensely popular).'[22]

The second response was to lessen dependence on OPEC oil: whilst Nixon's plan for energy independence was unrealistic, and whilst Carter failed to get his energy measures through Congress without almost complete loss of content, strategic stockpiles were built up and the International Energy Agency was founded in 1976 at Kissinger's instigation to co-ordinate a counter-OPEC policy. Non-OPEC states were encouraged to produce more. By 1981, the results of this quiet anti-OPEC policy were evident. OPEC's share of non-communist oil production fell from 65 per cent in 1973, to 62 per cent in 1979 and 35 per cent in 1982. US oil imports from the Gulf had gone from 2 million barrels a day to under one million. It was anticipated that by 1983 there would be no OPEC surpluses at all. Both these responses—the military and the economic—were evident from 1974, i.e. long before the political crises in the Persian Gulf which generated the Carter Doctrine. Schlesinger and Kissinger were threatening force against the Gulf from that time onwards, and Administration plans to expand facilities on the Indian Ocean island of Diego Garcia were drawn up in 1973. It was therefore an inter-capitalist contradiction, the challenge of OPEC, not the Iranian, Ethiopian or Afghan revolutions, which laid the groundwork for a new US interventionist capability in the Gulf region: in the very year of 1973 when the tenacious guerrilla forces in Vietnam had apparently forced the USA to withdraw its troops from the Asian mainland, the oil-producers of the Middle East were posing a different and in some ways equally threatening challenge to which the US adminstration responded by preparing new interventionist initiatives.[23]

The oil states' new position within the international capitalist system has rested upon geological accident, and upon the increased demand of the advanced states for oil. These states did not produce the wealth they

---

[22] *The Economist*, 17 November 1973.

[23] Marwan Buheiry, *US Threats of Intervention Against Arab Oil: 1973-1979,* Institute for Palestine Studies, Beirut 1980; Michael Klare, *Beyond the 'Vietnam Sydrome',* Chapter Three.

enjoyed: they were to all intents and purposes rentiers, living off a surplus transferred to them from the advanced capitalist countries, who could bear to pay, and the poor ones, who could not. Their own capacity to increase domestic production of other goods and services was extremely limited. The rise of the NICs was, by contrast, a challenge to the market shares of the major industrial producing countries and was the more remarkable because it occurred during the slump of the 1970s. In the period 1970–8 when industrial output in the advanced capitalist countries rose by 3.3 per cent per annum, the industrial output of the third world as a whole rose by 8.6 per cent per annum, while that of nine NICs rose by an annual rate of 15 per cent.[24] With all the accompanying distortions and other qualifications that can be noted, this burst of capitalist industrialisation was a striking development which posed a challenge both to the revolutionary states of the third world, whose economic records were rarely comparable, and to the developed capitalist countries, who saw goods being produced more cheaply and often with higher quality in the third world. In such products as textiles, footwear and shipbuilding the rise of third world output led to calls for protectionism: again the challenge from third world capitalist states was more directly felt and more immediately threatening than that from revolutionary states. The prospects were that in the 1980s the challenge of the NICs would be extended to high technology electronic goods.[25] This pressure by the NICs found its reflection in a harder official policy: as the US representative at a Latin American economic conference, John Bushnell, told delegates in May 1981, 'opinion makers in the United States have, in general, lost all interest in the old sterile debates on multinationals and the new (or old) economic order'.[26] The Cancún Conference of October 1981, called to co-ordinate a response to the demand of the poorer states, achieved nothing.

The USA had from 1974 onwards an overall deficit in manufacturing trade with the NICs and the challenge came in particular from five countries who accounted for 61 per cent of US imports from the third world in

---

[24.] Anthony Edwards, *The New Industrial Countries and Their Impact on Western Manufacturing*, Economist Intelligence Unit, London 1979, p. 9. The nine countries in question were: Hong Kong, Taiwan, South Korea, Spain, Mexico, Singapore, Yugoslavia, Brazil and Portugal.

[25.] *International Herald Tribune,* 25 August 1982.

[26.] *Le Monde*, 19 May 1981.

1981: Mexico, Taiwan, South Korea, Hong Kong and Brazil.[27] Their competition was particularly felt in steel, shipbuilding and textiles and in April 1981 new tariffs were imposed on some of their products. The strict challenge, felt by individual labour forces and enterprises, was a partial one: OECD countries as a whole benefited from the increased demand for their exports in third world countries.[28] The sectoral reverses were offset by the political advantages which this growth of capitalism reflected: many of the regimes presiding over such industrialisation were authoritarian right-wing governments who supported Cold War strategies and purchased large quantities of US arms. But what was beneficial to the macroeconomic and military-strategic interests of the west was perceived elsewhere in the USA as another erosion of US power to which the nationalism of the Cold War and the protectionism associated with it were a response.

The linkage between increasing economic contact with the third world and the need to preserve friendly capitalist regimes was evident in other respects. The third world was increasingly important as a source of repatriated profits for US companies. Most US foreign investment continued to go to developed capitalist countries. It was mistaken to see the prosperity of US capitalism as resting primarily upon the control of enterprises in the third world: but as a source of profits this latter source was by no means as negligible as it had been two decades before. US trade with the third world was equally significant: exports at $89 billion in 1981 were more than those to western Europe and Japan, and developing states bought almost 40% of all US manufactured exports.[29] On the other hand, the US financial community found itself involved in less easily managed operations in the third world where strategic and strictly economic considerations overlapped, namely through loans to right-wing governments. The mounting debt of such states as Turkey, Zaire and Brazil, who could not easily afford to meet their repayment schedules, emphasised the dangers for the US business community of these third

---

[27.] *The Economist,* 4 April 1981.

[28.] In 1977 manufactured exports from NICs to industrialised capitalist countries were still only two thirds of western manufactured exports to the NICs, giving the industrialised countries a surplus of $17bn. However, this margin was closing, and most of its was made up by a $10.4 billion Japanese surplus (Edwards, pp. 86-7).

[29.] *International Herald Tribune,* 19 October 1982.

world capitalist countries.[30] The defaulting of Mexico in August 1982 underscored these risks. For both these latter reasons—repatriated profits and government debt—the business community had an added interest in ensuring that the US maintained influence in these states and the ability to intervene where necessary to preserve that influence.

The Scare Over Strategic Resources

If the rise of OPEC and the increasing indebtedness of third world governments and private enterprises provided some reason for alarm about the increased links between advanced and third world capitalist states, this unease was greatly increased by a more general concern about the growing reliance of the US and other economies upon third world raw materials.[31] Whilst this was to some degree part of the concern about the rise of third world capitalist rivals, it is analytically distinct because of its special relation to military planning and deployment. It was stimulated in particular by two fears that received widespread diffusion in the late 1970s and which were used to legitimise an increased US intervetion capability: that the resources were not only finite but imminently exhaustible, and that the Soviet Union might be able to interrupt western access to these sources of supply during a war or as a preliminary to it.

Resource scares have served in the past to mobilise public and government opinion in the USA: they are in this respect a civilian equivalent of the missile gaps periodically invoked to justify increased military expenditure. Yet this new spate of alarmism has been particularly potent because of a number of convergent developments in the 1970s. Oil has provided the greatest boost: it is perceived as an issue by all consumers and it has signalled the apparent end of US economic self-sufficiency. In its political-psychological impact the growing US reliance on imported oil, to the point where this makes up half of US consumption, has been compared to the end of food self-sufficiency in Britain in the 1870s.

The impact of resource reliance takes a number of forms. First there is a 'national security' component: the fact that during the past two

---

[30.] From 1970 to 1980 medium and long-term loans to third world countries went from $60 billion to $450 billion, the chief borrowers being Brazil, Mexico and South Korea (Lewis and Allison, p. 120).
[31.] Michael Klare, *Beyond the 'Vietnam Syndrome'*, Chapter IV, Washington, Institute for Policy Studies, 1981, contains a succinct account of the development of this issue, on which I have drawn heavily.

decades the USA has become dependent on imports for certain minerals and metals which are vital to industrial and military power. Although three-year stockpiles of these are supposed to have been created, most are well below their prescribed limits. Among these raw materials are chromium ore, used in weapons alloys and tanks, 91 per cent of which is imported; cobalt, used in jet aircraft, 93 per cent of which is imported; 97 per cent of manganese, vital in steel production; 53 per cent of antimony, used in bullets and cannon shells; and over 50 per cent of tin, zinc and nickel.[32] A second component of the resource scare is speculation: as a result of great expansion over the past decade, international commodity markets turn over above $50 billions each year and have remained under the control of a few specialist companies.[33] The focus here has been on 'strategics', the minerals and metals used in military production, the trade in which has expanded over three times in the 1970s. The interest of these specialist firms is to promote the idea that their commodities are both scarce and vital to the US national interest, and other producers, notably South Africa, contribute to this alarm. US companies are also concerned by the erosion of their competitive position since the 1960s: by the nationalisations of oil and copper in the third world, and by the rise of new resource enterprises in Australia and Canada controlled by non-US firms. These companies form a common front with the promoters of 'national security' to foster alarm about 'strategics'.[34]

The third component of this scare is ecology. The ecologists are justified in their emphasis upon the dangers of atomic energy, the spread of pollution and the incidence of famine in the world. The depletion of the world's forests by capitalist enterprises is a very grave development. But the ecologists have contributed their own mite of ideology to the military and speculative determinants of the resource scare. Whilst politically quite distinct from these other forces, the ecological movement in the USA and Europe has reinforced the belief that the world is faced with imminent raw material depletion and dangerous scarcity: mixed

---

[32] Klare, p. 55, contains a listing of US import dependence, as does International Institute for Strategic Studies, *Strategic Survey 1981-1982*, p 44.
[33] James Ridgeway, 'The Play in Strategic Metals', *Metals Daily*, 15 October 1980; Richard Barnet, *The Lean Years,* London 1980, pp. 119-21; *Business Week,* 12 October 1981.
[34] Michael Shafer, 'Mineral Myths',*Foreign Policy*, no. 47, Summer 1982.

as it often is with a generalised hostility to the achievements of industrialisation, this romanticism so confuses the issues involved that it ends up by reinforcing the anxieties promoted on the right. The doomsday ideology and philosophic pessimism which are sometimes involved in the peace movement serve not to mobilise for purposive action against the Cold War, but rather to confirm the rationale of those who are promoting it.

The fourth, and *least* important, component of the scare is material reality itself. Whilst raw materials are of necessity wasting assets, there is little to confirm the generalised pessimism with which this issue is invested. Speculators know this rather too well, as, with the exception of oil, raw material commodity prices have been steadily declining since the early 1970s. Moreover, developments in exploration and excavation have as a whole lengthened the gap between resource availability and demand. The figures for 'known reserves' are always contingent and manipulated, since exploration is itself a function of demand; far more significant is the 'resource base', the volume of any raw material calculated to be in the earth. For non-fuel minerals life expectancies range from two hundred to five hundred years, if consumption continues to rise at 5 per cent per annum. If present consumption levels were sustained, the resources of the main non-fuel minerals—aluminium, copper, iron and nickel—would last for millions of years. The real problem lies in the domain of fossil fuels: at present consumption levels, oil will last for another hundred years, gas for 180, coal for much longer.[35] These limits require the development of other fuel and energy sources: but the situation is not as dire as much public discourse would indicate, and by the 1990s oil may make up a much smaller percentage of world energy supplies.

The combination of these four elements—national security, speculation, ecology, material fact—has produced the spectre of the 'resource war', the attempt by the USA's allies to cripple it by attacking its supplies. As with the Soviet 'superiority' in military power it is a theme not based wholly on imagination. But it is rather a distorted mobilisatory construct using certain real developments to legitimate a preconceived political end, in this case increased military appropriations for the US armed forces. The link between the ideology of the resource shortage and the New

---

[35.] Michael Tanzer, *The Race for Resources*, London 1980, pp. 38-9.

Cold War is then made in several ways. First, the general picture of competition for resources is used to stress US vulnerability, whether these resource wars are between east and west, west and south or advanced capitalist countries and third world revolutions. The very real prospects of famine in the third world are used not to induce compensatory food programmes but to heighten the sense of strategic alarm. Secondly, the vulnerability is indicated by pointing to the geographical location of the key resources, to the political problems associated with extraction and transport: the world's oil reserves are disproportionately located in the Persian Gulf, an area of great instability near the USSR; the greatest concentration of non-fuel fossils in the third world is to be found in what the geologists call 'High Africa', i.e. South Africa, Namibia, Angola, Zimbabwe and Zaire, a region producing uranium, chrome, diamonds, gold and cobalt.[36] No theory of international politics can rest upon a simple economism: but the dissonance of raw material supply and political stability evident in these two regions is a major concern to US strategists. The increased US military presence in the Arabian Peninsula region and the concern to harass Angola owe a lot to this material determination. This concern is accentuated by transport problems and by the prospect of interruption in time of war: the majority of the Gulf's oil passes round the South African Cape, so that a naval capability in this region is seen as a double raw material insurance.

The most vital link between the resource scare and the Second Cold War is provided by the place allotted to the USSR in this gloomy prospect. The Soviet Union is seen by western strategists as positioning itself to deny the west access to vital raw materials, by acquiring allies near the Gulf and High Africa. The USSR is also a major producer of gold, gas, chrome, manganese and titanium: it is said to be promoting a potentially fatal reliance of the west upon continued Soviet supplies. At the same time, the USSR is presented as being itself in quest of raw materials, purchasing grain and soon oil. It is therefore an increasingly desperate rival in international markets for those same commodities so needed in the west. This argument is one of the most confused of all those used to promote the Second Cold War: once again, it uses a Soviet threat as a means of legitimising a new US drive for hegemony.

[36.] Barnet, pp. 124-5.

First of all, it is true that the USSR is in a position to interdict or deny the west raw material supplies in the event of world war and it can be assumed that it would seek to do so if such a conflict broke out. The west would seek to blockade the USSR's sea and air communications as well. Whether such blockading would play the role in a short nuclear war that it did in the year-long world wars earlier in the century is debatable. But short of war the prospect is rather different. Through the past sixty years of east-west conflict it has been the west and in particular the USA which has used economic power as a means of putting pressure upon the USSR and the third world, not the other way around. The Russians know that to interrupt western access to oil from the Persian Gulf would be a cause of war, and unless such a war breaks out they are not going to attempt to do it. Indeed the Russians have a long record of maintaining economic ties to countries where political dictates might have suggested they desist: aiding the German state with wheat between the World Wars, supplying oil to Italy during the invasion of Ethiopia in 1936, giving aid to Turkey, a NATO state, and trading with the rulers of monarchist Iran and Morocco, not to mention collaborating with South Africa in arranging the world gold and diamond markets. The cases where the USSR has used economic pressure have been against other communist states— Yugoslavia, China, and Albania. In cases where interruptions have occurred in east-west trade it has been at the initiative of the west: the boycott of Cuban sugar and nickel after 1960 is a case in point. It is the USA which throughout its modern history has sought to use economic aid, and food, as instruments of political pressure upon the USSR, from the postwar manipulation of the Marshall Aid offer through the boycott of China and the blockade of Cuba to the 1980 boycott over Afghanistan and the sanctions imposed over Poland in 1981. The Reagan Administration has undertaken fresh studies to see how the US government can use its economic power to boost Washington's influence both over the east and in the third world. The use of trade and finance as means of pressure is a specialism of US foreign policy, against both capitalist and post-capitalist states.

A second distortion arises in this argument because of the ambiguity of the USSR's supposed relation to the raw material markets: at one moment the danger is said to be Soviet shortages, i.e. Soviet competition for world supplies, at another it is deemed to be the Soviet ability to export. Both are used to explain the motivations of Soviet foreign policy. The

Soviet shortages are said to be especially strong in the oil sector and the myth of a Soviet 'energy crisis' was promoted during the late 1970s as reason for assuming a Soviet drive to seize the Gulf. The generalised image of an economically weak and so more desperate Soviet Union is one widely held, on the left as well as in Cold War circles. It is untrue: the USSR is the only advanced industrial country that is self-sufficient in energy and indications are that it can remain so for years. The Soviet energy crisis has been shown to be an ideological fabrication[37]: a projection onto the USSR of problems internal to the west; and it has now been abandoned by those who first promoted it, the CIA. On the other hand, what is far more threatening is the opposite capacity, namely to supply international markets, and particularly Western Europe, with energy. This poses both a national security and an economic challenge to US interests; it is this fear, of the USSR as a source of energy supplies, which has underlain economic rivalry going back to the 1920s. In the interwar period the Soviet Union posed substantial competition to the oil monopolies, gaining around 15 per cent of world markets. After the war Soviet output increased considerably, as a result of Russia's pioneering new turbodrill techniques, more advanced than those available in the west. In 1960 the *New York Times* could write: 'Growing competition from Russian oil is casting a shadow over many of the markets of the free world that historically have been supplied by the international petroleum companies'.[38] The response was a series of boycotts against third world states that purchased Soviet crude for refining: Ceylon, India and most spectacularly Cuba. Indeed the break in US-Cuban relations in 1960 came when Havana decided to acquire Soviet oil at cheaper rates for its US-owned refinery.

In the 1970s this theme remained highly actual, even whilst others were using the supposed Soviet energy crisis for their cold war purposes. The prime target here had been a new Soviet-West European agreement under which gas would be piped to the west: whilst this agreement became a central issue in US-European relations during the Polish crisis of 1981–2, Poland served as a pretext for an intensification of US pressure that had been building up for a long time. As a result of this deal the EEC's dependence on gas from the USSR will rise from 9 per cent of its total

---

[37]. See Chapter Six, note 1.
[38]. Harvey O'Connor, *World Crisis in Oil*, London 1962, p. 390.

gas consumption to 19 per cent by 1990. Whilst opposed on the grounds
that it will give the USSR leverage over economies of Western Europe, the
agreement will threaten the position of US energy companies in a market
where, apart from France, they remain dominant. American coal interests have been particularly keen on blocking this challenge to their interests.[39] Yet the Germans, the main promoters of the agreement, may
remember that Stalin continued to supply food to Germany until the
very day of the 1941 invasion. The competition of the post-
revolutionary regimes in the world market is therefore far more as competitors in supply and as challengers to existing monopoly positions than
as exacerbators of resource shortages.

Increased Frequency of Inter-capitalist Wars

The three factors considered so far have involved the relationship between the Cold War and economic aspects of inter-capitalist conflict.
These aspects have been presented as aggravating an already existing
Cold War dynamic, that is, as encouraging a policy of confrontation with
the USSR, where such a confrontation is seen as providing a solution or at
least alleviation of the economic problems involved. There is, however, a
much more direct means by which inter-capitalist conflict can relate to
the Cold War, and this is probably the most ominous of all. If the danger
of war between the advanced capitalist states has receded since 1945,
that of conflict between capitalist states in the third world has greatly increased. This may produce situations in which conflict between third
world capitalist states itself embroils the great powers and thereby
generates the risk of local wars turning into nuclear ones.

The incidence of wars between third world capitalist states has been increasing with each decade since 1945, and, apart from the persistence of
existing conflicts, it seems probable that the factors underlying these will

---

[39.] A brief drawn up by the US State and Commerce Departments states: 'The United
States has attempted to convince its friends and allies that US coal represents an energy
source that is preferable to oil from instable Middle Eastern states, gas from the USSR or
coal from South Africa or Poland' (*International Herald Tribune*, 15 February 1982).
North America has 29 per cent of the world's recoverable coal reserves and provides 60
per cent of Europe's coal imports. However, if the USA were to be able to increase its coal
exports substantially, this would require large scale investment in port facilities on the
east coast (*The Economist*, 27 March 1982).

produce themselves in even more situations. The two classic third world conflict situations are the Israel-Arab and Indo-Pakistani disputes. The first wars broke out in the immediate postwar period: there have, in all, been five Arab-Israeli and three Indo-Pakistani wars, major confrontations by any standard. In addition to these there have been wars between Iran and Iraq, Tanzania and Uganda, Algeria and Morocco, Somalia and Ethiopia, Honduras and El Salvador, as well as the Turkish invasion of Cyprus, an indirect Turkish-Greek clash. There have also been many border confrontations which threatened to produce war: between Argentina and Chile, Peru and Ecuador, Libya and Egypt, Iraq and Syria, Pakistan and Afghanistan.

This increasing incidence of third-world wars involves the combination of two factors. On the one hand, there are the provision of arms by more developed societies seeking to derive financial profit by such supplies and the recruitment of these third world states into the alliance systems of the former.[40] On the other hand, there exist the increasing internal pressure for war from within the less developed states, born of rising nationalist sentiment, the diversionary use to which such wars can be put by insecure ruling groups, and the increased self-assertiveness of post-independence regimes. The ravages of the world recession have encouraged precisely those tensions within and between states that make wars more likely. Together this combination of external and internal factors suggests there will be not only continued wars in the third world, but also an increased risk that such conflicts will become internationalised; it is the tendency towards this internationalisation which is most dangerous for the world as a whole. The longer-established conflicts all exhibited such a tendency, whereby one state's alliance with the west led, whatever the internal social character of the other regime, to the latter's alliance with the USSR. Frequently such an alliance came only after the refusal by the west to arm the second local state: thus Egypt turned to the USSR in 1955, in its conflict with Israel; Afghanistan turned in the same direction after 1953 because of its dispute with Pakistan; Somalia became a military ally of the USSR's when the USA, committed to Ethiopia, declined to provide sufficient quantities of arms in the 1960s, and Ethiopia did so in 1977 when the USA cut off military supplies after the

---

[40.] For discussion of third world wars see Anthony Barnett, 'Iron Britannia', *New Left Review* 134, July-August 1982, Chapter V.

revolution which overthrew Emperor Haile Selassie, and began supporting Somalia.

So far, these third–world wars have not brought about direct great power conflict, but they have produced some of the tenser moments of postwar history and have yielded situations in which the threat of nuclear weapons has been made. The conflict areas of the third world are therefore the Balkans of today. During the 1956 Arab-Israeli war, in which Britain and France directly participated in support of Israel, Khrushchev threatened to launch rockets against London and Paris. During the 1967 and 1973 wars, the USA apparently believed that the USSR was considering the despatch of Soviet troops to the war zone, and it was during the 1973 conflict that Nixon ordered a world-wide nuclear alert by US forces to deter a supposed Soviet intervention in support of Egypt. During the 1977–8 Somali-Ethiopia war it was only intense US-Soviet diplomacy that prevented Ethiopia from counter-attacking into Somalia and thereby provoking a US intervention in support of Mogadishu. Fear of what a great power ally might do can act as a restraint on what a local enemy state does; but, by the same token, the more powerful allies, of east and west, can be drawn into situations where local conflicts have broken through into war.

This danger of internationalisation may go together with another problem, namely the increased likelihood of nuclear weapons being used in such contexts. This possibility arises in two situations: the use of nuclear weapons by an outside power, seeking to compensate for a local conventional weakness by using nuclear weapons, and the use of nuclear weapons by a local state that is facing defeat in a war with a neighbouring country. US government experts have on several occasions speculated on the possibility of using nuclear weapons in third world conflicts, and particularly in those of the Persian Gulf region.[41] The logic of first use in Europe, to offset a Soviet conventional superiority by battlefield nuclear weapons, applies even more in the regions south of the Soviet Union's Middle East frontier, where the conventional disadvantage would be much greater. The second possibility, of local states using nuclear weapons against their foes, has become much more likely as the limits on proliferation have broken down: both the technology and the materials

---

[41] Chris Paine, 'On the Beach: The Rapid Deployment Force and The nuclear Arms Race', *MERIP Reports*, no. 111, January 1983.

for manufacturing a nuclear weapon are within the reach of third world countries and there is no prospect that their present spread can be halted, let alone reversed. US intelligence experts estimate that by the year 2000 up to 31 nations will either have nuclear weapons or be able to produce them. Of the six states thought most capable of producing a nuclear weapon, four are locked in protracted regional conflicts: India, Pakistan, Israel and South Africa. The two others, Argentina and Brazil, are candidates for continental domination in their own region. Although both of the latter have signed the Treaty of Tlatelolco, banning nuclear weapons in Latin America, none have signed the Non-Proliferation Treaty of 1975. Other states, such as Taiwan, Iraq and Libya, may be further away from producing a bomb but could no doubt do so in the future, if their production processes are not interrupted by preventive attack from outside.[42] The use by an outside power of nuclear weapons may be more likely in cases of revolutionary conflict, but could also be envisaged as part of an intervention in inter-capitalist wars: if Saudi Arabia were attacked by Iran, the USA might resort to such supportive action. The possibility of a nuclear explosion in conjunction with an internationalised third world conflict involving east and west is, however, the more ominous, since it would draw in both sides into what could become, on the 1914 model, a global confrontation.

The pattern of capitalist development and conflict in the postwar era has therefore both abolished and restored the prospect of such inter-capitalist conflict bringing the world to catastrophe. It has abolished it in that the prospect of an allout war between major capitalist states, the kind of conflict that led to the outbreak of both the First and Second World Wars, is now a remote one. Whatever the extent of trade wars and diplomatic tensions they are unlikely to lead to military conflict between OECD states. Wars between first and third world capitalist states may occur, as happened over the Falklands in the spring of 1982: but these too are today unlikely to be protracted affairs. On the other hand, the persistence of inter-capitalist economic rivalries, produced in part by the very successes of capitalism in the postwar epoch, has reinforced the US search for a new Cold War discipline, just as the attempt to impose that discipline has aggravated intra-OECD relations.

[42.] *Strategic Survey 1981-1982*, pp. 111-15.

However, whilst the prospect of war between developed capitalist states has receded, that of war between third world capitalist countries has advanced, in a situation where these conflicts can be invested with both the strategic weight of east-west conflict and the destructive potential of nuclear weaponry. The continuation of the recession brings the danger of wars in the third world nearer. As with so many other artefacts of the advanced countries which they seek to export to the third world, the fundamental constituents of world politics have a new impact in the less developed countries. There the constraints of diplomacy and securely entrenched government may not apply.

8.
Retreat from Detente

The accumulation and interrelation of these five dimensions of world politics led to the onset of the Second Cold War of the early 1980s. The analysis of these factors shows that, as with any major historical development, Cold War II is the product of multiple contradictions, and that these have combined to determine east-west relations in a new international conjuncture: tempting as monocausal analyses may be, no single factor in the post-revolutionary or capitalist worlds can serve as an adequate explanatory device. Yet beyond stressing the multi-causal genesis of Cold War II, the analysis has also tried to suggest certain relationships between these causes, some hierarchy of determination that goes beyond the random assertion of several discrete influences. These relationships can be summarised as follows.

First the course of international politics is above all determined by the interaction of the global social conflict and the arms race. In practice, the arms race has become one of the dimensions through which the conflict of capitalism and communism is fought out, the others being economic competition between the blocs and the process of social and national upheaval in the third world. While both camps have sought to extend the social conflict to the home ground of their rivals, this has proved, as yet, to be a secondary factor in the global social conflict, compared to the arms race, economic rivalry and third world upheaval.

Secondly, the pattern of international conflict has been overlain by a series of developments internal to each bloc, which have in their own time and manner contributed to the emergence of the Second Cold War. These comprise the changes within us politics, the involution of the communist world, and the aggravated conflicts between western states. None of these is a primary cause of Cold War II, and each makes its own specific contribution: yet in conjunction with the accelerated arms race and the new wave of revolutions in the third world these internal processes must be counted amongst the major causes of the Second Cold War.

Thirdly both the USA and the USSR have made a contribution to Cold War II; but their contributions are identical neither in character nor in weight. Had the USSR accepted the US terms for Detente—military inferiority, third world abstention—then it is much less likely that relations would have deteriorated; had Soviet society and that of its eastern European allies evolved in a more democratic and prosperous manner then the west's ability to launch the Second Cold War would have been reduced. But the prime initiative lay in the west, and in particular with the USA, which reacted to the challenges of the 1970s by launching the Second Cold War. The bases of Soviet policy had been established in the 1960s, prior to Detente. It was in the USA, not in the USSR, that the sharp changes of mood and policy characteristic of the late 1970s can be seen. And it is the USA which then sought through the Cold War to reassert its dominance—over the USSR, its capitalist allies, and the third world.

This analytic account of Cold War II has involved the arrangement of historical events into thematic sections. What follows here is a more strictly chronological account beginning with the Nixon-Kissinger pursuit of Detente and ending with the Reagan victory of 1980. Because of the primary role played by US policy in the international politics of the 1970s, this account will focus on developments in Washington. Cold War II is above all else a US programme for waging the globalised social conflict, the Great Contest, a programme decided upon in the light of the failure of earlier strategies pursued with the same ends in sight.

The Republican Presidencies, 1969–1976

The policy aims of the Nixon-Ford period have been well articulated by Henry Kissinger, the President's National Security Adviser from 1969 to 1972 and then the Secretary of State throughout the remaining years of the Republican Administration. The foreign policy team who came to power in 1969 faced, in its eyes, four major problems and the strategy pursued was a multidimensional attempt to resolve all four. They were: the Vietnam war, the Soviet advance in strategic nuclear and conventional military capabilities, the weakened US economy, and rising domestic dissent.[1] To tackle these problems a set of policy goals was established: (1) to reach agreement with the USSR on limiting strategic nuclear weapons, and simultaneously to work for extension of existing US advantages in areas not covered by agreements; (2) to use the agreement on strategic weapons and on US-Soviet trade to disengage the Soviet Union from assisting its allies in the third world, and particularly in Vietnam—the policy of 'linkage';[2] (3) to withdraw from the direct involvement of US troops in Indo-China whilst securing the future of the South Vietnamese regime; (4) to pressure the USSR to assist an acceptable Indochina settlement by opening relations with China, offering Peking the enticements of trade and support against Moscow—whereas in the early 1960s US policy had sought to drive a wedge between Moscow and Peking by offering conciliation to the former and continued confrontation with the latter, the same division was now to be maintained by befriending China at Russia's expense; (5) to pursue negotiations with the USSR on European issues as a way of increasing pressure on the political fabric of Soviet and east European society.

This was therefore a comprehensive package designed to check the advances made by the Soviet Union and its allies—in the fields of nuclear weapons and in Vietnam—so as to preserve US interests. It was a programme for maintaining US superiority in which pressure upon the USSR, through China in the east and European negotiations in the west, was to be combined with inducements to Moscow to collaborate in recognising the US conditions for world peace. The policy programme was remarkable in several respects. First, it showed less concern for conventional anti-communism as far as dealings with Moscow and Peking were concerned. Nixon, despite his past, was quite willing to open relations with China and to toast Mao Tse-tung; his Presidency began only five months after what many saw as the most aggressive Soviet act since World War

---

[1] For a general overview see Walter LaFeber, *America, Russia and the Cold War, 1945-1980*, New York 1980; Tad Szulc, *The Illusion of Peace*, New York 1978; André Fontaine, *Un Seul Lit Pour Deux Rêves*, Paris 1981; Richard Barnet, *The Giants*, New York 1977. For Kissinger's interpretation see his *The White House Years*, New York 1979, covering the period 1969-72, and his *Years of Upheaval*, covering 1972-4. On Kissinger and Nixon's China policy see the shrewd analysis of John Gittings in *Superpowers in Collision*, p. 70-78.
[2] On linkage see *The White House Years*, pp. 129-30, and Marvin and Bernard Kalb, *Kissinger*, New York 1974, chapter six.

II, and the one most likely to prevent Detente, namely the Soviet invasion of Czechoslovakia. Even more striking was the fact that Nixon took these initiatives when for the first time since the Korean war US soldiers were being killed in large numbers by Soviet arms and with Soviet support in Indo-China; this was a situation that might have been expected to fuel the most virulent Cold War atmosphere in the USA.

Secondly, the Nixon-Kissinger strategy of Detente was a clear attempt to preserve US hegemony; this was never denied, whether such hegemony was over the USSR, the USA's allies, the third world or domestic dissidents. As Kissinger has explained it, SALT-I was designed to halt the race in the spheres of ICBMs and SLBMs at a time when the USA enjoyed a great advantage in warheads, and to give time for the development of other weapons systems not covered by the treaty—the Trident submarine, the MX missile, the B-1 bomber and the Cruise missile.[3] This meant that at its best Detente prepared the way for the means by which the USA would attain a new superiority. The development of these new weapons encountered some obstacles from within the USA at a time when opposition to the Vietnam war was at its height, and there were bureaucratic conflicts within the US state over priorities: but most of these programmes were implemented later, and in particular the Trident and Cruise. At the same time as the weapons systems were being introduced, new doctrines were being elaborated, most importantly the 'counterforce' doctrine of using increased missile accuracy to target military, i.e. 'force', sites in the enemy camp. First articulated in 1962, Kissinger had been advocating such a line of action since 1969; but it was enunciated as official policy by Secretary of Defense James Schlesinger only in 1974. In other words, at the height of Detente both the theory and the instruments for a new kind of nuclear warfare and for sustained US superiority were being developed.

This pursuit of a restored hegemony was duplicated in the economic field, where the Nixon measures of August 1971 were used to strengthen the dollar's position in international trade. It was even clearer in the third world, where new policies to offset the failure of the Vietnamese expedition were implemented. The Nixon Doctrine enunciated in July 1969 called for the delegation of military responsibility to third

---

[3.] Kissinger, *Years of Upheaval*, pp. 256-74.

world states; it suggested a new method of conducting counterrevolution in the third world, whether in Indo-China, where it ultimately failed, or in other parts of the world, where Iran, Brazil and Indonesia played their part and where, for a time, it succeeded. The USA expected the Soviet Union to desist from aiding its allies, but no such limitation was to be imposed on Washington. Indeed, the attempt to restrain Moscow and Peking from aiding the Vietnamese was coupled with the most ferocious bombing assaults of the war on North Vietnam, while in the Middle East the Shah was armed and encouraged to pursue a comprehensive regional policy of intervention.

The most eloquent instance of this one-sided interpretation of detente came in May 1972 when, on the very way back from signing the SALT-I agreement in Moscow, Nixon and Kissinger stopped over in Tehran. There, in a secret agreement, they pledged to back the Shah in his destabilisation of Iraq, a neighbouring state allied to the USSR. The purpose of the operation was to put pressure on the Iraqis to break their close ties with Moscow.[4] At the same time, in another part of the globe, the USA encouraged the Chilean army to prevent the Popular Unity government elected in 1970 from taking office and co-operated in political undermining of the government once it was in power.[5] Detente was a one-way street, designed to be to the Russians' disadvantage. As Bruce Cumings has shown, Washington sought to impose 'linkage' on the Russians whilst pursuing 'detachment' for itself.[6]

[4.] Szulc, p. 584.

[5.] There is as yet no evidence that the USA was directly involved in the execution of the 1973 coup against the Popular Unity government: there would not need to have been direct involvement, given the strength of the Chilean army, its backing from conservative social forces at home, and the weakness of the Allende government after months of harassment from the right. The USA was nonetheless implicated in the coup—it had tried to organise one in 1970, it had financed and encouraged the strikes by anti-government forces in 1972 and 1973, and it must through its intelligence sources have known in advance about the coup. In November 1970, i.e. even before Allende took office, Nixon and Kissinger had prepared a programme of economic warfare against Chile, embodied in National Security Decision Memorandum-93. This was designed to create economic conditions that would trigger a coup whilst the CIA maintained links with the military (Szulc, pp. 353 ff., 480 ff., 643.). Kissinger's protestations of innocence in his memoirs (*Years of Upheaval*, Chapter IX, especially p. 377) are not convincing. His observation of improved human rights under the junta is extraordinary—at least 15,000 people were slain by the military in the months after the coup, none by Allende's government.

[6.] Bruce Cumings, 'Chinatown: Foreign Policy and Elite Realignment', in *The Hidden Election*, p. 210; see also Richard Barnet, op. cit., p. 79.

The Nixon-Kissinger strategy had its successes. An agreement was reached with Vietnam and the peace accords were signed in January 1973, leading to the withdrawal of US forces later in the year. The opening to China was achieved with Nixon's visit in February 1972: this opened up a whole new area of potential vulnerability on Russia's eastern flank and stimulated the latent conflict between China and Vietnam. The SALT-I agreement was signed in May 1972 and passed by Congress. Discussions then continued for a second SALT treaty and preliminary agreement on some issues was reached when Ford met Brezhnev in Vladivostok in November 1974.[7]

The US position in the third world, apart from Indo-China, was not apparently threatened in the first years of the Republican Administration. In the Middle East, the USA received an unexpected victory when in 1972 Egypt expelled the Soviet military presence, the only substantial Soviet deployment outside the WTO, and after the 1973 war Kissinger was able to intervene as broker between Cairo and Tel Aviv, thus confirming the marginalisation of the USSR in the region. The 1973 Arab-Israeli war, seen by some conservative commentators as the first major breach of Detente by the USSR, was in fact the prelude to the greatest US triumph in the third world since the holocaust in Indonesia a decade before. By ousting the Soviet Union from Egypt, Washington, aided by the Saudis, deprived the USSR of its one significant set of air and sea bases in the third world. The Americans opened a period in which the Russians were denied any significant say in the diplomacy of the Arab world whose nationalist cause they alone sought to defend. Coincident with this triumph on the Nile, the Shah of Iran and Saudi Arabia were built up as the 'twin pillars' supporting western interests in the eastern region and particularly in the Persian Gulf.

In Africa it appeared that a placid decolonisation had taken place in the French and British colonies, whilst the Portuguese, Ian Smith and South Africa were holding their own in the south. In Latin America all guerrilla movements were defeated: the overthrow of Allende in

---

[7.] The Vladivostok Agreement was designed to come into force when SALT-I was no longer binding, i.e. from October 1977, and to last until December 1985. It was an agreement in principle on limiting the numbers of ICBMs and SLBMs. It recognised 'the principle of equality and equal security' and envisaged further negotiations, beginning no later than 1980-1, on a SALT-III Treaty to come into force in 1985.

September 1973 seemed to preclude the alternative path to change, through the ballot box.

US policy also met with successes in an area where less difficulty had initially been expected but where the 1970s presented new challenges, namely eastern and central Europe. One dimension of European policy was that of relations with the east, and on coming to office Nixon and Kissinger found themselves faced with the independent initiatives of West Germany. Ostpolitik, pioneered by Chancellor Willy Brandt in 1969 and 1970, promised to break down some barriers between eastern and western Europe and in so doing to lessen the dependence of each on the two major world powers. Brandt's visit to the German Democratic Republic and the signing of a Soviet–West German treaty in 1970 served, however, as the prelude to other arrangements in which the USA was directly involved and from which it derived benefit: the 1971 four power agreement on Berlin, which ended one of the original issues at stake in Cold War I, and the 1975 Helsinki Agreements, which brought the USA, Canada and thirty-three European states together to recognise the boundaries established in 1945. Whilst Ostpolitik and Helsinki brought benefits to the east, by somewhat relaxing tensions, they also provided new means for the west to wage ideological conflict against the communist countries. In addition, by the latter half of the 1970s the promise of a more independent German orientation had been abandoned in the pursuit by Helmut Schmidt, the German Chancellor, of the fateful NATO 'modernisation' that was to bind Bonn to Washington more tightly than ever before.

The Nixon–Kissinger Strategy Blocked

Yet the Nixon–Kissinger strategy was unable to meet all its goals and it was this failure which led to the alternative pursued under Carter. In fact, the failure of the Kissinger programme led to the emergence of two alternatives, one represented by Carter, and the other by the man who nearly secured the Republican nomination for Presidential candidate in 1976, Ronald Reagan. The Carter option was implemented first, and met its own nemesis; this then opened the way for the unchallenged execution of the alternative post-Kissinger policy which Reagan had been proposing from the mid-1970s onwards.

The most important weakness of the Nixon-Kissinger strategy was that although initially successful it ultimately failed to contain the challenges to US policy in the third world. Kissinger's approach had rested upon 'linkage', the belief first enunciated in 1969 according to which US willingness to negotiate with the USSR depended on Soviet 'behaviour' elsewhere in the world. In the periods of greater weakness lasting from 1945 through to the mid-sixties, the USSR had conceded this. Stalin had abandoned allies in Greece and Iran, and had tried to halt the advance of the Chinese communists. Khrushchev had not supported the Vietnamese in the early 1960s. But under Brezhnev the Russians had rejected 'linkage', both in the mild sense that they should refrain from aiding their allies, and in the stronger sense that they should intervene to prevent their allies from pressing the advantage when this became possible.

In Vietnam, the NLF and North Vietnamese authorities did sign the accords of 1972, which permitted the US-backed government to remain in Saigon. But when Thieu broke these accords in 1973 and 1974, the Vietnamese revolutionaries decided to take the initiative and in 1975 completed the reunification of their country. This was of course the aim which they had always set themselves; but Thieu's violation of the agreements between them, combined with the US's inability to intervene, opened the door to this final push for victory. Although fought out on the ground in Vietnam, the final outcome owed much to the international balance of forces at the time. Washington was paralysed by the aftermath of Watergate which made it impossible for the Administration to intervene directly. And this offensive was also reliant on Soviet aid: some of the weaponry used by the Vietnamese in the final assault had been captured from the Americans, but a significant portion had also been supplied by the USSR in 1974, and without Soviet aid it is doubtful if that victory would have occurred.

The conclusion victories in Laos and Cambodia coincided with this, as did, later in the year, the transfers of power in Africa to the groups that had been opposing Portuguese rule in the five countries then granted independence. The Angolan episode illustrated the lesson of the US role in Iraq: with an eye on what might happen when the Portuguese pulled out, Kissinger encouraged the CIA to give support to the pro-western UNITA and FNLA guerrillas in 1974. The Soviet Union had previously suspended aid to the MPLA, but once CIA aid began to flow the Russians and Cubans restarted support. In the end the Cuban forces intervened to support the MPLA against the right-wing guerrillas backed by Zaire, South Africa and the CIA. For Kissinger, this was perhaps the most important disappointment: he had expected the USSR to restrain its allies and its own activity, whilst allowing the USA to take its initiatives as in Egypt, Iraq, and Chile. No one had expected Cuba, apparently confined in the Caribbean by the failure of Latin American revolutions, to avenge Chile by such a daring intervention in Africa. Linkage had failed: it assumed a stability and degree of metropolitan control no longer possible in the third world, and it pre-supposed that the USSR would abandon any global role in return for the paragraphs of SALT-I and the benefits of US-Soviet trade. The key defeat was that of Vietnam, for the whole prestige and strategy of the USA in the third world had relied upon a successful, and in US terms 'honourable', solution in Saigon. Combined with the fall of other US-backed governments, and with Watergate, it destroyed the premises upon which Detente rested.

The early 1970s strategy failed in another area, one which Kissinger had hoped to ignore, namely that of economics. The Metternichian world view paid little attention to such matters as productivity and currency rates: as already noted, Kissinger had to receive instruction from a scion of British imperialism in these matters. His memoirs indicate the most reluctant interest in them. Yet economic pressures upon the USA grew in the 1970s despite the reduction of some US difficulties after the winding down of the intervention in Vietnam. One new problem was the rise of the OPEC states, whose manipulation of the oil price issue was only made possible by the increased US demand for oil. Of equal seriousness was the growing strength of Europe and Japan, both of which were as interested in Detente as was the USA. They resented the arbitrary nationalism that characterised Nixon's approach to international monetary matters, and even more so the brash style with which decisions were taken by the Secretary of the Treasury John Connally. With SALT-I settled and Vietnam apparently contained, Kissinger did proclaim 1973 the 'Year of Europe': but he could neither comprehend nor respond to the broader changes which were undermining US hegemony throughout the period of Detente.

Europe was the site of another failure in the Republican strategy, namely that which underlay the Berlin and Helsinki accords. The hope that such agreements could be used to influence the political systems of eastern Europe and the USSR proved to be mistaken. It is not clear how far the Republican leaders really believed in this possibility, but it was certainly one which they encouraged others to entertain at this time. Agreements were adhered to by the eastern bloc states where they concerned strategic and international issues; but the ruling parties east of the Elbe had no intention of diluting their domestic power in the name of Detente, or in return for arms agreements. Nor did the USSR simply halt its arms programmes as a result of SALT-I: it adhered to the limits imposed by the agreement, but expenditure continued to rise, steadily as it had done before SALT, and the Soviet Union sustained that technological progress which had been in train since the middle 1960s. In the USA Kissinger's critics alleged that he 'oversold' Detente, by implying that other linked issues would be resolved by SALT-I. But these illusions, fostered by Kissinger, were ones designed not to indulge the USSR, but merely to find the most convenient means then available for arresting the erosion of US power: his failure reflected the misconceptions of an offensive strategy, not unwarranted conciliation.

If Kissinger had made incorrect assumptions about the stability of the third world, and the ductility of Soviet policies, he had also believed that the politics of the NATO countries and of the USA would conform to expectations. In fact, after the 'Year of Europe', the European political balance was challenged by the Portuguese revolution of April 1974, the fall of the junta in Greece in July 1974, and the death of Franco in November 1975. Meanwhile in Italy and France the communist parties were apparently gaining ground, and it was widely believed that they could, in the foreseeable future, gain positions in coalition governments. This development encompassed more than 'Eurocommunism', a significant force in only Italy and Spain, and it appeared that the postwar stabilisation of western Europe upon which US strategy had relied was now in jeopardy. Ironically it was the Soviet invasion of Czechoslovakia in 1968, an event which Nixon and Kissinger were able happily to swallow, which had provoked the new independence and popularity of the Eurocommunist parties.

In the longer run, the changes in Portugal, Spain and Greece were not such as to weaken the hold of capitalism in Europe. Indeed, relatively stable parliamentary regimes emerged in all three countries, and as examples of political democracy these states were far more convenient allies of both the USA and the EEC than had been the fascist regimes that preceded them. The successful transition from dictatorship to capitalist democracy in these states must count as one of the great successes of the west in the 1970s, and was a gain which made it all the easier to fight the Second Cold War on the ideological terrain of freedom versus dictatorship. But this deeper trend was not evident in 1975 and 1976: then it appeared to Washington as if the fall of these southern fascisms had opened the door for a left-wing advance in Europe comparable to the victories of Indo-China and Africa.[8]

Even within the USA the programme of restabilisation did not succeed as hoped, and Kissinger, in characteristic overstatement, described his years in office as ones of 'near civil war'. The momentum for withdrawal from Indo-China had in part been designed to curb the domestic dissent it had generated: yet the 1972 accords were only partially successful in this. Whilst the protests on the streets died down, Congressional doves continued to oppose Nixon's more militaristic policies, and the newly emergent hawks were also on the move, winning their first major victory with the Jackson-Vanik Amendment of 1974 that linked US trade with Russia to the emigration of Soviet Jews. Moreover, the sense of self-imposed siege and Presidential paranoia of the Vietnam war period itself was to lead, with a lag of two years, to the internal crisis that reduced the executive's power further than anything that had preceded it, namely Watergate. The effect of this was to produce a general discrediting of the US executive which affected foreign as well as domestic policy. The anodyne approach of the Ford interregnum did something to staunch the loss of Presidential power; but the authority of the chief executive, essential for the pursuit of any consistent foreign policy, was far weaker when the Republicans were voted out of office in November 1976, than it had been when Johnson left office in the wake of the 1968 anti-war demonstrations.

By the time of the 1976 elections two alternatives for a global US strategy were already in evidence. Team-B, the Committee on the Present Danger and the other elements of the Republican right were calling then for a new Cold War. Kissinger stated publicly in the course of 1976 that he no longer used the word 'Detente': Angola was the reason he most frequently gave. Ford suspended talks on SALT-II in the runup to the election. Yet the domestic preconditions for a full-blooded Second Cold War Presidency were not yet mature. Vietnam was too recent, Watergate made a hardline Presidency inoperable, the New Right activists had not gained sufficient momentum. The alternative was to pursue a less

---

[8.] Henry Kissinger, *For the Record*, New York 1981, pp. 1-22, gives the text of an analysis he made in 1977 stressing the dangers of Eurocommunism.

overt restorationist policy, one that preserved Detente and postponed military expenditure, but which chose to counter-attack against the USSR on the ideological and political fronts, while consolidating a domestic consensus. This second option was as much as the first designed to reverse the trends of the previous decade. It was embodied in the person of the rather quixotic former Governor of Georgia, James Earle Carter.

The Carter Years, 1977–1980

Carter's policies rested upon a studied ambivalence, of liberalism and anti-communism, of traditional east-coast strategic management and a new southern approach, of conciliation and belligerency. While he presented himself as a man of peace, he reserved his greatest admiration among former Presidents for Harry Truman, the man who had launched Cold War I. In the 1976 election he criticised both the military emphases of his predecessors *and* the concessions made by Ford at Helsinki and in the Vladivostok memorandum on SALT-II. The expectation was that this studied ambivalence could be maintained, each part of it bringing advantage to the USA. If this did not succeed, then one or other side of the policy would have to prevail. Under the circumstances, there was little possibility of the more liberal and conciliatory element prevailing: and so it was that, in the latter half of his Presidency, Carter ushered in the Second Cold War. Watergate and the lingering effects of Vietnam may have postponed the new Cold War, but Carter's Presidency marked the transition to a greater militancy in US politics, a shift which itself prepared the way for the policy of the Reagan Administration. Carter was, as two British writers on the USA have pointed out, the first President in modern times to govern more conservatively than he promised.[9]

The foreign policy platform upon which Carter was elected reflected a liberal cold war response to the failure of the Nixon-Ford years. If it is mistaken to portray Carter as a straightforward proponent of Detente and to ignore his contribution to the Second Cold War, it would be comparably mistaken to see his policies as an unalloyed propagation of con-

---

[9.] Fawcett and Thomas, chapter 5. For overviews of Carter's foreign policy see K. Oye, D. Rothschild, R. Lieber, eds, *Eagle Entangled,* New York 1979; Holy Sklar, ed., *Trilateralism*, Boston 1980; Cummings, op. cit.; and Alan Wolfe, 'The Many Doctrines of Carter', *The Nation,* 6 December 1980. Also, Jimmy Carter, *Keeping Faith.*

flict with the USSR. Initially they were not so unambiguous: what resolved the ambiguity was the Democratic Administration's inability to sustain these policies, and above all the continued refusal of the rest of the world to behave in the manner which the US government hoped and expected. Many components of Carter's strategy derived from his association with the Trilateral Commission, the body of opinion-makers established in 1973. Their activities were important not just in framing Carter's initial programme, but in securing his nomination for the Democratic candidacy in 1976.[10] Carter had had no experience, no profile, in foreign policy: this was at first an asset, since it enabled him to befuddle his audiences at home and abroad and to embody widely contradictory expectations. Reality was later to impose greater clarity upon him, and it was a clarity which focussed his strategy in a more resolutely confrontationist mould.

The liberal elements in Carter's strategy can be summarised as follows: (1) continued pursuit of a SALT-II agreement, whilst agreeing that SALT-I remain in force, and with lower weapons totals than Ford had envisaged; matters not settled in the second agreement could be resolved in SALT-III: a SALT-II agreement was signed in June 1979—without the 'deep cuts' in strategic weapons which Carter had initially called for; (2) playing down of the confrontation with the USSR, what he termed 'an unhealthy obsession', in favour of emphasis upon north-south issues and relations with other capitalist countries—the core of the Trilateral philosophy; (3) a determined effort to reflate the US economy, with the support of other developed capitalist countries; (4) a vocal hostility to the more overt forms of militarism—arms exports, military budget increases, deployment of US forces abroad—and in particular a commitment to withdraw US forces from South Korea; (5) a distancing of the USA from repressive right-wing regimes, ones that were deemed to have violated human rights. In keeping with the liberal intent of this part of Carter's programme, his strategy was presented as a final break with the legacy of the Vietnam years, the militarism associated with it, and the style of Presidential government, imperial, secretive and mendacious, characteristic of the Nixon years.

Yet this new leaf was accompanied by the appointment of officials and by a set of other policies that reflected preparation for Cold War.

[10.] Sklar, op. cit., for details.

Although enunciated by Carter along with the liberal components of his policy, this Cold War element was more unambiguously associated with other prominent members of his Administration: National Security Adviser Brzezinski, a firm believer in linkage and in using non-military means to put pressure upon the USSR; Harold Brown, the Defense Secretary, who had been Secretary of the Airforce during the bombing of North Vietnam and who now oversaw the revamping of America's intervention forces for the third world and the establishment of an intelligence alliance with China; and James Schlesinger, the former Secretary of Defense and now Energy Secretary, who favoured an aggressive policy towards the USSR. Carter's inability to exert control over his officials was also evident in the personnel handling relations directly with the USSR; whilst his personal adviser Marshall Shulman favoured pursuing agreements with Moscow, the Ambassador in the Soviet capital itself, Malcolm Toon was a hawk, who privately opposed SALT-II.[11] The policies favouring Cold War covered several areas of foreign policy. Carter pushed ahead with important elements of the US nuclear programme. In June 1977 he announced a two-part decision: to cancel the B-1 bomber and go ahead with production of Cruise missiles. Whilst this was presented as a conciliatory decision, it was nothing of the kind, since the reason for the choice was the cost involved: Cruise missiles launched from modified B-52 bombers were judged to be a far cheaper and more invulnerable strategic nuclear deterrent than the B-1 bomber. Although not stated at the time, the B-1 cancellation was also offset by the programme to develop a new 'Stealth' bomber.[12] Similarly, whilst he postponed the actual production of the neutron bomb, amidst much publicity, Carter did so only to avoid European criticism. He nonetheless ordered launchers for the bomb to be prepared and certain components of the new weapon to be made ready.[13] The impression of an overall decline

---

[11.] For further analysis of the Carter foreign policy personnel see Cumings, op. cit., pp. 206-7.

[12.] *Keesings Contemporary Archives*, 7 October 1977, reports Carter as saying at his 30 June press conference: 'I think in toto the B-1, a very expensive weapons system, basically conceived in the absence of the Cruise missile factor, is not necessary'. Three reasons were given for this: (i) Cruise can be launched from B-52 bombers, submarines and ground launchers; (ii) each B-1 would cost $100 million, compared to a Cruise, which costs $750,000; (iii) the Cruise cannot be detected and is not vulnerable to attack, because it is mobile. See also *Keeping Faith*, pp. 80-83.

[13.] *Keesings Contemporary Archives*, 7 March 1980.

in US defence expenditure was deceptive: the restraints following Vietnam were over, and military outlays rose throughout his Presidency. For example, fighter plane expenditure continued to rise at the rate of 10 per cent per year throughout the 1970s.

In the SALT-II discussions Carter refused to meet requests to include European theatre weapons in the negotiations, as both the Russians and Helmut Schmidt proposed. This had been an issue in the negotiations with Ford in 1974–6 and the continued US refusal to discuss these weapons under SALT was conveyed to Moscow when Secretary of State Vance made his first visit there in March 1977. The fact of West German dissent from Washington appears to have led the Russians to pause, but once Schmidt had given way this refusal by Carter to discuss TNFs led to the Soviet decision to deploy SS-20 missiles in the latter half of 1977 and to the subsequent conflict over European theatre weapons.[14]

Carter's human rights policy was transformed into an anti-communist crusade in a new guise. He had in fact opposed the 1975 Helsinki Agreement on these grounds and the launching of a crusade on human rights, however accurate some criticisms of Soviet political dictatorship may have been, constituted an ideological whitewashing of the USA, of a brazenness only exhibited by the moralistic and religious politicians of Carter's ilk. It was in one move designed to obliterate the record of Vietnam, Chile, Indonesia and Iran and to rearm the USA for new ideological campaigns in defence of the 'free world'. The human rights policy had some positive impact in Latin America; but in Korea and Iran, countries of more strategic importance, Carter soon bowed to conventional realities. Carter also quickly asserted his belief in challenging the Soviet Union politically in a range of countries in the third world where he judged its position to be vulnerable. In a June 1977 address he named six of these: China, Vietnam, Somalia, Iraq, Algeria, Cuba.[15] As with his human rights policy, this new approach was presented as a contrast to the apparent fatalism of Kissinger, i.e. as a more vigorously anti-

---

[14.] Schmidt has given the following account of this matter: 'I criticised the Ford Administration, but not publicly, for not including medium-range nuclear weapons in SALT TWO. Then the Carter Administration tried to renegotiate SALT TWO, and I told them that SALT TWO must include Euro-strategic weapons as well as long-range ones. The Carter Administration, namely Zbig Brzezinski, told me this was none of my business' (*The Guardian*, 19 February 1982).

[15.] *International Herald Tribune*, 13 June 1977.

communist strategy than that of the preceding Administration. In the Middle East, this policy had considerable success especially after the Sadat visit to Jerusalem in November 1977 had opened the door to the Camp David agreement which consolidated the exclusion of the USSR which Kissinger's shuttle-diplomacy had begun. In the Far East Carter quickly went back on his commitment to withdraw US forces from South Korea.

Jimmy Carter came to office with the expressed aim of avoiding military involvement in the third world. But within a few months of his assuming responsibilities, Carter had laid the basis for a new counter-insurgency capability. An overview of US abilities, Presidential Review Memorandum Number 10, indicated a weakness in the realm of dealing with third world crises and as a result Carter in 1977 signed Presidential Directive Number 18 (PD-18) which called for the setting up of special forces for use in wars in the third world. Whilst not as well-known as its later companion, PD-59, which established a new counterforce commitment, PD-18 nonetheless set up the ground-work upon which Reagan and his Defense Secretary Weinberger were later to build.[16] In sum, the liberal Detente-oriented components of Carter's policy were from the start offset by other elements which prepared the way for the Second Cold War. Indeed some of the elements that were presented as breaks with the Vietnam-Watergate past were especially suited to the prosecution of the globalised conflict with the USSR under different forms.

Despite the presence of this Cold War component from the beginning, the changes in the world situation that occurred in the first part of Carter's Administration led to a marked shift further to the right in his overall policy, and this shift was accompanied by the gradual removal of those individuals associated with the liberal aspects of his policy: Paul Warncke, head of the Arms Control and Disarmament Agency, left in October 1978; Andrew Young, ambassador to the UN was dismissed in July 1979; and Cyrus Vance, Secretary of State, resigned in April 1980. Each departed some time after the policies they espoused had been defeated, but their demises confirmed the rise in influence of the man most actively promoting the Cold War within the Administration, Brzezinski, and coincided with the onslaught launched in Congress and the press from 1978 onwards in favour of the Cold War.

[16.] On PD-18 see Michael Klare, *Beyond the 'Vietnam Syndrome'*, p. 69.

Carter's Failures

The failure of Carter's initial strategy and the resolution of the ambiguity in his programme can be attributed to several factors.

Most importantly, he failed to overcome the recession. In 1977 he won some support at home by a small reflation, but this 'Locomotive' policy antagonised the Europeans and the Japanese because it exported inflation. US GNP continued to expand in 1978 and 1979 but despite fitful moves no sustained economic upswing occurred. By the last year of Carter's Presidency, growth in the USA was at zero level and inflation was over 9 per cent. The nomination of Paul Volcker to head the Federal Reserve Bank in July 1979 symbolised the triumph of a policy which relied on higher interest rates to manage the economy. It was this economic failure which, above all, discredited Carter, both amongst business leaders, and amongst the mass of the population. It laid the groundwork for the right-wing counter-attack in which a New Cold War, reasserting US power, was tied to the supposedly magical new formula of supply-side economics.

Carter's prestige as President was eroded by his own lacklustre performance as a chief executive and by his inability to control Congress. In 1978 the New Right made some ground in the mid-term Congressional elections, but the key changes came within the body of existing Congressmen who were moving steadily to the right under the influence of conservative pressure outside and of world events. The significance of the final vote on the Panama Canal Treaties was that Carter could get agreement only by conceding to the DeConcini amendments: under these US forces would be allowed to reoccupy the canal after the US withdrawal of 1999.[17] In the end, Carter, who needed a two-thirds majority, only just got this victory, by 68 votes to 32, and in achieving this

---

17. The issue of the Panama Canal Treaties first arose in the 1976 election, when Reagan raised it in the Texas and New Hampshire Republican primaries to advance his drive for the Party nomination. It played a symbolic role, as a talisman of conservative obduracy, comparable to that played by the question of the Kuomintang-held islands of Quemoy and Matsu in the 1960 election. Reagan's uncomplicated attitude was: 'We built it, we paid for it, and we're going to keep it.' Or, in the words of California Senator Hayakawa, 'We stole it, fair and square.' One element that contributed to the willingness of the US military to forego the Canal was the fact that its latest generation of battleships was 2 ins too wide to pass through the Canal: it has been planned to build another canal, to go through Nicaragua, but subsequent events made this less likely. For Carter's account see *Keeping Faith* pp. 152-185.

he used up credit which he was sorely to need when SALT-II came to Capitol Hill in the summer of 1979. The SALT-II debate provided the perfect occasion for prolonged assertions of how weak the USA had become, an unsubstantiated charge which had nonetheless gained widespread credence by the last years of Carter's Administration.

Carter antagonised the USSR by his human rights policy, by his abandonment of the initial agreement on the Middle East, by his Cold War initiatives. He was, as the Russians would say, *neseryoznyi*—'not serious', an unreliable negotiating partner who vacillated in his policies and could not deliver on agreements. Carter always denied that human rights was linked to SALT-II and there is no evidence to contradict this; but while it had some positive impact among Washington's third world allies, the preposterous nature of the campaign against the USSR, combined with continued military development such as the June 1977 Cruise decision and the refusal to include European theatre weapons in SALT-II, certainly angered the Russians. By mid-1977 they had turned against Carter. They began deploying SS-20s in October: however they may have justified this on the grounds that they were only redressing the balance against the Poseidons and other SLBMs in NATO's armoury, this was a mistake on Russia's part since no military advantage could compensate for the political damage which it caused. It gave NATO the ideal pretext for deploying Cruise and Pershing in Europe as an apparent reply to the Soviet action, and this move was decided upon by the summit of four heads of state who met in Guadeloupe in January 1979.

By the time Carter had secured a SALT-II agreement with Brezhnev, in June 1979, the anti-Soviet mood in the USA had reached such a pitch that Congress was not willing to pass the measure, except with a rerun of the DeConcini-style amendments that the Russians would almost certainly have rejected anyway. After their defeat in 1980, Carter's aides were ready to acknowledge that they had mishandled the issue of arms negotiations with the Russians and that had they pursued a more united and speedy policy in the first months of the Carter Administration they could have secured passage of SALT-II. Instead, the Administration mixed the public signals on arms talks with the issue of human rights. Rather than moving quickly to secure passage of a modified Vladivostok agreement, they began to talk of the need for 'deep cuts', which the Russians were in no mood to accept, and they allowed over two years to elapse before initialling SALT-II.

Failure to reach agreement with the USSR on nuclear weapons was matched by a rapid transition from conciliation to conflict on another front, namely the Middle East. Carter came to office committed to pursuing peace in the Middle East and he intended to work for a reconvening of the Geneva Conference in which the USSR would have participated. He also talked of the Palestinians in somewhat more sympathetic terms than any US President had done before, referring to their right to a 'homeland'. The result of this policy was that in October 1977 Secretary of State Vance signed a memorandum of understanding on the Middle East with Gromyko, in which the USA and USSR committed themselves to working together for a solution of the Arab-Israeli question. However, far from marking a step forward, this Soviet-US agreement soon became the occasion for a retreat, both in relations between the two powers, and in Carter's internal position: for it unleashed a powerful counter-attack, by pro-Israeli forces within the USA who feared a reduced backing for Tel Aviv and by governments in the Middle East, including both Israel and Egypt, who wanted to prevent any return by the Soviet Union to Middle Eastern diplomacy. Carter was soon told by his pollsters that continuation of this policy would ruin him domestically.[18] Sadat and Begin moved to arrange the dramatic visit of the Egyptian President to Israel a month later. The short-term result appeared to be favourable: Carter was able in 1978 to preside over the Camp David agreement between Israel and Egypt, hailed as his greatest foreign policy triumph. But whilst this achieved the success of bringing an Israeli-Egyptian peace withdrawal from Sinai in 1982, Camp David marked a major if temporarily hidden setback on other fronts: in relations with the USSR which no longer thought Carter a reliable interlocutor, and in dealings with US public opinion and pro-Israeli elements within his own Administration who had shown that Carter possessed neither the political will nor the solid base to hold the line on controversial foreign policy issues. The has-

---

[18.] In 1977-8 Carter's main electoral challenge came not from Reagan, whom few took seriously at that time, but from the challenger within his own party, namely Kennedy, a strongly pro-Israeli politician. Such advisers as Pat Cadell, his pollster, Stuart Eizenstat, his domestic affairs adviser, and Robert Strauss, a major fundraiser, are all believed to have urged Carter to reverse his policy. The difficulty of taking an independent stand on the Middle East was almost as great in the Republican Party: John Connally's campaign for the Presidency ended abruptly in October 1979 when he called for an equitable solution of the Arab-Israeli dispute.

ty retreat of October 1977 was therefore a portent of the surrenders that were to follow.

The shifting mood in the USA and the change in Carter's own policy were confirmed by developments on a front over which neither the USA nor the USSR had control, namely the third world. It was the revolutions there which made it impossible for the US political leadership as a whole to abjure the lessons of Vietnam, and which underscored that loss of control and power for which the decline in the US economic situation and the new military capability of the USSR were in fact mainly responsible. By strategic elision, the changes in the third world were ascribed to Soviet 'expansionism' and combined with the effects of the recession to provoke widespread chauvinistic mobilisation in the USA. The fact that the USSR was not responsible for instigating any of these upheavals, and that it was in many cases inactive, was irrelevant in a context where a demonic Soviet threat was imagined by most of Congress and the US press to be stalking the world. When Carter came into office the effects of Angola were still noticeable in public debate, and it was less than two years since Vietnam had been reunified. The reason why Angola aroused more alarm than Vietnam, despite the history of US involvement in the latter, was partly that there was nothing Washington could do about Vietnam—the defeat was final—and partly because US opinion was outraged by the vigorous role of the Cubans in confirming the truimph of the MPLA. Carter resisted appeals to aid UNITA openly, but the CIA did continue to provide assistance to it, via Morocco, and Carter refused to grant US recognition of Angola. In similar vindictive vein, he pursued a policy of denying aid to Vietnam, under the pretext of Hanoi's failure to collaborate over the US Missing in Action, and deliberately blocked further negotiations in 1978 in order to curry favour with Peking.

In 1977 the first rising in the Shaba province of Zaire occurred, but it was contained by the French and Moroccans. It was with the Horn of Africa crisis of 1977-8 that the third world came to play an active part in the gathering Cold War of the Carter period. The crisis was blamed on the USSR and Cuba, which stepped in to aid Ethiopia after the Somali attack of summer 1977. Yet the war there was something for which Carter himself was in part responsible: he had cut off military aid to Addis Ababa earlier in the year, because of human rights violations in Ethiopia, and had encouraged the Somalis to believe that the west would support them if they seized the Ogaden, part of Ethiopia's territory which they claimed as theirs.[19] Brzezinski's later assertion that Detente 'lies buried in the sands of Ogaden' ignored two basis facts: the first is that it was Washington which helped to precipitate the crisis; the second is that the Russians and Cubans were acting in a quite legal fashion, as they had been in Angola, by assisting a sovereign state to repel invasion. They also complied with a US request to limit the impact of the war by preventing Ethiopian counter-attacks into Somalia.

The Horn crisis of February 1978 gave way to the second Shaba uprising in the spring of 1978 and then to the twin upsets of central Asia, Afghanistan and Iran, in April 1978 and January 1979 respectively, which were themselves followed by the crisis over North Yemen, and the Grenadan and Nicaraguan upheavals later in that year. By early 1979 Carter was being widely assailed within the USA for his inability to handle the third world, and for his apparent weakness where others could and would, it was claimed, have acted with unspecified decisiveness. The latter part of 1979 saw heightened anti-Soviet hysteria in the USA, brought on by the ludicrous issue of the Soviet 'combat brigade' in Cuba supposedly discovered by US intelligence in July of that year.[20]

The spate of 'third wave' revolutions discussed above would have constituted a major problem for any US President and would have led to renewed calls for pressure on the USSR. Yet the manner in which it contributed to the Second Cold War was accentuated by additional factors promoting a widespread bellicist sentiment in the USA. First, there was the image of Carter as a weak-kneed, 'Pollyannish', incompetent president, whose one military venture, the attempt to rescue the US hostages in Iran, ended in disaster. Here again the combination of suppressed bellicosity with the drive for a Cold War was evident. Secondly, sustained inflation combined with the prominence of OPEC brought the issues of the third world much closer to the US public than had previously been the case: Vietnam could be left behind, but the impact of Saudi and

---

[19.] See Fred Halliday and Maxine Molyneux, *The Ethiopian Revolution*, London 1982, pp. 225-31.
[20.] The issue of the Soviet forces in Cuba was given particular emphasis for two reasons: first, the State Department wanted to highlight it as a way of discrediting Cuba in advance of the forthcoming Non-Aligned Summit in Havana; secondly, two Senators accused of excessive liberalism and now running for re-election, Stone of Florida and Church of Idaho, found in this issue a means of projecting a more resolutely anti-communist image. Both failed to secure re-election.

Libyan decisions was felt in every home. Thirdly, the Iranian hostages affair which began in November 1979 was an instrument by which chauvinistic sentiment could be mobilised by the US right in favour of intervention in the third world: the question of captives has a long history of ideological potency in the USA—from the case of the first attack on Africa, what later became Libya, to rescue US captives in 1809, to the concern over the POWs in the Korean and Vietnamese wars and in the *Pueblo* incident of 1969. This episode, publicised on TV and with a Central Castings opponent in the person of Khomeini, was deployed to considerable effect by all sections of the right. The role of the Russians in Afghanistan, and of the Cubans in Angola and Ethiopia, seemed to confirm the impression of a concerted Soviet drive through the third world designed to weaken America. These events combined to produce a shift to the right in US politics from the middle of 1978 onwards, in both popular sentiment and Administration policy. At the same time, the Administration felt its own position strengthened by the progress in developing a closer relationship with Peking. If a date for the onset of Cold War II has to be set, it is 1979. Yet this onset took a double form: a resolution of the inherent ambiguity of the Carter programme in favour of Cold War components; and a larger wave of Cold War mobilisation which swamped Carter altogether in 1980 and so swept Reagan to power in January 1981.

Initiating Cold War II

The shifts in Carter's policy were the opening rounds in the Second Cold War: whilst not identical to the policies pursued by Reagan, they certainly marked a break with the more ambiguous and cautiously confrontationist policies of the first period and laid the way for the 1981 Reagan offensive.

From 1978 onwards Carter authorised an increase in US military expenditure. In January 1978 he called on all NATO countries to implement 3 per cent increases in the coming years, and the FY 1979 allocations were up by 9.4 per cent, equivalent to a 6 per cent real increase. He committed himself to further increases in FY 1980 and FY 1981 and to continuing rises if he was re-elected. This buildup applied to both strategic and theatre nuclear weapons. Whilst the B-1 was shelved in favour of Cruises launched from B-52s and whilst the Trident programme inherited from Nixon was continued, the third component of the strategic 'Triad' was boosted by the decision taken in June 1979 to go ahead with the development and deploymnet of MX missiles in the Utah and Nevada deserts. In December 1979 the NATO countries agreed to the stationing of Cruise and Pershing-II missiles in Europe, a move long prepared by NATO and Congressional forces favourable to such a development, but made all the easier by the deployment of SS-20s in 1977 and the prevailing Cold War atmosphere. The USA had decided to go ahead with it in 1978 and the four main NATO countries had accepted this at the Guadeloupe Conference of January 1979. The delay for 'consultation' with the main NATO allies countries was of a purely cosmetic nature.

The deployment of theatre land-based missiles in Europe was more than a return to the policies of the early 1960s, when the Thor and Jupiter had been stationed there; the new missiles were not only more invulnerable, because mobile, but they were also far more accurate. It was in the context of this new accuracy that public attention focussed in 1980 upon the emergence of the 'counterforce' strategy as a part of NATO's current war plans.

As discussed in Chapter Three, the possibility of greater accuracy in targeting missiles led to the shift from the 'countervalue' approach, aimed at cities and economic targets, to one aimed at specific military targets, i.e. 'counterforce'. Although under discussion for many years, and first enunciated in 1962 by then Secretary of Defense MacNamara, it was officially propagated in 1974 by then Defense Secretary Schlesinger. It became central to official policy in July 1980 when Carter signed Presidential Decree 59, a document ratifying this new approach to nuclear warfare. Whilst there was no guarantee that this was now the sole US policy, it did, like all military planning documents, establish 'counterforce' as an option and so make the possibility of some commanders envisaging a limited war all the greater. For a USA with only a quarter of its ICBMs on land, as compared to three-quarters for the USSR, and with a 'limited' war threatening the Soviet Union's land area and not the USA's, the advantages of such an approach were self-evident. Whilst most attention was focussed on strategic and conventional weapons for use in surface combat, the Carter Administration was also taking steps to increase the USA's capacity to use outer space for military purposes. This was until the 1970s a marginal domain of competition, but in the course of that decade space became a central concern of military planners. The US-Soviet Partial Test Ban Treaty of 1963 had banned explosions in outer space, and the 1967 Outer Space Treaty banned the placing of nuclear weapons there, as well as the establishment of military facilities on celestial bodies. But no treaty regulates the use of outer space for reconnaissance satellites or for the installation of anti-satellite offensive weapons: more than 1,700 reconnaissance satellites were launched in the 1970s and talks on anti-satellite warfare limits were abandoned by the Russians and Americans in 1979 at Washington's initiative. In 1974 the US had begun an unpublicised programme for setting up anti-satellite systems, to offset the 89 Soviet military satellites estimated as scheduled to be in place by 1981 and to prepare to attack the killer satellites which the Russians might deploy against US reconnaissance equipment in orbit.[21] Such satellites are much more economical ways of hitting enemy satellites—coming at $18 million per satellite, compared to $100 millions for a Titan rocket. In the mid-1970s the US authorities had also begun preparing for the Space Shuttle which eventually went through its first flight in April 1981: although presented as a civilian scientific venture in most coverage, the Shuttle is also a Department of Defense venture with substantial military implications. Around 40 per cent of its initial tasks were military ones.[22] In December 1978 Defense Secretary Harold Brown authorised the construction of a new integrated anti-satellite system and Carter set 1985 as the target date for this to become operational, using miniature homing vehicles against Soviet satellites. As with the Nixon decisions of the early 1970s, which bore fruit with the Cruise and MX, so Carter's decisions on space war have prepared the ground for a new race in space in the 1980s.

Together with its increased nuclear capability and adoption of a counterforce strategy, the Carter Administration began to develop US conventional forces for new third world interventions.[23] Carter opposed such interventions at the time of his election, but as early as August 1977 the Department of Defense began preparations for a Rapid Deployment Force for possible use in the Middle East. The Iranian revolution

---

[21.] *Economist Foreign Report,* 6 August 1981.

[22.] SIPRI *Yearbook 1981*, p. 138.

[23.] For a comprehensive overview see Michael Klare, *Beyond the 'Vietnam Syndrome'.*

accelerated this process, both because it removed the Shah as regional power and because of the hostages seizure. The April 1980 mission may have failed, but Carter had already in January proclaimed the Doctrine that bears his name, which authorised future US deployments in the Gulf if it was felt the USA's interests were threatened. Presidential Decree 18, of 1977, had laid the groundwork for what was later to be the Rapid Deployment Force: Presidential Decree 51, of 1980, allowed for the use of tactical nuclear weapons in the event of Soviet advances into the Persian Gulf.[24] Although publicly justified by the seizure of the hostages and the Soviet intervention in Afghanistan, the Carter Doctrine in practice predated these developments. NATO leaders had been talking for some time about the development of an extra-European capacity for the Alliance and NATO had acted in the Shaba uprisings, in aiding Somalia, and in developing relations with the Arab states of the Peninsula long before January 1980. Deployment in the Indian Ocean had been steadily increasing since plans to build up Diego Garcia were laid in 1973 and in November 1979 the US government decided on new expansion there, including the lengthening of the runways to accommodate B-52 bombers. Brzezinski had always advocated the projection of US forces into what he called 'the third strategic zone'. Desert warfare exercises in the Mojave Desert in California, begun in 1974, were increased in 1979 and in the Caribbean a new US task force was stationed at Key West in October 1979.

A similar reversal of policy occurred in the Far East, with regard to South Korea. Carter not only abandoned his initial commitment to withdraw US ground forces from there, but he flew to Seoul in June 1979 to toast President Park Chung Hee. The similarities with Carter's praise of the Shah were more than symbolic, since four months later Park was assassinated. But his place was taken by another brutal dictatorship that proceeded to kill many hundreds of its own people after demonstrations in the city of Kwangju in April 1980. Far from protesting, the US Administration continued to give its support and the local US commander had in fact released Korean troops under his command for operations against the insurgent population. At the same time, Carter retreated on one of the most original planks of his 1976 campaign, namely his opposi-

---

[24.] On discussion of the use of tactical nuclear weapons in the event of Persian Gulf conflict see Klare, p. 78, and Cumings, p. 208.

tion to arms sales to the third world. The Administration had initially declined to sell arms to Morocco until it showed willingness to negotiate a solution of the Sahara war, but in February 1979, immediately after the Iranian revolution, arms sales to Morocco resumed. In 1980, in the wake of the Sandinista triumph in Nicaragua, deliveries to El Salvador began again. Overall, US arms sales continued at a high rate throughout the Carter Presidency. They stood at $10.3 billion in 1979, compared to $10.6 in 1976.

This new US militancy in the third world and towards the USSR was accompanied by closer ties with China, both in the direct military sphere, where China was used to spy on the USSR and encouraged to attack Vietnam, and in the strategic sphere where the 'China Card' was brandished by those in Washington intent upon placing maximum pressure on the USSR.[25] Relations had been stalled since Nixon's visit in 1972 and, for fear of antagonising the USSR, US Administrations were reticent about developing their ties with Peking. China's poverty and administrative inefficiency dulled early hopes that a new China market was waiting to be opened up, and uncertainty about the policies of Mao's successors, following his death in September 1976, also played their part. So, at first, Carter was cautious about China: Secretary of State Vance's visit in August 1977 yielded no progress but in the first half of 1978 relations between the two states improved, and following the crisis in the Horn of Africa, Brzezinski visited Peking in May 1978. Full diplomatic relations were established in December 1978. The deteriorating situation in Indo-China (Vietnam invaded Cambodia in December) and the new acerbity in Soviet-Chinese relations associated with this formed the background to Teng Hsiao-ping's visit to Washington in January 1979, itself followed by the Chinese attack on Vietnam. There had been a wide-ranging policy debate in the USA during the mid-1970s about how far to play the 'China Card': but the onset of the Second Cold War resolved this. As one expert has written, China was more important than SALT.[26]

In August 1979 Vice-President Mondale visited Peking and it was then that the USA and China signed a secret agreement under which China would permit the USA to install an electronic listening facility at

---

[25.] On the 'China Card' see Cumings. op. cit., and Banning Garrett, 'China Policy and the Strategic Triangle', in *Eagle Entangled*.
[26.] Cumings, op. cit., p. 212.

Aksu, in Sinkiang province on the Soviet frontier. Defense Secretary Brown visited Peking in January 1980 to discuss further military agreements, including for the first time the supply to China of US (non-lethal) military equipment. The effects of this process on the USSR would seem to have been contradictory: anxiety about a Peking-Washington axis, as perceived in late 1978, may have encouraged the Soviet Union to go for an agreement on SALT-II in 1979, even though this did not cover European theatre weapons; but later the US decision to aid China militarily, expecially in the Mondale and Brown visits, antagonised the USSR and, combined with the stalling of SALT-II and the NATO decision on Cruise and Pershing-II, certainly hardened Soviet resolve in the weeks prior to the decision to send troops to Afghanistan. It is debatable whether the USSR would have abstained from sending troops to Afghanistan even if relations with the USA had not worsened. But the deterioration must have swayed some in the Soviet leadership and provided a Cold War II backdrop for what was later seen in the west as the USSR's most provocative move in the 1970s. The Soviet Union even at the height of Detente would have been unwilling to see the Afghan communist regime overthrown: yet the timing and manner of the Soviet intervention to support the regime may have owed a lot to the Cold War that had already begun.[27]

The issue of US relations with Peking is frequently phrased in terms of a particular option, a 'China Card', which the USA may or may not take up in its conflict with the USSR. The threat of playing this 'Card' against the Soviet Union is one that Washington supposedly held in reserve throughout the 1970s. It is true that the alliance with China was part of a US strategy of weakening the USSR, but the 'Card' analogy is in certain respects a misleading one. The most important impact of China on US-Soviet relations was that registered in the late 1950s and early 1960s, not as a result of US wooing of Peking, but of the strains imposed upon

---

[27.] A number of Soviet commentators have implied that the military intervention in Afghanistan itself might not have taken place if the Cold War had not by then begun. The intervention was, in the words of Georgi Arbatov, head of the Institute for the Study of the USA and Canada, '*both cause and consequence*' of the worsening in east-west relations (my italics). This is a dubious claim, since it suggests that under other circumstances the USSR would have allowed the communist regime in Kabul to be overthrown. The timing, justification and level of the intervention might have been different under other conditions but it is hardly conceivable that Moscow would ever have allowed its Afghan allies to be overrun.

the Sino-Soviet alliance by the US wooing of Moscow. This, more than anything, changed the strategic context within which the Soviet Union operated, and it reflected continued Cold War in US relations with Peking. In the late 1970s, there were, moreover, substantial obstacles to the establishment of a fully-fledged Washington-Peking alliance. On the Chinese side, the limits of its economy precluded it from offering major openings to US businesses, whilst the Chinese armed forces were so badly equipped that it would have required US aid on a gigantic scale to turn China into an operational military ally. Within the USA, there was disagreement on whether to encourage China against the USSR, opinions varying on whether such encouragement was expected to produce positive or negative results in Moscow; such a debate characterised the Carter Administration. But there was a deeper, more atavistic debate, on whether to support Peking at the expense of Taiwan, an issue that resurfaced with the advent of Reagan to office.

The 'China Card' was never therefore a question of a single once-and-for-all option, so much as a set of options which themselves depended in part on factors beyond Washington's control. This was not, of course, how it was seen in Moscow: there the development of a US-China alliance with military implications was a cause of considerable alarm and made its contribution to the hardening of Soviet resolve in the late 1970s. While there was no decisive China ace to be played, Carter's rapprochement from 1978 onwards served nonetheless to confirm the trend towards the Second Cold War. The development of relations with Peking served as a counterpoint to relations between the USA and another state long present in Washington's perspective, namely Vietnam. During the negotiations on a withdrawal from Indo-China Nixon had offered in a secret letter to provide economic reconstruction funds to Vietnam, to the tune of $3.25 billion. An economic agreement was to be signed in July 1973. But the US unilaterally broke talks off: this sum had never been paid, and diplomatic relations had not been established. Talks on recognition did, however, continue until the latter part of 1978, when the USA broke these off. The reason for the US move has been quite openly stated: it was to gain favour with Peking.[28] But it coincided not only with the US-

---

28. Thus Jimmy Carter: 'The China move was of paramount inportance, so after a few weeks of assessment I decided to postpone the Vietnam effort until we had concluded our agreement in Peking' (*Keeping Faith*, pp. 194-5). Derek Davies, editor of *Far Eastern*

Chinese rapprochement, but also with worsening relations between Vietnam and China's South-East Asian ally, Cambodia. China encouraged Cambodia in its attacks on Vietnam, with military and diplomatic aid. The effect of these two pressures—abandonment of the prospect of US aid on the one side, military harassment by China's junior ally on the other—was to push Vietnam decisively towards the Soviet Union. Whereas in the first period after the unification of the country in 1975, Vietnam had resisted Soviet pressure to ally with it and to join Comecon, and had offered favourable terms to western firms wishing to invest in Vietnam, the polarisation of 1978 placed Hanoi firmly on Moscow's side. It joined Comecon and signed a twenty-year friendship treaty in late 1978. The Vietnamese invasion of Cambodia in December 1978, and the punitive Chinese attack on Vietnam in February 1979 then followed—all consequences of the US policy of using the conflicts of the Far East as a means of placing pressure upon the USSR. In the words of one authoritative observer: 'Post-war Vietnam's watershed year was 1978—the year in which its comparatively liberal internal policies and its relatively conciliatory foreign policies met with consistent failure and were transformed into today's hard-line attitudes'.[29] As the same author points out, the Vietnamese were mistaken in thinking that Washington would be more conciliatory than it was, and in waiting too long to drop their conditions for the normalisation of relations. But the primary responsibility must lie with the combination of US malice and Chinese provocation that forced Hanoi into Moscow's arms and provoked the two Indo-Chinese wars of late 1978 and early 1979.

Economic Review, reported: 'There is perhaps an element of vengefulness against the country which had the temerity to beat the Americans. Discussing the Vietnamese hope for increased assistance along multilateral channels, one senior American official commented: "Let them stew in their Soviet juice. Hanoi hasn't paid its dues; we aid those countries which we defeat, not those countries which defeat us"' (*Far Eastern Economic Review*, 25 December 1981).

[29.] Davis, *FEER*, ibid. It is debatable how far Washington actually encouraged China to attack Vietnam in February 1979. Carter states in his memoirs (pp. 206-9) that Teng Hsiao-ping informed the Americans of China's intention to attack during his trip to the USA in early 1979, and that Carter advised Teng against this course. The USA had, nonetheless, helped to bring the war about—by cutting off its own talks with Vietnam, and thus signalling the latter's isolation in August 1978, and by openly wooing China when Peking was stoking the Cambodian-Vietnamese conflict. Nor did the USA condemn China's action.

By early 1980 the evolution in Carter's policy was complete, and the Cold War II policies propounded by Brzezinski were being implemented. Brzezinski had never concealed his intention of forcing the Soviet Union into an economic and military competition that would exacerbate its internal weaknesses, real or imagined.[30] In private, he is believed to have welcomed the Soviet involvement in Afghanistan because this provided the west with a convenient propaganda tool. This policy of strategic harassment went together with an overt belief in the possibility of winning nuclear war and of the need for a more agressive US presence in the Middle East. His view of nuclear war was expressed in an interview with the *New Yorker*: 'It's inaccurate thinking to say that the use of nuclear weapons would be the end of the human race. That's an egocentric thought. Of course it's horrendous to contemplate, but in strictly statistical terms, if the United States used all of its arsenal in the Soviet Union and the Soviet Union used all of its against the United States it would not be the end of humanity. That's egocentric. There are other people on the earth.'[31] Whilst he was not as concerned with the third world in its own right as other Trilateralists, he stressed the need for the USA to 'project' its military power in the Gulf region and was active in fostering an Indian Ocean/Gulf presence well before the Soviet intervention in Afghanistan. He was also a strong proponent of the theory of linkage earlier elaborated by Kissinger. In the last days of the Carter Administration he stressed: 'I have argued consistently for four years that Detente, to be viable, has to be reciprocal and based on the principle of restraint. I argued that, unless we insist on reciprocity in practice and unless we react strongly to Soviet lack of restraints, detente would be undermined. I believe the Soviets have shown such lack of restraint— first, indirectly, in Ethiopia, then more directly in Afghanistan. It is because of the lack of restraint that Detente today is in poor shape.'[32] The result of this posture was that Brzezinski attempted to portray the end of Detente as something independent of the Adminstration's own decisions, and once it had been generally accepted, Carter launched the

---

[30.] In the words of a close collaborator or Brzezinski's: 'Brzezinski's own instinct is to stand up, be tough, outproduce them economically and militarily. His view is that we are coming out of a bad time and they have to be shown some things. There is an almost systematic toughness in Zbig's writing and thinking' (*New Yorker*, 1 May 1978).
[31.] *New Yorker*, 1 May 1978.
[32.] *Trialogue*, No. 25, Winter 1980/81.

Second Cold War in the last period of his Administration. If the Soviet intervention in Czechoslovakia in 1968 had been a prelude to Detente, that in Afghanistan was used to justify its abandonment.

Such was the change in US policy brought about during Carter's Presidency that Brzezinski was later to rebut the criticisms of the Reagan camp by showing how the Democratic Administration had initiated the Second Cold War. 'I have to take issue with your implied hint,' he told an interviewer in 1981, 'that the Carter Administration was somehow "soft" on the Soviet Union. It was President Carter who, for the first time in peace-time, increased the defence budget. It was President Carter who ordered the creation of a Rapid Deployment Force. It was President Carter who decided on the deployment of the MX missile. It was he who shaped a regional security framework in the Persian Gulf.'[33]

The evolution of the Second Cold War was not, however, only a matter of bureaucratic infighting in Washington or a response to events in the outside world. It also reflected those changes in the US political scene to which Carter had to respond if only to attempt to secure re-election. By late 1979 and in particular during the debate on SALT-II, the right was in full cry. Whilst SALT-II was being considered in Congressional committees there was unbridled speculation about supposed Soviet military superiority, an alleged 'Window of Vulnerability' in the 1980s, the Soviet 'Combat Brigade' in Cuba and much else besides. The prevailing climate induced a replay of the phantasmagoric debate on the Panama Canal Treaties, although on a more global and important issue, namely east-west relations. While Carter was by now pursuing a Cold War policy, the perception of him as a weak president remained pervasive, rooted as it was in the problems of the domestic economy, but reinforced by the Iranian hostages affair. Specific constituencies of importance to any Democratic President seeking re-election lost sympathy for him, the Jewish vote because of Carter's overt dislike for Begin, and the black vote because of the recession and his dismissal of Andrew Young. White working-class opinion turned against him for both racial and economic reasons. The stage was set for the fullblown Second Cold War, under Ronald Reagan.

[33.] George Urban, 'A Conversation with Zbigniew Brzezinski', *Encounter*, May 1981.

9.
The Great Contest in the 1980s:
Limits of Confrontation

In the preceding chapters, three issues have been discussed: the constituents and character of Cold Wars (Chapters One to Two); the major causes of Cold War II (Chapters Three to Seven); and the chronological onset of the Cold War during the 1970s (Chapter Eight). Whilst necessarily schematic, for reasons of space and available knowledge, this analysis has attempted to provide a general and proportional account of the different factors and events that brought Cold War II into being. This concluding chapter must, of necessity, be even more provisional. It will confine itself to outlining the major features of US and Soviet policy in the early 1980s, together with an indication of those factors which may inhibit the continuation of Cold War II.

Reagan's Initial Programme

The First Cold War lasted for seven years, beginning in 1946 and ending in 1953 as a result of the changes attendant upon the death of Stalin and the stalemates in Korea and Indo-China. In Cold War II, Reagan has faced greater difficulties at home than anticipated, and the new Soviet leadership under Andropov has taken new initiatives in seeking agreement on arms limitation. But the fear of nuclear war, the political impasse in Soviet-US relations, the divisions in the west, the capitalist recession, and the problems of Eastern Europe, epitomised by Poland, have continued to grow. The Second Cold War has therefore found its own momentum since 1979.

The triumph of Reagan in the November 1980 election brought victory to those in the west who had been calling for an allout Cold War. Despite Carter's initiation of the Second Cold War, Reagan's presidency marked a new level of confrontation with the USSR and of the subordination of US foreign policy as a whole to this objective. The tenor of relations with the USSR changed from that of even Carter's last months in office, to one of reasserting US power on a global scale, confronting the USSR, advocating an increased US military profile in the third world and predicting the breakup and ultimate disappearance of the communist camp. At once symbolising and implementing this new mood was the expansion of military outlays for the period 1981-6, bringing expected expenditure for those years up to at least $1,600 billion, and, if some unpublished Pentagon estimates are to be believed, up to 50 per cent higher than that.[1] Expenditure for Fiscal Year 1983 at $216 billion was 17 per cent up on 1982 and $34 billion higher than the target fixed by the Carter Administration for this period. This represented a rise for 1982 of 13 per cent in real terms, with the commitment to an average real rise of 8.3 per cent over the coming five years.[2]

To justify this arms drive, the administration mobilised the rhetoric of 'rebuilding' America's strength after the years in which the Carter Administration had apparently allowed US defences to fall into 'disrepair'. The patriotic note struck by Reagan served both to reassert traditional values at home and to promote the military programme and an assertive foreign policy. This new orientation was expressed in a spate of individual initiatives. Sales of weapons abroad were boosted; restrictions on the export of nuclear technology were lifted; the CIA's budget was increased—by 25% in 1983 alone; a concerted campaign against Soviet 'proxies' and against states accused of aiding 'terrorism' was launched. The favourite states of the New Right—Israel, South Africa, Taiwan—were at once given more favoured treatment. Interest in alleviating the economic problems of the third world decreased even further. The main emphasis of the Reagan Administration lay on what it termed 'rearmament', the constituent elements of which became clearer

---

[1.] In January 1982 two Pentagon specialists calculated that it could cost up to $750 billion more for the administration to implement its military objectives than the $1.6 trillion already allocated (*International Herald Tribune*, 9 March 1982). The official calculations for 1983 also assumed a 5.2 per cent real growth in the economy and 7.9 per cent unemployment.

[2.] Presidential Budget Message, January 1982, as quoted in *San Francisco Chronicle*, 31 January 1982.

as the Reagan Administration got further into its term of office. These elements can be summarised as follows:

In a Pentagon document revealed in May 1982, *Fiscal Year 1984-1988 Defense Guidance*, and in a document presented to the National Security Council in August 1982, the administration developed what was implicit in Carter's Presidential Directive 59.[3] This involved preparation for a protracted, six-month, nuclear war with the Soviet Union, a war which the USA now thought it could win. Special emphasis was laid on two aspects of the strategy, both of them made possible by the technical advances of the 1970s: one was 'decapitation', i.e. the elimination of centres of Soviet military and political command by the use of counter-force weapons; the other was communication between US command centres in the period after the initial Soviet attack. The adoption of this policy reflected the full maturing of the counter-force doctrine, with its assumption that victory of some kind is now possible in a nuclear war. Despite the attempts of administration officials to mute the import of this outlook, by saying they wished only to 'prevail' over the USSR, this development represented, to a degree not previously seen, the abandonment of deterrence and the return to a quest for superiority.

In October 1981 Reagan revealed the outlines of a new strategic arsenal, the components of which were elaborated over the following year.[5] The three main elements were the MX missile, the B-1 bomber, and improved long-ranged communications. The justification for the 100 MX—Missile Experimental—missiles was that they would replace the existing ICBMs, Titans and Minutemen, which had supposedly become vulnerable to a Soviet first strike through the 'Window of Vulnerability'. After considering several siting possibilities, it was decided in late 1982 that the MX would be located in what were called Dense Packs, conglomerations where the very concentration of missiles would mean that most incoming Soviet ICBMs would be deflected when the first bomb exploded. Since the MXs were to be in specially hardened silos, the majority

---

[3] Robert Scheer, *With Enough Shovels: Reagan, Bush and Nuclear War*, London 1983, pp. 7-12.
[4] *New York Times*, 30 May 1982, for details of 1984-1988 Defense Guidance; *The Guardian*, 17 August 1982, for the new nuclear war strategy.
[5] *Strategic Survey 1981-1982*, pp. 39-40.

of them would not be hit and could therefore be used for a retaliatory strike. The US counter-force capability would, therefore, be preserved.[6]

Congress rejected the Dense Pack solution and Reagan was forced to search for other basing systems. But underlying this dispute lay the fact that, despite its appearance of scientific credibility, this programme was more a reflection of political and emotional than of strictly technical concerns.[7] The degree of vulnerability of the existing ICBMs to a Soviet first strike was, as already indicated in Chapter Three, greatly overrated. On the other hand, if the Window arguments were to be accepted, then the Dense Pack solution was no solution at all: the impact of even one ICBM would create a crater so large that no amount of silo hardening could protect the other missiles. Lying behind the MX programme was a belief that the USA would abandon the SALT-I Treaty of 1972, which prohibited anti-ballistic missiles, and construct a new ABM system to protect the MX, at a cost of $25 billion. Even the timing involved in 'closing' the Window was suspect: the MX would be in place at the earliest in 1986, whilst by that time the Trident submarines would be in operation, providing the USA with a sea-borne counter-force capability that nullified the need for the MX. The conclusions could only by ominous: (a) that if the administration believed its Window rhetoric, the MX would have to be fired first—i.e. as part of a US pre-emptive first strike; (b) that a serious MX programme would involve scrapping the ABM treaty; (c) if it did not believe the Window rhetoric, it was installing the MX in response to political pressures at home, and in accordance with the ideology of superiority that became so explicit in the 1980 election.

The motivation for the B-1 bomber was even more obviously symbolic: the B-1 will add little to the bomber part of the strategic triad. It is subsonic, cannot penetrate Soviet air defences, and can only launch Cruise missiles as the B-52 could before.[8] A decision was also taken to go ahead with the Stealth bomber, embodying new radar-avoiding technology: but this would come into operation only after the MXs had been positioned. On the other hand, the purpose of the improved communications is to strengthen the second-strike capability, in accordance with the new doc-

---

6. On new US counter-force accuracies see Steve Smith, 'MX and the Vulnerability of American Missiles', *ADIU Report*, vol. 4, no. 3, May/June 1982.
7. Steve Smith, as above.
8. Congressman Les Aspin in *International Herald Tribune*, 3 February 1982.

trine, since communication with deeply submerged Poseidons and with command posts has been one of the weaknesses of the US strategic force till now. These three components of the strategic modernisation were, however, to be accompanied by another striking expansion in the nuclear arsenal, namely a 70 per cent increase in the number of warheads. Under a programme signed into action by Reagan in March 1982, the Department of Defense was to produce another 17,000 warheads to add to the 23-25,000 operational warheads already in existence. Under the programme this would bring the total of warheads that could be launched immediately against Soviet targets from 12,000 to 20,000.[9]

A new European battlefield capability also featured in Reagan's plans. On top of Carter's plan for the introduction of the Cruise and Pershing II missiles came the decision of August 1981 to develop the neutron bomb, an artillery shell with enhanced radiation to be used against enemy tank formations. The neutron bomb is not needed to restore any balance on the European front: that already existed with NATO's superiority in anti-tank weapons and battlefield tank quality. The purpose of the neutron bomb is to give NATO even greater superiority in Europe and a weapon that could be used in the third world as well. An equally controversial addition to the European battlefield arsenal was the new chemical warfare weaponry authorised by Reagan in January 1982. The USA has signed a pledge not to be the first to use chemical weapons, and there had been a moratorium on production since 1969. But amidst claims that the USSR was developing its capabilities in this field, and was even using them in third world arenas such as Laos and Afghanistan, Reagan authorised production of artillery shells containing two liquids which, when combined, produce a nerve gas.

Reagan has laid great stress on an enhanced third world deployment and intervention capability. The greatest increases in the military budget have come in expenditures on conventional forces that can be used in third world confrontations, whether with local forces there or with the Soviet Union. This has involved organising troop manoeuvres in the Middle East and increasing military aid to third world allies, noticeably in Central America. It has also led to the use of threats against third world foes—Cuba, Nicaragua, Libya—and a contempt even for the previous administration's selective concern with human rights. But the

---

9. *The Guardian*, 1 March 1982; *International Herald Tribune*, 23 March 1982.

core of the new programme has been the buildup of the navy, under which the number of combat ships will rise from 455 to 600. This increase includes two new nuclear-powered aircraft carriers and 58 new major combatant ships.[10] The aim was to give the USA undisputed naval superiority in the event of any conflict, local or global, but also to provide the means for projecting the troops ear-marked for immediate intervention in areas of third world upheaval. In January 1983 a new Central Command—*Centcom*—was set up to oversee US deployments in nineteen countries of the Middle East and West Asia.

Development of space weapons has been expanded. In an extension of the Carter Administration's military space programme, the Department of Defense opened a Space Command in September 1982. The main function of the Command was to oversee the military use of the space shuttle, and nearly half of the shuttle payloads between 1982 and 1984 were to be military ones. While some critics talked of the dangers inherent in the militarisation of the National Aeronautics and Space Administration, pressure was growing for an allout programme to develop a capability for space war. One of the major lobbyists for the militarisation of space pointed out: 'The shuttle gives us a strategic edge over the Soviet Union and their masses of missiles and submarines.' The long-term goal was for orbiting platforms with directed energy weapons, either charged particle beam or killer laser capabilities that could hit Soviet planes and missiles as these carriers circled the earth: once installed, such a system could in theory destroy all Soviet weapons systems in just two orbits. These were prohibited under the 1972 SALT agreement and the technical problems and costs involved in this were still judged to be prohibitive; it was estimated that hundreds of billions of dollars would be needed to place such a system in space, and it would need the equivalent of ten power stations to direct a beam powerful enough to knock out a target on earth. Moreover, such platforms would be rather vulnerable to attack by enemy killer satellites. But even while doubt subsisted on whether the full space panoply could be deployed, the Administration was proceeding with the more limited programme of killer satellites begun by the previous administration.[11]

---

10. *International Herald Tribune*, 6 July 1981.
11. *International Herald Tribune*, 23 June 1982; Robert Aldrige in *The Nation* 18 October 1980.

The buildup in military forces has been accompanied by a more aggressive approach to arms negotiations and an emphasis upon the need to negotiate with the USSR from 'strength'. The first director of the Arms Control and Disarmament Agency, Eugene Rostow, a veteran of the foreign policy advisory group most responsible for the war in Vietnam, stressed: 'We are not waiting to rearm'.[12] Rostow laid particular stress upon the fact that MIRVing and the mobility of missiles now make satellite reconnaissance more difficult: the USA has had such advantages for years, but it is now that the USSR is introducing them that US officials begin to talk of the need for on-site inspection, something the USSR is unlikely, for political reasons, to accept. On-site inspection was an issue raised in the 1950s and 1960s but was rendered less important by the increased precision of satellite photography.

Although the USA agreed to enter into negotiations with the Soviet Union on both strategic and intermediate missiles, the opening proposals made were ones the Russians could not conceivably accept. In the first case, the USA proposed a reduction of ICBMs, landbased missiles, to 850 on each side: the Russians rejected this because these ICBMs represented a much higher percentage of their total strategic force. In the intermediate missile talks, the American position was to propose what they called the 'Zero Option', whereby they would withhold the Cruise and Pershing missiles in return for dismantling of the Soviet SS-4s, SS-5s and SS-20s. This the Russians found unacceptable because it left out of account the other components of the NATO intermediate arsenal, i.e. those bombers, landbased missiles and, most importantly, submarine-based missiles, which were aimed at the USSR. The US 'arms control' proposals were therefore unusually blatant attempts to force Soviet acceptance of US superiority and the negotiations were used to buy time for the development of new US capabilities.

Economic warfare was given much higher priority by the new Administration. In the initial period, Reagan indicated that he would apply the policy of linkage, albeit in a tougher form. Lists of places where the Administration demanded a Soviet retreat or 'good behaviour' were announced, the threats being two: that the USA would not enter into arms talks unless these conditions were met, and that it would sever economic

---

12. Eugene Rostow, Lecture at Royal Institute of International Affairs, London, 1 October 1981. He was later dismissed for being too doveish.

ties.[13] However, this policy was not developed, and Reagan dropped these geopolitical conditions for arms talks which began regardless. On the other hand, the Administration abandoned linkage in the other direction when it developed a comprehensive, and *unconditional*, policy of economic warfare, designed to reduce all contacts with the Soviet bloc and to do the utmost in its power to aggravate the economic problems of the east. Thus, initial policy on sanctions involved an apparent use of linkage after the declaration of martial law in Poland in December 1981: the imposition of banking sanctions and the attempt to prevent construction of the Soviet gas pipeline to Western Europe. But it soon became evident that what was envisaged was an indiscriminate and permanent overhaul of links with the east, with the explicit aim of weakening its economies. Poland was but a pretext. In his statement to Congress in February 1982 Defense Secretary Weinberger made this clear. 'The infusion of new technology from the West helps preserve the Soviet Union as a totalitarian dictatorship,' he stated, arguing that the reduction of economic ties would both reduce the USSR's military capabilities and undermine its social system.[14] Some US officials even talked of an 'economic window of vulnerability' through which the west could force military and political concessions on the Soviet Union.

Reagan's policy is an unambiguous drive for strategic superiority over the USSR, tied to a general re-establishment of hegemony over Europe, the third world and the US domestic population. It is therefore a third alternative, after those of Nixon and Carter, to the problems faced by successive US administrations ever since the late 1960s. In addition to the pursuit of superiority over the USSR, this is a wide-ranging attempt consciously to reimpose the controls which the USA had been losing over the previous two decades within the capitalist world itself. Cold War II is being used to pressure other NATO countries and Japan into higher military

---

13. For example see 'US Poses 2 Tests for Soviet Relations, Moscow's Response to Initiatives on Afghanistan, Cambodia Called Key', *International Herald Tribune*, 4-5 July 1981. According to this report US Secretary of State Haig told Soviet Ambassador to the USA Dobrynin that the administration would regard Soviet responses to US proposals on Afghanistan and Cambodia as 'a test of future East-West relations'. Other leaks from the US government mentioned possible test cases as including Ethiopia, Angola and South Yemen.

14. Caspar Weinberger, Report to the Congress for Fiscal Year 1983, 8 February 1982, *Survival*, March-April 1982. For analysis see Michael Klare, 'The Weinberger Revolution', *Inquiry*, September 1982.

expenditures, to secure their agreement to tougher policies in the third world and towards the USSR, and to coerce them into opening up their markets to US products. Within the USA the new military expenditure has gone together with a concerted attempt to reallocate wealth to the rich, through the reduction of welfare programmes and the onslaught of supply-side economics.

The Administration used increased military outlays as the pretext for substantial cuts in other branches of government expenditure designed to bring down inflation. Many of the ideological concerns of the New Right, school prayer and limits on abortion, are being given official support. By 1982, the Equal Rights Amendment had been defeated. The Second Cold War therefore has a domestic political rationale far beyond the realm of boosting the military industries. It is an encompassing class and ideological project, on both the international and national levels.

Obstacles to Cold War II

Yet, despite the dynamism and apparent ideological coherence of the Reagan programme, it is worth examining the conditions under which it may be blunted and the Second Cold War ended. The Cold War II strategy is beset with serious difficulties. Whether these lead to greater aggressivity and militarism, including the outbreak of war, or to a backing away from the confrontation of the early 1980s onslaught, remains to be seen. It is, none the less, possible to discern certain obstacles which the Second Cold War will encounter, and certain changes which may help to limit the continuation of Cold War II.

The domestic economic strategy upon which Reagan has placed the main emphasis since coming into office has encountered growing obstacles and could inhibit his foreign and military policies. Far from balancing the budget by 1984, his initially proposed target, Reagan will in fact increase the deficit. Original estimates of a FY 1982 deficit of $44 billion were far below the final $110 billion, and the 1984 figure may reach $175 or $200 billion. His initial promise to cut taxes had been reversed by the summer of 1982. Any semblance of managerial coherence behind the budget cuts evaporated in November 1981 when David Stockman, the Director of the Budget, stated that the government had no control over what it was committed to spending or cutting. Projections for the US GNP and inflation have done little to confirm prognoses of a quick revival of US economic strength: by the end of Reagan's first year in office Wall Street was evidently sceptical about the new administration's plans and only 22 per cent of those polled in March 1982 said they had full confidence in Reagan's management of the economy.[15] At the same time, the cuts in welfare had generated opposition from unions and urban unemployed: whilst Reagan had won substantial support amongst blue-collar workers in 1980, a contrary swing was evident by the November 1982 mid-term elections. The ultimate consequence of Reagan's programme may therefore be to rekindle domestic dissent, to exacerbate the USA's internal problems, just as the defence spending boom itself may increase inflation and so make military spending a matter of domestic controversy within the USA as it had been in the closing period of the Vietnam war.

Reagan's victory was not so sweeping a political triumph as appeared from the number of states he won. While 44 of the 52 states fell to him, he acquired only 51 per cent of the total vote on a turnout of 55 per cent: in other words he was voted in by 28 per cent of the total electorate. 116 million of the 160 million eligible voters did not come out to support him.[16] Reagan's coalition was also a very wide one, the constituents of which were potentially contradictory and not equally represented in the new Administration. Although the New Right, *stricto sensu*, was represented in Congress it found little representation in the Administration itself; the control of foreign, intelligence and defence jobs by more traditional members of the Republican right meant that the potential for division between these factions was considerable. On the other side, Reagan faced a challenge from the regrouped forces of east-coast internationalism, who objected to his alienation of the European allies and to the intensity of his military programme. By early 1982 they were criticising the administration for its provocation of the Europeans, well before the dispute over the Soviet gas pipeline produced the crisis in Altantic relations. A surprisingly vocal faction of the foreign policy establishment spoke out against the nuclear arms programme, and in April 1982 four senior members called openly for the rejection of first

---

15. *The Guardian*, 29 March 1982.
16. Walter Dean Burnham in Thomas Ferguson and Joel Rogers (eds), *The Hidden Election*, pp. 99–100.

use of nuclear weapons by the USA.[17] Encouraged by Reagan's incompetence domestically, and anxious at the trend in US foreign policy, this faction of US semi-official opinion was more vocal than any comparable group in Europe and linked into the much wider current of concern at nuclear weapons that emerged in the freeze movement of 1982.

The impact of Reagan's policies on the USA's allies was to sharpen resistance to Washington, despite initial politeness in the European capitals and Tokyo. The NATO countries will not follow the levels of US expenditure increases on arms which are now projected at 8 per cent per annum in real terms. Real defence spending by the USA's NATO allies rose 2.1 per cent in 1982—the US figure by 13 per cent. Nor will these allies easily accept the new economic nationalism being displayed in Washington over trade matters. The attempt to enforce a boycott of the Soviet gas pipeline in 1982 produced the greatest division for two decades and Reagan had in the end to back down. Above all, these allies face increased pressure at home by movements urging nuclear disarmament and disengagement from the military alliances with the USA; if only to protect their domestic constituencies, they will have to demonstrate some distance from the policies pursued by Reagan.

Macroeconomic consequences aside, the USA faces severe limits on its ability to build up its military forces in the manner planned. Stockman's summary of the Pentagon programme was clear enough: 'The whole question is blatant inefficiency, poor deployment of manpower, contracting idiocy'.[18] The shortages of skilled personnel within the existing service plans will be accentuated, and the example of the first Trident to be launched—three years late, 40 per cent over cost—will be repeated throughout an armaments industry that is unable to meet the demands placed upon it. The Pershing II missile, scheduled for 1983 deployment in Europe, is giving major technical problems.

The attempt to reimpose control on the third world may well lead to greater bloodshed and horror. While it will present additional difficulties for the revolutionary movements and states there, the sweeping approach pursued from Washington has not succeeded: in Central America there has been no quick solution to the wars in El Salvador or

---

[17.] McGeorge Bundy, George Kennan, Robert McNamara, and Gerard Smith 'Nuclear weapons and the Atlantic Alliance' *Foreign Affairs*, Spring 1982.
[18.] *International Herald Tribune*, 12 November 1981.

Guatemala, and Mexico and Brazil have refused to follow Washington's policy dictates. Cuba has remained defiant, and the long-term prospect of an upheaval in Mexico, a second Mexican Revolution, haunts the USA's southern horizon. The projection of a 'strategic consensus' onto the Middle East underestimated Arab hostility to Israel, as previous US administrations have done. The attempt to unseat Qaddafi did not, at least initially, succeed. The USA is also tying itself to a collection of dictatorial regimes, republican and monarchical, where social and political tensions continue and where the US's allies could be challenged by mass threats from below or from within their own state apparatuses. In the Far East, the governments of South Korea, the Philippines and Thailand all face considerable opposition: South Korea is the most significant of these, given its proximity to North Korea, and the presence there of US forces equipped with nuclear weapons. From the Himalaya to the Atlantic there are at least ten countries which the USA is now investing with military support and which could involve Washington in unwelcome imbroglios—Pakistan, Oman, Bahrain, Saudi Arabia, North Yemen, Sudan, Somalia, Egypt, Tunisia, Morocco. In none of these countries is there a likelihood of direct Soviet intervention, and the potential causes of revolt are internal to them: but the risks of conflict threatening US allies are considerable.

The aim of the Reagan Administration has been not just to contain the advance of revolutionary forces, but in some degree to reverse it. This is sometimes phrased in terms of the need to 'go to the source', i.e. to hit at revolutionary states said to be assisting rebel movements in countries where the outcome is still not clear. It is sometimes argued that after the series of defeats and humiliations of the 1974–1980 period, the USA 'needs' a victory to re-establish its internal morale and command respect abroad. A similar process was evident in the period of the First Cold War when, under the name 'Rollback', attempts were made to overthrow a number of pro-Soviet regimes, most notably in Albania. The Second Cold War has been accompanied by much planning for 'spoiling operations' against Soviet allies, this time in the third world. Cuba, Grenada, Nicaragua, Ethiopia, South Yemen and Afghanistan have all been mentioned as possible targets. Covert action by the CIA is known to have increased greatly. Yet in reality such reversals, as distinct from harassment and economic warfare, are extremely difficult to achieve: Washington has been able to overthrow nationalist or reformist regimes with covert action, but not revolutionary ones. Even in Afghanistan, with a widespread Islamic opposition movement, willing to fight and enjoying legitimacy in the west, the Reagan Administration has found it difficult to mount any effective action. Short of provoking a major international crisis by using US forces overtly, there is a limit to what covert action can do against established revolutionary regimes where these enjoy military backing from the USSR. The CIA would clearly like, as it sees it, to emulate the KGB in overthrowing enemy allies: but it is precisely this misinterpretation which ensures the CIA's failure. For it is not the KGB but socially rooted movements which overthrow governments and it is these roots, strengthened by post-revolutionary consolidation of military apparatuses, which lessen the room for manoeuvre of counter-revolution.

One of the greater surprises of the Reagan period has been the continued opposition of a majority of US public opinion to direct US military involvement in the third world. Reagan, despite initial hopes of a new interventionism on the part of the right, was not able to send troops to Central America. But no such inhibitions affected the USA's allies, who did show that in the early 1980s the use of force in third world conflicts can pay off. Britain's assault upon Argentina was a reminder of what European imperialist states could do in crisis situations. South Africa's repeated attacks on Angola and Mozambique harassed two of the most radical states in Africa. Israel's invasion of Lebanon in June and July 1982 was a major bonus for the USA, since it humiliated two Soviet allies—Syria and the PLO—and provided new opportunities for US diplomacy in the region and for the deployment of US forces in a peacekeeping role. The balance-sheet of the third world, therefore, shows that the power of the USA to intervene is still constrained by domestic factors, and that some of the initial rhetoric has not been translated into practice. But the climate of bellicosity and interventionism diffused by Washington has encouraged other, junior, allies to seize their opportunities.

Perhaps the greatest falling of the new Administration has been in relations with an important ally, namely China. After the rapprochement of Carter's later years, Reagan has antagonised Peking by fostering closer ties to Taiwan and in particular by proposing to sell substantial quantities of arms to Taipeh. Initially this did not lead to a breach in Peking-Washington relations between China and the USSR. But Reagan's traditional right-wing Republican espousal of Taiwan and the increased strength of the Taiwan lobby in the USA deprived Washington of an important supporter in its worldwide campaign against the USSR.[19] It must have increased the longer-run possibility of a revision in Peking of its stance on the dispute with the USSR.

So far, the limits to the Cold War strategy considered have been ones within the capitalist world, in Sino-American diplomacy, or in countries where the USA has come into conflict with third world revolutionary states. Yet, as indicated at the beginning of this study, the central axis of international conflict lies in the conflictual relations between the USA and the USSR, the Great Contest, and in the manner in which this relationship is focussed and affected by the question of nuclear weapons. By the early 1980s the arms race between the USA and the USSR had become not only an issue of major objective importance, but also the object of widespread public debate as opinion in Western Europe and the USA became more alert than was ever previously the case to the dangers inherent in the military policies of both blocs. It is therefore here, in the course of Soviet-US relations and in the manner of controlling the arms race, that the outcome of Cold War II would appear to be decided. In particular three major dimensions of the international situation can be identified: significant change in the situation of any of these would have an impact on the continuation of the Second Cold War. These dimensions are: the Soviet response to the US offensive; the evolution of Sino-Soviet relations; and the progress of the disarmament movement.

The Soviet Response

When Reagan first came into office, the Soviet government appeared to hope that its own firmness, combined with the limits of US power, would halt the Cold War offensive. Moscow also believed that the European allies, especially West Germany, might quell Reagan's enthusiasms.

---

19. The bases of support of the Taiwan Lobby within US politics might appear to be obscure, for Taiwan possesses none of the resources which that other tenacious ally, Israel, can deploy. Three contributory elements can, however, be discerned: the economic factor—Taiwan trades with the USA more than China does; the ideological factor—Taiwan has projected itself as a success story of vibrant free enterprise; and the historical factor—the generation that holds senior positions in the US foreign policy establishment of the early 1980s was formed in the immediate postwar period, at the time of the Chinese revolution and the Korean war.

This soon turned out not to be the case. Despite the hesitations, personnel conflicts and professional incompetence of Reagan's foreign policy team, a decisive policy did emerge, in which the new Administration emphasised the need for confrontation with the USSR and for a military build-up. Indeed military expenditure grew *more* than Reagan had promised. Reagan himself, while corresponding tentatively with Brezhnev, took the occasion of his address to the UN Special Session on Disarmament in June 1982 to make one of his most militant attacks on the Soviet Union. By mid-1982 the Soviet Union appeared to have decided that there was little to be gained from negotiations with the United States, whilst at the same time believing that it would be damaging to be seen as the side which had decided to break off talks. It was in this spirit that the USSR entered into the two series of Geneva talks, on strategic and intermediate nuclear missiles. The initial positions of the two sides, at least, were quite irreconcilable, and there was none of the optimism that had preceded the SALT-I and SALT-II negotiations, which formed part of Detente.

At the same time, the USSR seems to have decided that war could still be avoided, and that it was possible for the Soviet Union to wait for a more amenable US Administration to come into office.[20] In military terms, the Soviet Union announced that it would match US weapons developments and was prepared to make the economic sacrifices which such a competition entailed. There is no information on Soviet military plans for the 1980s comparable to that available for the USA: but the general picture, of a sustained Soviet pursuit of parity from a position of technological inferiority, continued to hold. In the third world context, the USSR supported allied states already in existence and ignored calls for retreat in Afghanistan, South Yemen, Ethiopia or the Caribbean. But Moscow also sought to avoid further involvement in third world crises, both because its own resources were stretched and because these might afford the USA the occasion for a confrontation that was favourable to the latter. Soviet commentary on events in Central America, Lebanon and southern Angola was hostile to the west, but did not suggest any major counter-moves. Moscow denied all involvement in the July 1982 Somali-Ethiopian border clash, even though this began with a Somali attack on Soviet oil prospecting personnel inside Ethiopia. Aid to Vietnam

---

20. Georgii Arbatov, Director of the Institute of the USA and Canada, 'US Policy in a Dreamland', *Pravda*, 16 July 1982, as translated in *Soviet News*, 21 July 1982.

was reduced in 1980 and 1981.[21] Cuba was enjoined to proceed cautiously. In the most spectacular case of all, the USSR watched two of its Arab allies, the PLO and Syria, suffer humiliating defeat in Lebanon at the hands of the Israelis in the summer of 1982. The Israeli siege of Beirut and the subsequent expulsion of the Palestinians were a blow to Soviet prestige. But the Russians were prepared to pay this price because they did not wish to risk confrontation with the USA.

This caution in the third world, designed to avoid conflict with the USA, went together with a persistence in other policies that had contributed to the development of Cold War II. It was possible that Brezhnev's successor, Andropov, would in some measure alter these, but there was no great expectation that this would be the case. The Russians were not going to be forced into policy concessions by the USA: the US belief in the efficacy of economic warfare as a form of pressure on Moscow was unfounded. This policy persistence on the part of the Soviet Union was particularly evident in two respects: the arms race and control of internal dissent. While in military matters the Russians followed behind the USA in arms policy and capability, their public stance was less distinguishable. The USSR took major disarmament initiatives in the period after Reagan came into office; chief amongst these was the commitment not to be the first to use nuclear weapons and the announcement of a unilateral freeze on the deployment of SS-20s. But the impact of these moves was reduced by the Soviet insistence that the USSR was pursuing parity, i.e. by the underlying threat that it would develop a destructive potential aimed at Western Europe and the USA comparable to that which the USA was aiming at the territory of the USSR. Locked as it was into the logic of maximum deterrence and strategic parity, the Soviet Union was unable to break the mould of the arms race and appeal directly to the populations of the west in a distinctive voice.

The control on internal dissent within the Soviet bloc continued to attract attention internationally and to confirm the Cold War image of the USSR. The most pertinent case of this within the USSR itself was the action taken in June and July 1982 against the Group for Establishing Trust Between the USSR and USA, an eleven-member unofficial body set up in Moscow. Although at first allowed to issue their statement, the members of the Group were then subjected to house arrest, after which

---

[21.] *Far Eastern Economic Review*, 27 February 1981.

at least one was held in a psychiatric hospital. There could have been no clearer indication of the inability of the Soviet authorities to see the link between internal freedom and opposition to the Cold War. On a much more dramatic scale there was the continuing crisis in Poland, following the rise of Solidarity as an opposition trade union movement in August 1980 and the imposition of martial law in December 1981. The repression of Solidarity, although it took place without the direct involvement of any Soviet forces, was the occasion for the worsening of the cold war climate: the USA used the declaration of martial law as the issue upon which to declare an economic war it had been planning to implement. Public opinion in Western Europe and the USA saw that the Soviet Union supported the imposition of martial law and that the martial law government was seeking to re-establish a centralised control similar to that which prevailed in the USSR itself. The paradoxical consequence of the Polish crisis was therefore that, whilst the Soviet role and the level of bloodshed were less than in Czechoslovakia in 1968, the altered international climate was such that, if anything, the USSR suffered even more from this reassertion of official control.

The second anniversary of Reagan's election, in November 1982, coincided however with the death of Brezhnev and the advent of Andropov to power. Stalin's death in 1953 had been a major factor in the ending of the First Cold War, since the new party leadership had been willing to take initiatives that the dead leader had eschewed. Soviet forces were withdrawn from Austria and one faction, led by KGB chief Lavrentii Beria, was willing to contemplate abandoning East Germany. The leadership transition in 1982 offered some similar opportunities and Andropov was quick to press the pace of the nuclear weapons negotiations by making a series of conciliatory offers to the west. But the situation was also, in many ways, a different one. First, the 'Thaw' in 1953 came after an almost complete standstill in east-west discussions, whereas in the 1980s the Cold War continued despite the fact that talks were going on. Secondly, the modification of Soviet foreign policy went together with a liberalisation internally, an important factor in making Soviet policy more attractive in the west: Andropov's accession to office was accompanied, if anything, by a tightening up on political and social deviance within the USSR. Most importantly, it was hard to see what major territorial concession the USSR would make to win western attention. Afghanistan was not a country occupied in a world war, as Austria and

Korea had been, and because the ruling party had come to power in the capital and claimed to rule the whole country it could not now be partitioned—this being the obvious compromise solution of the 1950s kind.

Neither the Soviet record in the first phase of the Reagan Administration, nor the underlying assumptions of Soviet policy which appeared to be shared by Brezhnev and Andropov, suggested that the Russians would, in fact, take those initiatives by which they themselves could reverse the process of Cold War. While they sought a return to Detente and were prepared to sit out the Reagan Administration, they avoided those changes in their policy which would have challenged the overarching logic of Cold War into which the military and political policies established for two decades had drawn them. They did seek to lessen the impact of Reagan's policies by their own offers, but the best hope for a reduction in tension lay in a combination of Soviet flexibility with a weakening of Reagan's support at home.

Sino-Soviet Relations: A Thaw

The importance which China's conflict with Russia played in the growth of Cold War II has been analysed in Chapter Six, and in the narrative of the 1970s in Chapter Eight. It was, therefore, of considerable importance that the intensification of the Cold War under Reagan was accompanied by changes in China's position which threatened to weaken the USA's offensive in the vital East Asian area. For China became increasingly antagonised by the US support for Taiwan and by the time of the Twelfth Congress of the Chinese Communist Party, in September 1982, the Peking leadership had effected a clear if partial break with the USA. The 'super-power' policies of Washington were once again condemned, and the Twelfth Party Congress placed US policy on a par with that of the Soviet, as an equal threat to world peace.

This cooling of relations with the USA was accompanied by a slow improvement in relations with the USSR, and Yuri Andropov emphasised hopes of an improvement in relations as soon as he came to office. The first signs of this trend were seen in 1977, soon after the death of Mao.[22] In that year, Foreign Minister Huang Hua visited the Soviet embassy in

---

22. Allen Whiting, *Siberian Development and East Asia, Threat or Promise?*, Stanford 1981, Chapter 6, 'The China Factor'.

Peking on the occasion of the anniversary of the Bolshevik revolution, and an agreement was reached on navigation in the Amur and Ussuri rivers that formed part of the frontier between the two states. But the Vietnam-China war of February 1979 set back any such reconciliation, as did the Soviet intervention in Afghanistan in December. Border talks continued without progress and trade sunk in 1981 to $240 millions, compared with a figure for US-Chinese trade of $5.6 billions and $10 billions in Sino-Japanese exchanges. The Chinese declined to renew the Thirty-Year Treaty of Friendship, Alliance and Mutual Assistance signed by Mao and Stalin in 1950.

From the statements of the two main leaders to speak on this issue in 1982, Brezhnev in Tashkent in March, and general secretary Hu Yao-bang at the Twelfth Party Congress in September, it appeared that five major issues still divided the two states: defining the border, the stationing of troops on the frontier, inter-party relations, Afghanistan and Indo-China.[23] The Russians stated that they had no territorial claims on China: the Chinese still contested parts of their joint 4,650 mile frontier. China did not actually ask for the return of any Soviet territory, only for an admission that that the treaties ceding land to Russia in the past had been 'unequal'. But less emphasis was laid on this than by Peking in the past and it did not appear to be the major stumbling block. The question of troop concentrations worried the Chinese, since between 500,000 and 725,000 Soviet troops, or up to one-fourth of the Red Army, were believed to be along the Chinese frontier with Russia or in Mongolia. However, although the Russians had appeared to menace China during the 1979 Sino-Vietnamese war, neither side expected a full-scale war: the Russians, because their superior arms and air power guaranteed battlefield superiority, the Chinese, because they believed that a major war with them would expose the Soviet Union in Europe.[24] A mutual reduction of forces would, none the less, constitute an index of improved relations.

Inter-party relations had been at the core of the conflict of the early 1960s, especially as both Moscow and Peking sought to organise sup-

---

[23] Brezhnev's Tashkent speech in *Soviet News*, 30 March 1982; Hu Yao-bang's Report to the 12th Party Congress in *Beijing Review*, 13 September 1982, esp. pp. 29-33. A fascinating Chinese account of east-west relations is given in Zhang Zhen and Rong Zhi, 'Some observations on Soviet Detente', *Beijing Review*, 18 October 1982.

[24] Whiting quotes a Chinese official as telling him in 1975: 'The Soviet Union won't attack us until after they have defeated NATO', p. 163.

port within the international communist movement for their respective policies. But the Chinese failed almost completely to do so, and the Russians also exercised decreasing disciplinary control over the European parties after 1968. As part of their general reduction in claims to rectitude after the Cultural Revolution the Chinese announced that no party could claim full correctness and they added that the question of 'revisionism', the main initial accusation against the Soviet Party, was only an internal matter of each party. By the time of the Twelfth Congress, the Chinese abandoned any claim to be organising an International and both the Russians and the Chinese insisted that they believed in noninterference in the internal affairs of other parties (although the Russians insisted on their right to continue criticising aspects of Chinese foreign policy which they considered to be in contradiction with socialist principles, and the Chinese in practice continued their attacks on Soviet 'hegemonism' and 'expansionism', even if after 1980 they no longer charged the USSR with 'social-imperialism' or being a capitalist country). An important, if unspoken, element in the Sino-Soviet thaw was their common position on Poland: China had supported the Soviet intervention in Hungary in 1956 and had denounced the invasion of Czechoslovakia in 1968. Given their own hostility to independent opposition movements, the Chinese leadership evinced no sympathy for Solidarity and tacitly endorsed the declaration of martial law in Poland. They thereby removed from the agenda an issue in Sino-Soviet relations that could, if the Chinese so chose, have reanimated the inter-party polemics of the 1960s.[25]

More serious and intractable were the questions of Afghanistan and Indo-China. They were more serious because here Russia and China were indirectly in military conflict with each other; they were more intractable because they involved third parties over whom neither side had complete control. The Chinese had opposed the communist seizure of power in Kabul in April 1978 and had begun even then to send arms to the guerrillas, via Pakistan.[26] The Soviet intervention of December

---

[25]. Chinese commentary on Poland stressed that the problems of the country should be solved by the Poles themselves—hence the military takeover of December 1981 was not condemned. China had little sympathy for independent trades unions, and the right to strike was removed from the new, 1982, constitution.

[26]. Yaacov Vertzberger, 'China and Afghanistan', *Problems of Communism*, May-June 1982; Peter Niesewand, *McLeans* magazine, 30 April 1979.

1979 occasioned even more virulent polemics: whilst the Chinese never admitted to sending arms to the Afghan rebels, they did say that providing military assistance to them was 'not inconsistent with the principle of non-interference in the internal affairs of other countries'. At the Twelfth Party Congress Hu Yao-bang insisted that the Soviet presence in Afghanistan was a threat to China's security. As long as prospects for any resolution of the Afghan war itself remain remote, the only solution would be if the Chinese decided to downgrade the issue.[27] But to do so would appear to Peking to be legitimating a Soviet military takeover of an Asian state, setting precedents elsewhere.

By far the most difficult issue dividing the Soviet Union and China is Indo-China, with the Vietnamese and Cambodian governments allied to the USSR pitted against the Pol Pot guerrillas in western Cambodia. The latter are supported by Thailand, with whom China has an active alliance. The importance of Indo-China as an ideologically sensitive issue in the west is paralleled by its importance in the east, and the conflict between Russia and China over Vietnam in particular goes back to the early 1960s. Indo-China is much more of a real geographic concern of China's than Afghanistan, since Indo-China is the one area of the world where China can exercise the influence of a great power, and the defeat of Peking's Cambodian allies in 1979 by the Vietnamese intervention forces was a substantive humiliation for Peking. In contract to Afghanistan, however, some resolution on the ground may come about, through the final victory of the Hanoi-Phnom Penh forces over the Chinese-, Thai-and US-backed guerrillas and through a broadening of the Cambodian government. Peking would then be faced with the choice of sacrificing its relations with Moscow by backing a lost cause, or accepting a defeat which an improvement in its own relations with Vietnam would make somewhat more palatable. In such a situation, strong Soviet backing for Peking's claim to Taiwan, a point that Brezhnev emphasised in his Tashkent speech, might weigh more than continued attachment to the Khmer Rouge.

These five issues do not in themselves constitute the full range of problems dividing Russia and China. Beyond such specific questions there lies a history of accumulated resentment and interest. The death in

---

[27.] For indications that China would accept a pro-Soviet Afghanistan provided Russian forces left, see *Le Monde*, 19 November 1982.

September 1976 of Mao, who was opposed to any reconciliation with the USSR, certainly made it easier for the Chinese to lower the level of hostilities. But the Chinese leadership, far more than the Soviet, derives major internal and international benefits from the confrontations. It provides both revolutionary and patriotic sustenance to the regime at home, since hostility to the Soviet Union has been an important ingredient of the regime's claim to legitimacy for two decades. The conflict also has important external benefits: it provides the main rationale for US interest in supporting Peking, and it gives China credentials as a non-aligned power in the third world. Russia too derives benefits, although these are less significant, in its dealings with countries suspicious of China— Mongolian and Vietnam. Overall, the pattern of responsibility has been constant since the mid-1960s: the Russians have wanted a reconciliation more than the Chinese. While the Chinese for a long time claimed that Russia was a capitalist country, the Russians always analysed China as a socialist one, albeit deformed. If, following the indications of the Twelfth Party Congress, there were to be a significant improvement in Sino-Soviet relations it would mark a major shift in world politics. It would weaken the USA, greatly reassure the USSR and in so doing lessen the dynamic underlying the Second Cold War.

Progress of the Disarmament Movement

The early period of Cold War II coincided with the emergence of a major popular movement against nuclear weapons in both Western Europe and the USA. During Cold War I, there had been a movement for peace: yet although this attracted many who were not subordinated to Stalin's policies, it remained a movement linked to the official communist parties.[28] This alliance of pro-Soviet and peace positions lasted through the early 1950s, until the entry of Soviet tanks into Budapest in 1956 terminated the hopes upon which this juncture had rested. Yet no sooner was this peace movement discredited than there arose in one European state, namely Britain, a mass movement calling for unilateral nuclear disarmament. From 1958 until 1962 this mobilised tens of thousands of

---

[28]. A prominent instance of such non-party support for the Soviet position was Jean-Paul Sartre's *Communists and Peace*, published in 1952. For Sartre's reasoning on why he adopted this stance, and why he later criticised the USSR see *Between Existentialism and Marxism*, London 1974, p. 119.

people, and at one time commanded the support of the majority of the Labour Party. But CND failed to hold the Labour Party, which reverted to its Atlanticist loyalties, and it lost its mass appeal: the defeat of unilateralism in the Labour Party in 1961, the apparent progress in US-Soviet negotiations marked by the July 1963 Nuclear Test Ban Treaty, and, later, the wave of opposition to the US role in Vietnam all placed CND in a secondary position. In no other major capitalist country, with the exception of Japan where it remained a permanent issue, was the question of nuclear disarmament posed as a prominent public topic.

In retrospect, it is striking that there was so little concern throughout the late 1960s and most of the 1970s about nuclear weapons. The accumulation of warheads and refinement of delivery systems continued, and so the levels of potential destruction were increasing every year. The movement of the early 1960s had received particular impulsion from the issue of fallout from atmospheric explosions, something the 1963 US-Soviet Treaty ended. Another factor may have been that Detente encouraged a belief that nuclear war had become less and less likely and that the best solution to the problem lay in bilateral agreements between Moscow and Washington rather than in mass pressure from below. Many on the left, sickened by the Soviet invasion of Czechoslovakia and the Chinese courting of Nixon, disregarded the east-west conflict altogether and instead concentrated on issues pertaining to the third world or to politics within their own specific countries. Many scrutinised the Paris Peace Accords on Vietnam, few the texts of SALT-I. Because it was deemed to be conducted in a hypocritical manner, the Soviet-US conflict was also felt to be unreal, something that could without complications be ignored. There may also have been a certain fatalism about the nuclear arms race, a feeling that, once it had passed a certain stage, it could not be arrested: the devil of nuclear fission had been released from its cage, and the best hope lay in seeking political solutions to those problems, in Europe and the third world, which, if unsolved, might unleash a nuclear confrontation. Yet the depth of apathy about such a hideous and man-made Damoclean sword hanging over the world is, in retrospect, surprising.

The growth of the peace movement in the advanced capitalist countries can be seen against the background of the shifting fortunes of the left. As already discussed in Chapter Six, the early 1970s witnessed a change in the political climate in the developed capitalist countries that was, in one respect, an enabling condition of the Second Cold War. For, after a clamorous few years epitomised in the events of 1968, the socialist and left opposition forces underwent a significant retreat. This was true both for the organised working class movement, whose advance was halted in this period, and for the less organised and much less proletarian forces that had emerged around 1968, in independent social movements in Europe and anti-war protest in the USA. The exceptions were the women's movement and, to a lesser extent, the ecological movement, neither of them prominent in 1968 itself. This ebbing of the opposition forces of the late 1960s, which, for all its country-by-country variation, was common to all the advanced capitalist countries, was not offset by the fact that in some countries established right-wing forces were ousted from power. In the three south European states—Portugal, Spain, Greece—the left made initially strong moves after the fall of the fascist dictatorships, but was later confined for the rest of the 1970s by more astute conservative opponents. By the time the Greek and Spanish socialists were able to win governmental power they had discarded their more militant economic and foreign policies and had re-established their loyalties to Washington. Portugal's Soares had already been the spearhead of capitalist restabilisation in his country. In northern Europe, the tenures of social democratic parties in Germany (from 1969 onwards), Britain (1974-9), France (1981 onwards), Holland and Denmark offered no radical break with the domestic or international policies of the right. A complacent stewardship replaced the pursuit of a markedly different alternative.

Why then did the peace movement emerge when it did, in 1980, and on such a widespread scale? In autumn 1981 up to two million people participated in demonstrations against nuclear weapons in Europe. In June 1982 hundreds of thousands of Americans took to the streets of New York to protest at their own government's policies. In Europe the focus was on opposition to the Cruise and Pershing-II and on support for European Nuclear Disarmament, from Portugal to Poland, an aim proclaimed in the END manifesto of April 1980. There were many proposals for smaller nuclear-free zones. In the USA most attention centred on the call for a freeze—that the USA seek to negotiate an agreement with the USSR on halting the testing, production and further deployment of nuclear weapons in a way that both sides could verify. In Eastern Europe conditions were different: official controls sought, with varying degrees of repression, to contain those who called for disarmament on both sides, and there appeared, on the basis of the impressionistic evidence available, to be some popular antipathy to the END programme—ranging from general support for their own government's policies in the USSR to sympathy for Reagan's confrontation with the Russians on the part of many Poles. But, both at the level of official peace committees and in the acts of the independent groups, there was also response in Eastern Europe to this sudden re-emergence of the nuclear question.

Three immediate factors played their part in bringing this issue to the fore. One was the proposed or actual introduction of new intermediate-range missiles on land: the SS-20s by the USSR, and the Cruise and Pershing II, by NATO. Although there was a long prehistory of such intermediate weapons in Europe, this visible escalation, particularly that by NATO, involving deployment of new missiles on land, acted as a catalyst that reopened European concern about the future of the continent. The intermediate range weapons which NATO planned to deploy aroused fears that the USA was now willing to fight a nuclear war in Europe at the latter's expense and so save continental USA from attack. This was, in fact, neither new nor probable: the possibility of an exchange limited to battlefield weapons had existed since the late 1950s, while any use of the new NATO weapons against the territory of the USSR would, as the Russians insisted, invite a riposte against the USA itself.[29] But the fact that these weapons would be under sole US command, and the technical impression they gave of exempting the USA from retaliatory attack, aroused European hostility. A second factor was the increased level of east-west confrontation that accompanied the latter part of the 1970s, from Angola to the Afghan, Iranian and Central American crises. The danger points in the world were not so manageable or remote as had appeared in the 1960s and early 1970s. Thirdly, there was the fact that the policy statements of both the later Carter and Reagan Administrations laid much more stress than had been the case since the Kennedy period on the need to build up a military potential for possible east-west confrontations. The modish Washingtonian belief in the possibility of fighting a nuclear war, ironically given greatest prominence by the writings of an expatriate Englishman, Colin Gray, alarmed many in Western Europe.

---

29. On the impossibility of limited nuclear war in Europe see Michael Howard, 'Surviving a Protest', *Encounter*, November 1980.

In particular the glibness of Ronald Reagan in the face of possible disaster confirmed this unease.[30]

There were, however deeper reasons for the revival of the peace movement in Europe. One was the very survival of that left and of that ecological movement that had been placed on the defensive since the early 1970s. Faced with the accommodations of Schmidt and Callaghan, many young people turned to nuclear disarmament as they had turned to support for Vietnam in the period of the Wilson government in Britain after 1964. Far fewer on the left now placed their hopes on 'model' socialist states far away. The recession also played an important part. It underlined the class-specific character of decisions on budget allocation taken by governments throughout Europe, often at the behest of the USA: while social services were being cut and unemployment was growing, more money was being spent on weapons. But the recession had another significant consequence, in that it weakened one of the foundations of the alliance, namely the appeal of capitalism and its epitome, the USA. The prosperity and dynamism of the 'Free World' that marked the 1950s was no longer as strong. The USA itself was not only the embodiment of a system that offered less respect and hope, but it was seen to be beset at home by crime, racism and other tensions that greatly diminished its appeal. The most specific image associated with Reagan, that of the cowboy, had now become a menacing one, not the reassuring stereotype of the 1950s. In a Europe where the combined GNP now equalled that of the USA and where the superiority of US consumer and political values was no longer so easily accepted, the movement to reject US domination in the field of military matters reflected a much wider mood of cultural and economic assertion that had been growing on both left and right since the latter half of the 1960s.[31]

The movement in the USA began somewhat later and, of necessity, from different roots. Whereas European public opinion had long accepted

---

[30.] For a general account see Scheer, *With Enough Shovels*. Apart from Reagan's own admission that he could consider a nuclear war limited to Europe, and the statements by many administration officials on winning nuclear war (see p. 52-3), there was the remark by Presidential Counsellor Edwin Messe that 'nuclear war is something that may not be desirable' (*Time*, 29 March 1982).

[31.] For discussion of disarmament in Europe see E.P. Thompson and Dan Smith (eds), *Protest and Survive*, London 1980; Alva Myrdal et al, *Dynamics of European Nuclear Disarmament*, Nottingham 1981; Mary Kaldor and Dan Smith (eds), *Disarming Europe*, London 1982.

the reality of nuclear war, even while downplaying it, US debate had allowed of the problem far less and it was only in 1981 that a major public concern came into being. Although the USA has a long pacifist tradition, the cause of peace had a small place in US political culture in recent years. Some of the factors that applied in Europe did, however, operate here too: Reagan's insouciance frightened many, as did the growing influence of the Pentagon and its soft-spoken evil genius Caspar Weinberger, within the Administration. The recession pressed the issue of alternative budgetary allocations home to many. The reserves of opposition amongst young people also came into play. But in the USA there is an additional factor not present so much in Europe, that has brought the issue much more decisively into the centre of debate, namely the role of sections of the foreign policy establishment and the church in criticising official policy. The calls from Catholic bishops, former ambassadors and presidential aides for a freeze and for a no-first-use pledge, minimal appeals in themselves, are none the less a novel feature of the US political scene, as was the placing of the freeze proposal upon the ballot papers of nine states in November 1982, in eight of which it passed. There is no immediate overall majority for this policy and anti-Soviet sentiment is as strong as ever: but a breach in the previously serene complacency of US public opinion has been opened, encouraged by and linked as it is to the emergence of the peace movement in Europe.

Despite its appeal, however, the peace movement on both sides of the Atlantic faces major dilemmas and difficulties. In the USA the freeze proposal is in no way a measure for disarmament, only a move to halt further increases in nuclear weaponry. It is opposed by powerful sections of the US government, allegedly because it would make permanent a supposed Soviet advantage, actually because it would hinder the US pursuit of superiority. And the call for verification in the freeze proposal raises substantial questions, of a kind already encountered in direct Soviet-US talks. The movement in Europe is uncertain about which weapons it is talking about—END refers to all nuclear weapons, others oppose only the new intermediate range missiles, the SS-20s, Cruise and Pershing. There are also disagreements about the attitude to adopt to official and unofficial bodies in Eastern Europe. Beyond the regional nuclear free zones, there is doubt as to which geographical areas to choose, three candidates suggesting themselves: from Portugal to Poland (the END position); from the Atlantic to the Urals (the French government position); and from the mid-Atlantic to the Urals (the Soviet position, designed to include submarine-based missiles).

But the central question about the European peace movement is one avoided by many involved in it for a combination of tactical and ideological reasons, namely the question of political power. Put starkly, the question is in which countries there will come to office a government committed to enforcing the full rejection of nuclear weapons from its national territory and waters. Britain and France have nuclear weapons of their own. Britain, Germany and Italy are to have Cruise and Pershing II on their soil in 1983. All NATO countries could have US nuclear forces deployed in them in time of war, whatever guarantees were given in peacetime. If they fail to stop the 1983 deployment, can they compensate for this later? In such a context, one of the strengths of the peace movement has also became a weakness: for the very forces that rally to it tend to be ones that side-step the issue of state power and party organisation, either from a permanent left reflex that sees electoral triumph as unattainable or from a belief that somehow nuclear disarmament can be brought about by circumventing normal political channels, without government power, by local action, 'challenging existing structures' and alternative forms of political practice. The long march from 1968 has educated rather too few in lessons of political reality and state power which the incumbent governments and the NATO generals know only too well. For all its problems, however, the European peace movement has become capable of challenging the nuclear arms race; but this challenge rests not just on the mobilisation of protest and goodwill but on a political change in Europe by parties that will implement a complete rejection of nuclear weapons.

Unmaking Cold War II?

A rapid end to the Cold War is almost impossible to imagine for the simple reason that the deep causes of this development still persist. There is still a vocal constituency in the USA for expansion of the US nuclear arsenal and conventional forces, although its dynamism has been somewhat lessened by the economic weaknesses of the US economy. The third world remains a site of many conflicts and new sudden eruptions and clashes are always possible. The right wing within the USA understands the logic of power well and has no intention of allowing the victory of

1980 to be quickly or easily reversed. For its part, the new Soviet leadership is determined to maintain its pursuit of parity with the USA and its repression of dissent and pluralism at home. Trade and financial disputes between the major capitalist states, and between first and third world countries, remain as acute as ever. These, the five main factors which brought on Cold War II, persist as important forces in world politics.

Yet there are tendencies at work which can mitigate the Cold War and return the world if not to Detente than at least to the stop-go situation of the early 1960s. A combination of Soviet concessions in negotiation and American retreat from its original stance could produce some agreement on arms limitation at Geneva; whilst this would not remove the danger of war, or end Cold War II, it would be a symbolic lessening of tension with possible repercussions in other areas. At the same time, the economic difficulties of the US government and the advance in anti-nuclear sentiment in the USA could modify what any Presidential candidate would propose in 1984, whether Republican or Democrat. A shift in the position of both major powers is therefore possible, as both realise the dangers of persisting in the position from which they began earlier in Cold War II.

It is in this context that the peace movement in Europe has a major contribution to make. Even if it fails to place a party in power in any NATO country that will reject the Cruise and Pershing-II, it has produced a popular movement that governments cannot ignore, in western Europe and the USA. One of the factors pushing the USA towards negotiation with the USSR at Geneva is the calculation of what failure there will mean for western Europe. The real results of any Geneva agreement, whether on strategic or intermediate range missiles, will be far less than the peace movement envisages, but it will be the latter's activity that has made a major contribution to even this symbolic concession by the major powers.

Yet the potential of the peace movement concerns more than the issue of nuclear weapons: beneath the challenge to NATO on this issue lies a much broader challenge to the Atlantic link as such. Most of those in the peace movement avoid this question, believing it is preferable to focus on the single and immediate issue of nuclear weapons. But it is obvious that a country which is part of a nuclear alliance, as NATO is, is both morally implicated in the use of these weapons and is a target for nuclear attack by the enemy even if the country in question does not possess weapons itself.[32] There are others who argue against a challenge to NATO on the grounds that this will upset the existing balance in Europe. Such is the argument of the Italian Communist Party.[33] Yet this presupposes that a balance now exists—when in fact there is a great imbalance, militarily and economically, in NATO's favour—and it is also assumed that main- tainance of the existing situation is the best route to keeping the peace.

The opposite position can, in fact, be advanced: namely, that what is needed is a challenge to the existing bloc system, a move that deliberately seeks to break the existing balance in Europe. It is here that the prospect of an independent western Europe becomes relevant. For such a Europe would subtract from the major powers factors which are so useful in the prosecution of the arms race and of Cold War, and it would constitute a new independent and non-aligned force in the world.

It would, in the first instance, weaken the ability of the USA to wage a world-wide Cold War against the Soviet Union, because it would with- draw a significant part of the alliance upon which US power increasingly lies. It is always alleged by NATO that such a sundering of the Atlantic link is a primary goal of Soviet policy: but the political price to the USSR of such a breach would be enormous. It would weaken the rationale by which the Soviet Union justifies its grip on Eastern Europe, a control which in no country appears to command majority support. A European break with NATO would therefore increase the prospects for liberalisation in Eastern Europe, and hence, by example, in the USSR itself and it would lessen Soviet fears of a nuclear attack. The effects of such a change would not, however, be confined to Europe but would bring a new and powerful actor into play on the world political stage, one with more economic and

---

[32.] States within NATO that do not process nuclear weapons can in the normal course of events have other, US, nuclear weapons on their soil, or in their territorial waters. Even when a state prohibits the presence of such weapons, there is the possibility that in the event of war NATO commanders will ignore this ban. And even when there really are no nuclear weapons present, such installations as tracking and signals stations form part of the overall alliance military structure and may, therefore, be bombarded by nuclear missiles.

[33.] Thus the PCI's foreign affairs expert Giorgio Napolitano: 'Ten years ago we changed our position on the question of whether Italy should withdraw from NATO. We concluded then that relations between East and West had become so complex and dangerous that any unilateral withdrawal either from the Atlantic Alliance or from the Warsaw Pact would alter the balance of power between the two blocs and would not serve the cause of detente and not even the cause of a gradual overcoming of both military blocs' (*In These Times*, 30 June 1982).

political potential than either China or the divided membership of the Non-Aligned Movement itself can deploy. Whereas hitherto European states have acted as imperialist allies of the USA, a new Europe would be able to provide an independent source of economic and diplomatic backing to states in the third world, which have till now been pulled in opposing directions by the magnetic force of the great power conflict. As Lucio Magri has written: 'Western Europe to-day possesses—as it did not thirty years ago—the economic, technological and cultural resources to assert its own political autonomy and to help sustain another path of development for the Third World'.[34] The emergence of such an independent and non-aligned Western Europe would, therefore, challenge the Cold War in three central respects—by reducing the strategic power of the USA, by undermining the legitimation for the Soviet hold on Eastern Europe, and by loosening the bipolar dynamic that grips the third world. Such a prospect raises many difficulties the solution to which can only be suggested now. An independent Europe would have to find forms of unified political decision-making that would in practice bring a single state into being: difficult as this may be, it will be made easier by the removal of the Atlantic link that has given the USA such a say in European affairs. The new Europe would also have to develop forms of defence able to protect it against both major powers: since the presupposition of a break with the USA is a rejection of nuclear weapons, nonnuclear forces would have to be developed. As recent research has shown, an adequate military posture can be constructed without nuclear weapons, provided such postures are intended to be *defensive*.[35] Yet the greatest contribution to world peace that Europe could make lies not in the rejection of nuclear weapons alone, but in the development of an alternative social model that defies both east and west.

A socialist Europe, which pioneered a new democratic model of society, would undermine the political legitimacy of both the USA and the USSR, and so do more than anything to challenge the underlying political logic of the Great Contest as it has been fought out since 1945. The immediate question is therefore one concerning the Cold War and the role of the European peace movement in helping to lessen it, by putting

4. Lucio Magri in *Exterminism and Cold War*, p. 132.
35. On non-nuclear defence see Ben Dankbaar and Anders Boserup in *Disarming Europe*, and Robert Neild, *How to make up your mind about the bomb*, London 1981.

pressure on NATO governments. The longer-run possibility is that, however this Cold War is ended, greater European political independence can provide a new international focus, disruptive of the Great Contest itself. It can, together with changes in the third world and within the two major powers themselves, lead to a new pattern of international politics, in which the infernal bonding of Great Contest and nuclear arms race can be broken. This bonding has already brought two Cold Wars and has threatened to bring us the ultimate Hot War. If Europe can play a role in lessening the tensions of Cold War II, it can also assume the larger responsibility of projecting a social alternative that will make the recurrence of Cold Wars less likely.

The potential for such a break in the established geography of eastwest conflict goes beyond the immediate balance of forces in western Europe in the midst of Cold War II. For, as of early 1983, the political map of the European NATO states did not show signs of imminent revision. In West Germany, the return of the Christian Democrats to power in the March elections promised to strengthen NATO in its pursuit of a hard line in the Geneva negotiations. In Britain, the Thatcher government had a strong chance of being re-elected. The Eurosocialist governments of France, Spain and Greece were, despite some gestures of independence from Washington, entrapped within the strategic constraints of the North Atlantic alliance, and the economic bonds of a capitalist system they sought only to modify. The prospects for a major change in western Europe lay not in the intentions of governments but in the sustained mobilizations of the peace movement, which the periodic consultations of the electoral process alone could not deflect, and in the continued underlying conflict between the USA and a group of countries that now had the economic and political weight to assert an independence which had been impossible in the circumstances of Cold War I.

What was most striking about the progress of Cold War II was that it was to a considerable extent disaggregated. In the Middle East and southern Africa, the USA's two major allies, Israel and South Africa, were emboldened to adopt intransigent positions because of the indulgence of Washington and the vulnerability of the countries they confronted. In central America, the tenacity of the guerrillas in El Salvador denied Reagan that counter-revolutionary victory that was so important to the revived interventionism of the USA. In Asia, on the other hand, a widespread process of Thaw was underway. In contrast to Cold War I, when Europe witnessed a certain relaxation of tension as East Asia remained a site of conflict, what now occurred was a comprehensive process of negotiation in which animosities that had preceded and grown with the early stages of Cold War II began to subside: between Russia and China, China and India, India and Pakistan, Pakistan and Afghanistan, even China and Vietnam, dialogues and initial negotiations were taking place. If the most important global conflict, that between the USA and the USSR, continued to take its toll in most areas of the globe, the tentative Thaw between Russia and China encouraged a countervailing process in that part of the world where it had been the predominant source of division for over two decades.

The difficulties faced by Washington in its pursuit of Cold War II did not temper the vigour with which Reagan pursued his policies and in March 1983, perhaps emboldened by the results of the west German elections, the American President reiterated the themes and the tone of his electoral campaign of 1980: denouncing the godless and evil nature of communism in a speech in Orlando, Florida, calling for a new programme of research to enable the USA to mount a space-based anti-missile system over two decades, and making a supposedly flexible offer on intermediate range missiles that the Soviet Union would not even discuss. But the forces capable of resisting such a sustained Cold War campaign had also survived the initial Reagan years: El Salvador remained defiant, China was more antagonized, US domestic opinion was restive, the Soviet attitude had hardened, and European hostility to Reagan was as strong as ever. In attempting to impose a new confrontationist line upon Europe, Reagan may in fact have strengthened those tendencies that seek to reject the Atlantic bonds that have persisted for so many years.

Selected Bibliography

Books and Articles

Aldridge, Robert, *The Counterforce Syndrome*, Washington 1978
Amin, Samir, Arrighi, Giovanni, Frank, André Gunder, Wallerstein, Immanuel *Dynamics of Global Crisis*, London 1982
Anderson, Perry, 'The Left in the Fifties', *New Left Review*, 29, January-February 1965

Barnet, Richard, *The Giants*, New York 1977
____, *The Lean Years*, New York 1980
____, *Real Security*, New York 1981
Barnett, Anthony, 'China and the New Cold War,' IPS Pamphlet, Washington 1979
____, *Iron Britannia*, London 1982
____, 'Surviving Between the Superpowers', *New Statesman*, 12 February 1982
Barraclough, Geoffrey, *From Agadir to Armageddon*, London 1982
Blechman, Barry, and Kaplan, Stephen, *Force Without War: US Armed Forces as Political Instruments*, Washington 1978
Brandon, Henry, *The Retreat of American Power*, London 1973
Buchan, Alistair, *Change without War*, London 1974
Buheiry, Marwan, *US Threats of Intervention Against Arab Oil 1973-1979*, Beirut 1980

Carter, Jimmy, *Keeping Faith*, London 1982
Chaliand, Gerard, *Revolution in the Third World*, London 1977
Chomsky, Noam, *Towards a New Cold War*, London 1982
____, Steele, Jonathan, and Gittings, John *Superpowers in Collision: The New Cold War*, London 1982

268

Claudín, Fernando, *Eurocommunism and Socialism*, London 1978
____, *The Communist Movement*, London 1975
Cox, John, *Overkill*, London 1981
Crawford, Alan, *Thunder on the Right*, New York 1980
Davies, Derek, 'Caught in History's Vice', *Far Eastern Economic Review* December 1979
Deutscher, Isaac, *Russia, China and the West*, London 1970
____, *The Great Contest*, London 1960

Ellsberg, Daniel, 'Call to Mutiny' in US edition of Smith and Thompson (eds.), *Protest and Survive*,
____, 'First Strike', Interview, *Inquiry*, 13 April 1981

Fawcett, Edmund, and Thomas, Tony, *America, Americans*, London 1983
Ferguson, Thomas, and Rogers, Joel, *The Hidden Election*, New York 1981
Fontaine, André, *Un Seul Lit Pour Deux Rêves*, Paris 1981
Frank, André Gunder, *Crisis in the Third World*, London 1981
____, *Crisis in the World Economy*, London 1981
____, 'From Atlantic Alliance to Pan-European Entente', Department of Economics, University of Amsterdam, Research Memorandum, October 1982
Freedman, Lawrence, *Arms Control in Europe*, London 1981
____, *The Evolution of Nuclear Strategy*, London 1981
Gittings, John, *The World and China, 1922-1972*, London 1974

Halliday, Fred, *Threat from the East? Soviet Policy from Afghanistan and Iran to the Horn of Africa*, London 1982; also published as *Soviet Policy in the Arc of Crisis*, Washington 1981
Holloway, David, *The Soviet Union and the Arms Race*, London 1983

Kaiser, Karl, Lord, Winston, de Montbrial, Thierry, Watt, David, *Western Security: what has changed? what should be done?*, London 1981
Kaldor, Mary, *The Baroque Arsenal*, London 1982
____, *The Disintegrating West*, London 1978
____, and Smith, Dan (eds.) *Disarming Europe*, London 1982
Kaplan, Fred, *Dubious Spectre: a Second Look at the Soviet 'Threat'*, Washington 1978
Kaplan, Stephen, *Diplomacy of Power: Soviet Armed Forces as a Political Instrument*, Washington 1981
Kissinger, Henry, *For the Record, Selected Statements 1977-1980*, Boston 1981
____, *White House Years*, London 1979
____, *Years of Upheaval*, London 1982
Klare, Michael, *Beyond the 'Vietnam Syndrome'*, Washington 1981
____, *War Without End*, New York 1973

LaFeber, Walter, *America, Russia and the Cold War, 1945-1980*, New York 1980

Lippmann, Walter, *The Cold War*, London 1947

Mandel, Ernest, *Europe versus America?* London 1970
_____, *From Stalinism to Eurocommunism*, London 1978
_____, 'Peaceful Coexistence and World Revolution' in Robin Blackburn (ed.) *Revolution and Class Struggle*, Hassocks 1978
_____, *Revolutionary Marxism Today*, London 1979
_____, *The Second Slump*, London 1978
Mandelbaum, Michael, *The Nuclear Question*, London 1979
_____, *The Nuclear Revolution*, London 1981
Mayer, Arno, 'The Cold War is Over', *Democracy*, vol 2. no. 1, January 1982
Mayer, Martin, *The Fate of the Dollar*, New York 1981
Medvedev, Roy, *Leninism and Western Socialism*, London 1981
Muravchik, Joshua, *The Senate and National Security: A New Mood*, Washington 1980
Myrdal, Alva, and others, *Dynamics of European Nuclear Disarmament* Nottingham 1981

New Left Review, ed., *Exterminism and Cold War*, London 1982
Nixon, Richard, *The Memoirs of Richard Nixon*, London 1978
_____, *The Real War*, New York 1980
Parboni, Riccardo, *The Dollar and Its Rivals*, London 1981
Podhoretz, Norman, *The Present Danger*, New York 1981

Scheer, Robert, *With Enough Shovels: Reagan, Bush and Nuclear War*, London 1983
Schell, Jonathan, *The Fate of the Earth*, London 1982
Schurmann, Franz, *The Logic of World Power*, New York 1974
Shaw, Eric, *Cold Peace: Soviet Power and Western Security*, London 1978
Short, Philip, *The Dragon and the Bear*, London 1982
Sklar, Holly, ed., *Trilateralism*, Boston 1980
Smith, Dan, *The Defense of the Realm in the 1980s*, London 1980
_____, and Thompson, Edward, eds. *Protest and Survive*, London 1980
Smith, Hedrick, *The Russians*, London 1976
Stockholm International Peace Research Institute, *World Armaments and Disarmament Yearbook*, 1981
Szulc, Tad, *The Illusion of Peace*, New York 1978

Tanzer, Michael, *The Race for Resources*, London 1980
Therborn, Göran, 'From Petrograd to Saigon', *New Left Review* 48, March-April 1978
Thompson, Edward, *Beyond the Cold War*, London 1982

USA, Department of Defense, *Soviet Military Power*, Washington 1981
USSR, Ministry of Defence, *Whence the Threat to Peace?* Moscow 1982

Warren, Bill, *Imperialism, Pioneer of Capitalism*, London 1980
Westoby, Adam, *Communism Since World War II*, London 1981
Wolfe, Alan, *America's Impasse*, New York 1981
____, *The Rise and Fall of the 'Soviet Threat'*, Washington 1979

Periodicals

ADIU Report (UK)
Beijing Review (China)
The Economist, (UK)
END Bulletin (UK)
Foreign Affairs (USA)
Foreign Policy (USA)
International Affairs (UK)
International Affairs (USSR)
International Security (USA)
MERIP Reports (USA)
The Nation (USA)
New Left Review (UK)
Problems of Communism (USA)
Race and Class (UK)
SAIS Review (USA)
Soviet News (UK)
Survey (UK)

List of Abbreviations

AFL–CIO	American Federation of Labor-Congress of Industrial Organisations
CIA	Central Intelligence Agency
CND	Campaign for Nuclear Disarmament
CPSU	Communist Party of the Soviet Union
CSCE	Conference on Security and Co-operation in Europe
EEC	European Economic Community
END	European Nuclear Disarmament
ERA	Equal Rights Amendment
FEER	*Far Eastern Economic Review*
FNLA	National Front for the Liberation of Angola
FRELIMO	Front for the Liberation of Mozambique
FSLN	Sandinista National Liberation Front
FY	Financial Year
GDP	Gross Domestic Product
GNP	Gross National Product
ICBM	Intercontinental Ballistic Missile
ITV	Independent Television
JVP	People's Liberation Front
KGB	Committee for State Security
MBFR	Mutual and Balanced Force Reductions
MIRV	Multiple Independently-Targetable Re-entry Vehicle
MPLA	Popular Movement for the Liberation of Angola
MX	Missile Experimental
NASA	National Aeronautics and Space Administration
NATO	North Atlantic Treaty Organisation
NIC	New Industrialising Countries
NLF	National Liberation Front
OECD	Organisation for Economic Co-operation and Development
OPEC	Organisation of Petroleum Exporting Countries
PAC	Political Action Committee
PCI	Communist Party of Italy
PD	Presidential Directive
PDPA	People's Democratic Party of Afghanistan

PKI	Communist Party of Indonesia
PLO	Palestine Liberation Organisation
POLISARIO	Popular Front for the Liberation of Seguiet el Hamra and Rio de Oro
SALT	Strategic Arms Limitation Talks/Treaty
SIPRI	Stockholm International Peace Research Institute
SLBM	Submarine-Launched Ballistic Missile
TNF	Threatre Nuclear Forces
UNITA	National Union for the Total Independence of Angola
WTO	Warsaw Treaty Organisation
ZANU	Zimbabwe African National Union
ZAPU	Zimbabwe African People's Union

Index